€1999

D1135778

RIOTOUS
ASSEMBLIES

CLARE COUNTY LIBRARY

WITHDRAWN FROM STOCK

Leabharlann Chontae an Chláir

CL184590

RIOTOUS ASSEMBLIES

Rebels, Riots & Revolts in Ireland

Edited by

WILLIAM SHEEHAN & MAURA CRONIN

CLARE COUNTY LIBRARIES

MERCIER PRESS

Irish Publisher – Irish Story

MERCIER PRESS

Cork

www.mercierpress.ie

© Individual authors, 2011

© Introduction: William Sheehan & Maura Cronin, 2011

ISBN: 978 1 85635 653 4

AN
303.623

10 9 8 7 6 5 4 3 2 1

A CIP record for this title is available from the British Library

This book is sold subject to the condition that it shall not, by way of trade or otherwise, be lent, resold, hired out or otherwise circulated without the publisher's prior consent in any form of binding or cover other than that in which it is published and without a similar condition including this condition being imposed on the subsequent purchaser.

No part of this publication may be reproduced or transmitted in any form or by any means, electronic or mechanical, including photocopying, recording or any information or retrieval system, without the prior permission of the publisher in writing.

Printed and bound by ScandBook AB, Sweden.

TO OUR FAMILIES,
FRIENDS AND COLLEAGUES

Contents

Acknowledgements   9

The Contributors   10

Abbreviations   15

Introduction   17

1   **Disorder and Commotion**   22
    Urban riots and popular protest in Ireland, 1570–1640
    Clodagh Tait

2   **The Dublin Parliamentary Elections, 1613**   50
    Stephen Carroll

3   **'We are not yet safe, for they threaten us with
    more violence'**   64
    A study of the Cook Street riot, 1629
    Mark Empey

4   **The 1830s Tithe Riots**   80
    Noreen Higgins-McHugh

5   **The Great Protestant Meeting of Dungannon,
    1834**   96
    Daragh Curran

6   **Collective Action and the Poor Law**   110
    The political mobilisation of the Irish poor, 1851–78
    Mel Cousins

7	**Recovering the Cargo of the *Julia***	127
	Salvage, law and the killing of 'wreckers' in Conamara in 1873	
	John Cunningham	

| 8 | **Riots in Limerick, 1820–1900** | 153 |
| | *John McGrath* | |

9	**'A centre of turbulence and rioting'**	175
	The republican movement in Limerick, 1917–18	
	John O'Callaghan	

10	**'Notorious Anarchists?'**	191
	The Irish smallholder and the Irish state during the Emergency, 1939–45	
	Bryce Evans	

11	**'Conditional Constitutionalists'**	210
	The reaction of Fianna Fáil grass-roots to the IRA border campaign, 1956–62	
	Stephen Kelly	

12	**Belfast, August 1969**	228
	The limited and localised pattern(s) of violence	
	Liam Kelly	

13	**When is an Assembly Riotous, and Who Decides?**	242
	The success and failure of police attempts to criminalise protest	
	Eałáir Ní Dhorchaigh & Laurence Cox	

| **Notes** | | 263 |

Acknowledgements

Firstly, we would like to thank the Mercier Press team who have supported this project over the last year. A sincere thanks, too, to Liam Irwin, the Head of History at Mary Immaculate College, and to our colleagues, Michelle Mangan, Sarah McNamara and Ursula O'Callaghan, and the Mary Immaculate College staff for their help and support at the 'Riotous Assemblies' conference held at the college in September 2009, from which this book grew.

Finally, we wish to express our gratitude to all the contributors to the conference and the book, giving special mention to Professor Peter King of the Open University who, as the conference's plenary speaker, shared some remarkable insights into the 'riotous' Irish in eighteenth-century London.

Maura Cronin
William Sheehan

THE CONTRIBUTORS

EDITORS

DR MAURA CRONIN is Senior Lecturer in History at Mary Immaculate College, Limerick. Her research interests centre on nineteenth-century Ireland and include popular politicisation, popular song, labour organisation, agrarian movements and the evolution of towns. She is co-ordinator of the Oral History Centre at Mary Immaculate College, which collects memories of Irish working lives and social change from the 1930s onwards. Her publications include *Country, Class or Craft: the politicisation of the skilled artisan in nineteenth-century Cork* (1994), *The Death of Fr John Walsh at Kilgraney Bridge: community tensions in pre-Famine Carlow* (2010) and *Agrarian Protest, 1750–1950* (2010).

DR WILLIAM SHEEHAN is a military historian and has lectured on the MA in Military History and Strategic Studies programme at the National University of Ireland (NUI), Maynooth. He is an associate lecturer of the Open University and a member of its Empire and Postcolonial Studies Group. Dr Sheehan is a graduate of University College Cork (UCC), the University of Limerick, the Open University and Mary Immaculate College. He has published four books: *British Voices from the Irish War of Independence* (2005), *Fighting for Dublin* (2007), *Images of Sarsfield Barracks* (2008) with Denis Carroll, Michael Deegan and Stephen Kelly, and *Hearts and Mines: the British 5th Division in Ireland, 1919–1921* (2009). His doctoral thesis will be published in 2011 under the title *A Hard Local War: the British army and the guerrilla war in Cork, 1919–21*. Dr Sheehan wrote the article on General Sir Peter Strickland, the British commander in Cork, for the *Oxford Dictionary of National Biography*. He is one of the leading historians on the Irish War of Independence and an expert on the British army's campaign in Cork from 1919 to 1921.

WRITERS

STEPHEN CARROLL is pursuing a PhD in Trinity College, Dublin and is currently in his second year of research. He is working under the supervision of Dr Robert Armstrong and the title of his thesis is 'Violence and popular protest in Ireland, 1603–1633'.

DR MEL COUSINS has written extensively on aspects of social history in nineteenth- and twentieth-century Ireland, including *The Birth of Social Welfare* (2003). He is currently based at Glasgow Caledonian University where he is completing research on the Poor Law in nineteenth-century Ireland.

DR LAURENCE COX is a lecturer in sociology at NUI Maynooth. He has particular research interests in social movement theory and methodology, the contemporary 'movement of movements' against neo-liberalism and working-class community organising. He is co-editor of the online social movement studies journal *Interface* (www.interface.net).

DR JOHN CUNNINGHAM is a lecturer in history at NUI Galway. He has published widely on Irish labour and social history. In 2010 he published *Unlikely Radicals: Irish post primary teachers and the ASTI*.

DARAGH CURRAN is a PhD student at NUI Maynooth and is currently researching County Tyrone Protestant society in the pre-Famine period. Central to this research is the study of Orangeism, electoral politics and the role of the lower classes in both of these areas.

DR MARK EMPEY is an Irish Research Council for Humanities and Social Sciences postdoctoral fellow at the University College Dublin (UCD) Humanities Institute of Ireland. His fellowship is held in conjunction with a three-year research project entitled 'Protestants, print and Gaelic culture, 1567–1722'. His current interest focuses on the seventeenth-century historian and antiquary, Sir James Ware, in addition to the broader study of the Protestant contribution to Gaelic culture in early modern Ireland. He also specialises in the political and religious history of Britain and Ireland.

DR BRYCE EVANS is an *Ad Astra* Doctoral Research Scholar based at the Humanities Institute of Ireland and the School of History and Archives, UCD. His most notable research is on Ireland during the Emergency (1939–45) and the life and career of Seán Lemass. His doctoral thesis was entitled 'Farewell to Plato's Cave: "Moral Economy" in Emergency Ireland, 1939–1945'. He is working on a new biography of Lemass, to be published in 2011.

NOREEN HIGGINS-MCHUGH is currently a PhD student at the Department of History, UCC. Her thesis topic is 'The tithe war in Ireland, 1830–38', which enlarges on her single-county study for an MA in History and Local Studies from the University of Limerick in 2000 and the publication *Tipperary's Tithe War, 1830–38* (2002). She has also published various historical articles in the *Tipperary Historical Journal*.

Liam Kelly is a third-year PhD candidate at the Institute of Irish Studies, Queen's University, Belfast. His doctoral research aims to produce a 'thick descriptive' historical case study of Belfast between 1968 and 1970, with particular interests in issues relating to space, identity, territory, violence and parading.

Dr Stephen Kelly is currently Post Doctoral Research Fellow (IRCHSS funded) at the UCD International Centre for Newman Studies. His research interests are contemporary Irish history and politics, Anglo-Irish relations and European nationalism.

John McGrath has BA and MA degrees from Mary Immaculate College. He is currently completing a PhD investigating the development of organised labour in Limerick city in the nineteenth century. His previous publications include 'Music and politics: marching bands in late nineteenth-century Limerick', *North Munster Antiquarian Journal*, no. 46 (2006) and 'An urban community: St Mary's Parish, Limerick and the social role of sporting and music clubs 1885–1905', in J. Kelly and R. V. Comerford (eds) *Associational Culture in Ireland and Abroad* (Dublin, forthcoming).

Ealáir Ní Dhorchaigh is a postgraduate research student in sociology. Her research focuses on issues of accountability and governance, and is funded by the Irish Research Council for the Humanities and Social Sciences.

Dr John O'Callaghan lectures in modern Irish and European history in the Department of History, University of Limerick. His primary research interests lie in the area of twentieth-century Ireland. His previous publications include *Revolutionary Limerick:*

the republican campaign for independence in Limerick, 1913–21 (2010) and *Teaching Irish Independence: history in Irish schools, 1922–72* (2009). Among his current projects is a contribution to Mercier's Military History of the Irish Civil War Series, *The Battle for Kilmallock*. He is also co-editing a volume entitled *'Subversive Voices': oral history and the occluded Irish diaspora* for Peter Lang's Reimagining Ireland series.

DR CLODAGH TAIT is a senior lecturer in the Department of History, University of Essex. She is author of *Death, Burial and Commemoration in Ireland, 1550–1650* (2002) and co-editor of *Age of Atrocity: violence and political conflict in early modern Ireland* (2010). She has also published articles on religious culture, funerary monuments, martyrdom, riot, childbirth, baptism and naming, and is completing a book on the social and cultural history of the early modern British and Irish Isles.

Abbreviations

BMH	Bureau of Military History
Cal. Carew MSS	*Calendar of Carew MSS preserved in the archiepiscopal library at Lambeth, 1515–1624*, ed. J. S. Brewer and W. Bullen, 6 vols (London: Longman, 1867–73)
Cal S.P. Ire.	*Calendar of the State Papers relating to Ireland, of the reigns of Henry VIII, Edward VI, Mary and Elizabeth*, ed. H. C. Hamilton (vols 1–5), E. G. Atkinson (vols 6–10) and R. P. Mahaffy (vol. 11) (London: Longman/HMSO, 1860–1912)
Carte MS	Carte manuscript, Bodleian Library, Oxford
CSO	Chief Secretary's Office
DAA	Dublin Archdiocesan Archive
DFA	Department of Foreign Affairs
DT	Department of the Taoiseach
HC	House of Commons
HMC	Historical Manuscripts Commission
HMSO	Her Majesty's Stationery Office
ICOS	Irish Co-operative Organisation Society
IRA	Irish Republican Army
NAI	National Archives of Ireland
NAUK	National Archives, United Kingdom
NLI	National Library of Ireland
ODC	Order of Discalced Carmelites
OFM	Order of Friars Minor (Franciscans)
OSA	Order of St Augustine
PRONI	Public Record Office of Northern Ireland
RP	Registered Papers

RUC	Royal Ulster Constabulary
S.P.	State Papers Domestic, National Archives, London
TD	Teachta Dála [Member of Dáil Éireann]
UCDA	University College Dublin Archives

INTRODUCTION

This book grew from a conference held at Mary Immaculate College, Limerick, in September 2009. The question underlying the conference theme was simple: why have people in Ireland become involved in rioting? A simple question, it led us in the course of discussion to many other questions. Why did riots occur? Who rioted? What was the government response to public disorder? When did a riot or public violence have legitimacy and who defined legitimacy? How can we as historians restore the voices of 'ordinary' people, as expressed in these events, to the grand narrative of history?

History is perhaps no longer written by and for the great. Many generations of historians have recalled the voices of the forgotten to enhance our understanding of the past. This volume, as the different chapters show, offers a contribution to that ongoing work. As relatively few 'ordinary' people have left behind full and complete accounts of their lives, records of rioting or public action by crowds are often the only evidence we have for the grievances or fears of these ordinary people. One of the key problems of this type of historical recovery is that as historians we have to rely on official or semi-official sources as the basis of our analysis of these past events, since the poor and unimportant leave little behind for historians to explore. But as many of the chapters in this book so skilfully show, even these sources can be read against the grain, allowing those submerged voices to speak once more.

This book ranges across a wide spectrum of Irish history. Clodagh Tait explores urban rioting and disorder in early modern Ireland, as does Stephen Carroll in his examination of the 1613

Dublin parliamentary election. Noreen Higgins-McHugh focuses on the rural scene with an analysis of collective violence during the tithe war in Munster. Daragh Curran revisits the O'Connellite age of monster meetings, but details the phenomenon from an Orange and loyalist perspective through the analysis of a meeting in the Tyrone town of Dungannon. Mel Cousins brings us back to urban Ireland, and shows that violent protest was not simply a matter for the street but something that could occur within the walls of the workhouse, while John McGrath explores the pattern of urban disorder in Limerick City over a wide sweep of the nineteenth century. John Cunningham takes us west, with a unique micro-history which explores a conflict in Conamara surrounding the shipwreck and salvage of the *Julia*.

Subsequent chapters extend into twentieth-century Ireland. John O'Callaghan provides an intriguing study of political street fighting in Limerick just prior to the outbreak of the War of Independence. Bryce Evans and Stephen Kelly explore various Fianna Fáil governments' fears of, and attempts to control, public violence within the Irish state. Liam Kelly's chapter sheds new light on the history of the Northern conflict and reminds us of the importance of locality in the emergence of protest in 1969. Finally, Eálair Ní Dhorchaigh and Laurence Cox bring this volume right up to date by exploring the responses of the modern Irish state to 'riotous assemblies'.

Many common themes link the chapters. One such theme is the role of local rivalry in fomenting disturbances, particularly in the urban context, as in nineteenth-century feuding in Limerick (McGrath) and the role of space and place in the outbreak of violence in late 1960s Belfast (Liam Kelly). A further theme explored by many contributors is the theatricality of public violence, whether the election-related attempt in 1629 to undermine the mayor's authority by snatching the king's sword (Empey) or the carnivalesque 'reclaim the streets' protests of 2002 (Ní Dhorchaigh and Cox). Many of the actors, too, reappear again and again over the course of the period. Women were active rioters in Dublin in 1629 (Empey), in workhouse protests in Dublin in the 1850s (Cousins) and in Limerick street violence in the 1840s and 1890s (McGrath). As Tait and O'Callaghan show in very different periods, relations between soldiers and citizenry have almost always been fraught, while the potential for youth to engage in activities ranging from rhetorical rejection of authority to the fomenting of riot is as visible in local Fianna Fáil party cumainn reaction to the border campaign of the 1950s (Stephen Kelly) as it was in Lord Claud Hamilton's fomenting Orange protest in 1830s Tyrone (Curran) and the Limerick City youths' rowdy game that became a riot in 1599 (Tait).

The incidents sparking disturbances, too, seem to recur over time, many riots occurring when small communities come into conflict with outside forces – billeted troops and enforcers of cess in Waterford in the 1570s (Tait), tithe-collection enforcers in Kilkenny in the 1830s (Higgins-McHugh), custom officials interfering with wreck salvage in Conamara in the 1870s (Cunningham), compulsory tillage inspectors in Leitrim in the 1940s (Evans), and police and pipeline workers in Mayo in the early 2000s (Ní Dhorchaigh and Cox). Nor did violent or potentially violent protest necessarily involve large numbers: the individual yet explosive animosity shown towards tillage inspectors in Leitrim in the 1940s (Evans) was the tip of an iceberg of popular hostility towards government policy.

Rioting is often seen as the act of the underclass, yet as Carroll, Curran, Higgins-McHugh and Empey suggest, more elite elements could frequently be involved, either as active rioters or –

more usually – in orchestrating protest that they were sometimes unable (as in the Dungannon case) to fully control. Elites could also provoke rioting through their very efforts to control it – a question explored in considerable depth by Ní Dhorchaigh and Cox in relation to the early twenty-first century, but equally relevant in O'Callaghan's discussion of the Limerick Catholic clergy's condoning of anti-military rioting in 1918, and in Carroll's treatment of the dubious handling of the Dublin election of 1613. Considerable skill was needed on the part of those in authority to prevent the mutterings of discontent from becoming something more violent. Perceptive officials in the 1940s went some way to countering high-handed government orders on the matter of compulsory tillage (Evans), whereas the sidelining of an equally perceptive customs official in favour of less sympathetic individuals in 1873 hastened the explosion of violence surrounding the wreck of the *Julia* (Cunningham).

So, one is left with the question: what caused people to riot during the 500 years that form the time span of the present book? And, more fundamentally, what *was* a riot? When a crowd (large or small) exploded into violence in reaction to some unpopular event or individual, its suppression or placation on the one hand, or on the other its escalation into a riot, depended on the accompanying circumstances. Ní Dhorchaigh and Cox conclude that 'an assembly is riotous when the authorities say that it is' and while this may not be the whole story, its emphasis on the indefinable nature of the riot does echo many of the other contributions to this book.

Riots were usually spontaneous explosions of resentment, but sometimes they were long gestating. They were not entirely plebeian in their social composition, representing something of a cross-section of society, from lay and clerical elites at the top to the (usually) anonymous 'nobodies' at the bottom. They were usually but not always violent; they involved some, or several, grievances – reflecting local fear of outside forces, animosity between rival groups and localities, and resentment against change. Even if the causes, course and consequences of rioting vary considerably from one period to the next, many aspects of Irish rioting over the past 500 years, though expressed in the archaic terminology of past times, are familiar to today's readers. When put under the microscope, as they have been by the contributors to this book, they not only make for fascinating reading but will hopefully encourage more research in this area.

Maura Cronin
William Sheehan

1

DISORDER AND COMMOTION

Urban riots and popular protest in Ireland, 1570–1640[1]

CLODAGH TAIT

In May 1577 there was a disturbance in Waterford. The lord president of Munster, William Drury, rushed in a state of indignation to meet Lord Deputy Henry Sidney at New Ross, 'to complaine of the disorder and commotion of the Cittizens of Waterfforde in assaltinge the Quenes howse holde, where my La[dy] of Thame his wyffe, children, and some of his familys lay'. Lord Barry was hot on the president's heels, to protest at the taxation ('cess') imposed on his lands to pay for Drury's garrison and household in Munster.

In the same letter in which he noted his pacification of Drury and Barry, Sidney reported that rumours were circulating of an imminent invasion by James Fitzmaurice, leader of the first Desmond rebellion, aided by France, Spain and the pope, and that 'his confederates here are in dayly expectauncye of his arryvall'. Further, he claimed that agitation against cess in Dublin 'hath wrought soche an opinion amongst the common sorte as many refuse to pay cesse, which otherwayes, most willingly would have'.[2] Though we have no further details of the proceedings at Waterford, or their consequences, we can guess from this context that, like their counterparts in Dublin, the citizens' actions probably largely derived from their objections to the burden of paying for the billeting of both soldiers and the households of senior officials at a time of heightened tension in the country.

In recent times, historians have strongly challenged the assumption that politics in the early modern period was a matter engaged in largely by elite men. It is increasingly clear that, throughout the islands, people of all social backgrounds knew a lot about current affairs and ongoing debates about government, law and justice. There was a variety of means by which all sections of society, both men and women, might engage in meaningful 'popular politics'. As well as discussing issues and grievances among themselves, they could also seek to influence those in authority for personal, communal and political gain, and to resist changes and policies they perceived to be disadvantageous to them. It also seems they had an acute sense of the options open to them, as John Walter states, 'to take advantage of the law or to avoid its consequences'. Elsewhere, Walter reminds us of the 'fragile relationship between rulers and ruled' in early modern societies, and 'the obligation it forced on the government to enter into a dialogue with the people'.[3] Despite the rhetoric they might resort to, subjects 'were never merely the passive victims of a process that they were powerless to affect', and they could be articulate and proactive in local politics, finding a variety of ways by which to lobby those with influence and attempting to manipulate the decisions and behaviour of both officeholders and those involved in central governance.[4]

Steve Hindle points out 'the fragility of sanctions open to the government, especially when it was confronted with subtle, creative and communal resistance': even brute force was of little use against certain forms of opposition.[5] Tactics, ranging from non-cooperation, petitioning, rumour, slander and libel, to riot, violence and rebellion, were the means by which populations could attempt at least to make their voices heard when they felt their interests were being compromised. They engaged in various gestures of protest, and exploited the weaknesses of the state and the threat of disorder and violence to achieve their aims. This was as much the case in Ireland as in Britain.

The Irish Resisting the Toll at Roche's Castle, Cork, by J. Fitzgerald, c.1880,
depicting a seventeenth-century scene.
Courtesy of the Port of Cork Company.

It is, however, less straightforward to investigate such issues when it comes to Ireland. There are a number of reasons for this. Though historians like Raymond Gillespie have begun to get at popular political attitudes during the period, the grand narrative of conquest, coercion and rebellion has focused attention primarily on 'high politics', on the shifting political landscapes of the Irish lordships and on attempts to make sense of the inconsistent policies applied to the Irish situation by successive chief governors.[6] Large-scale revolts such as the Kildare, Baltinglass and Desmond rebellions, the Nine Years' War, the 1641 Rising and subsequent Wars of the Three Kingdoms have supplied so much conflict to be getting on with that smaller-scale demonstrations, riots and disputes risk passing 'under the radar'.

The paucity of surviving documents from the period is also a major difficulty. Rarely is it possible even to attempt to imitate the kinds of forensic micro-historical examination of episodes of rioting and protest that have been used so fruitfully by colleagues in France and Britain. Such examinations enable us not only to consider the causes and immediate context of crowd actions, but also to explore how protestors exploited factors such as space, gesture, language, notions about gender roles, and knowledge of the law to maximise impact while, at the same time, minimising the potential consequences of their actions for individual participants.

There was a limited native print-culture, and Ireland just does not possess the kinds of legal documents, for example, that historians of England have used so productively: rioters there were often taken to court and their stories are recorded, however partially, in court records, allowing us to pick through the differing opinions and self-presentation of the various protagonists. Irish records were less carefully kept and many were lost in the Public Record Office fire in 1922. The partial and piecemeal nature of what survives also makes it particularly difficult to compile adequate biographies of the background to crowd actions. Street demonstrations and riots were usually the final acts in a series of verbal and other clashes as grievances simmered up and boiled over, but most if not all of this context is usually lost. Mayors and corporations of towns might have a vested interest in failing adequately to record or even investigate incidents of riot, while the increasing use of provosts marshal and commissions of martial law meant that troublemakers might be dealt with informally and often quite harshly.[7]

To justify heavy-handed measures, there was a strong tendency on the part of the authorities to lump together everything from local riots and the depredations of bandits to fights between groups of retainers and outspoken protests at the activities of soldiers as 'rebellion', while the word 'riotous' was used to describe an array of threatening actions. For example, the state papers indicate that there were significant disturbances in the midlands and north of Ireland in mid to late 1628 and early 1629, related to grievances over the activities of garrisons and food shortages caused by a dearth that affected Britain as well as Ireland. However, the use of martial law to quash these disturbances, and the tendency universally to refer to the protagonists as rebels, serves to obscure the scale and nature of the activities and intent of the protestors. The records of the Court of Castle Chamber are full of people doing things 'riotously and routously', but as this was a catch-all phrase designed to indicate a large degree of force, it is often impossible to distinguish protest actions from assaults, affrays and other disagreements.[8]

Despite this, it is possible to catch glimpses of the inhabitants of Ireland taking to the streets to protest about a variety of issues. I focus on some of the kinds of crowd actions that occurred in urban areas, particularly between 1570 and 1640. In this period, most of Ireland's towns were comparatively small, in both area and population. It has been estimated that Dublin's population in 1600 was about 5,000; cities like Galway, Cork, Waterford and Limerick had 2,400 to 4,000 people, and Youghal, Kinsale, Kilkenny, Clonmel and others had about 2,000 inhabitants each. In most of these urban centres, the limited group of freemen (citizens entitled by birth, marriage or completion of apprenticeship to trade within town walls and to participate in the political life of the civic community) was dominated by a small coterie of families of wealthy merchants and craftsmen. These families were knit together by ties of marriage and business, and they provided the bulk of the candidates taking positions as aldermen, mayors, sovereigns or other officials. They also dominated the trade and craft guilds that were increasingly set up in the sixteenth and seventeenth centuries. The charters extended to the Irish towns often granted them privileges far wider than those possessed by their counterparts elsewhere, reflecting the crown's reliance on them as outposts that were to some degree amenable to co-operation with the central administration.[9] As was the case for other early modern towns, such privileges were jealously defended against threatened encroachment by the state or by local gentlemen and peers.

However, ordinary conflicts might be exacerbated in Ireland by particularly acute clashes of interests. Great vigilance and skill was required to negotiate the smoothest path between the financial good and safety of town communities and the influence of local magnates whose concerns often differed quite starkly from those of the monarchs who granted town charters and might also find reasons to revoke them.[10] Fissures grew as it became evident that most towns had majority Catholic populations, despite the fact that they were counted on to be the most 'civil' parts of Ireland and most amenable to cultural influences from England.[11] The perils inherent in their situation became especially acute during times of warfare and rebellion, when trading with their hinterlands might leave town populations open to charges of treason, while refusals to co-operate with local rebels might raise more immediate threats to the townspeople's livelihoods and property. The example of Youghal may have been an instructive one: it was sacked by the Earl of Desmond's troops in 1579, and subsequently punished by the loyalist Earl of Ormond, then president of Munster, who hanged the mayor for his lack of backbone in allowing the rebels access to the city to collect some wine.[12] But, apart from Youghal in 1579 and Kinsale in 1601–2, the fact that no other major town was captured by, or capitulated to, rebels before the 1640s is testimony to their special character and the skill with which their leaders and citizens managed to balance competing claims on their allegiance and maintain a large degree of independence. In this context of closely guarded privileges and closely packed spaces, intermittently closely watched by the agents of central government, urban crowd actions, ranging from small, relatively peaceful demonstrations to larger, more violent incidents of riot, represented in microcosm some of the larger issues of the time.

One of the most frequently reported provocations of crowd actions in early modern Ireland was the activity of soldiers. Times of outright rebellion and warfare, especially in the latter half of Elizabeth's reign and the 1640s and 1650s led to increased recruitment of troops from England, Wales and further afield, but greater or lesser numbers of soldiers were deployed in various parts of the country throughout the sixteenth and seventeenth centuries.[13] It was rarely the case that local strongholds had the capacity to house anything other than small numbers of men, or that the infrastructure of the state was adequate to keep them clothed, paid and fed. More often, travelling companies were authorised to exact food and lodgings from the areas through which they moved, while the towns and cities were obliged to provide for the needs of garrisons either directly, by billeting them in their houses and providing for them, or indirectly through levies of money or foodstuffs (cess or purveyance). Repayments for these services were usually inadequate or tardy. As we have seen in the case of the attack on William Drury's family, the households of officials also needed to be supported, and soldiers often extorted or commandeered far more than they were officially entitled to.[14]

Not surprisingly, a variety of grievances might arise on all sides, civilians resenting the calls on their financial resources and food stores and the behaviour of their visitors, and the soldiers finding fault with provisions that were often grudgingly given or with the general attitudes displayed towards them. Armed soldiers were in a position to back up their claims and grievances with the threat of force, while in a highly militarised society their hosts and opponents were equally prepared to defend their own interests violently. Furthermore, differences between the protagonists in political viewpoints, social status, ethnicity and religion might heighten tensions. In a series of riots in Limerick in 1599, for example, many of these kinds of issue came to the fore. On two occasions, complaints by soldiers about the unsatisfactory provisions they received led to retaliation by the townsmen and resulted in street brawls and casualties. An all-out assault by the citizens on the church being used as a vantage point by the army ostensibly resulted from a disagreement between the soldiers and the young men of the town who had been whiling away the evening with a game called 'fox to hole'. However, the rhetoric of the attackers revealed a host of other provocations – contempt for the 'English churls' (the Old English townspeople of Limerick on other occasions expressed their opposition to the garrisoning there of the Earl of Thomond's native Irish troops as well); the idea that they were 'defiling' the church by their presence; and, perhaps most importantly, the claim that they were being fed 'fatt on bread and milk' in a time of food shortages. Moreover, these incidents occurred within the wider context of an ongoing conflict over jurisdiction between the town and local gentlemen, particularly the Earl of Thomond, and partly as an expression of frustration aimed at the government for its lack of response to complaints about the erosion of the mayor's authority when attempts were made to implement martial law within the city in criminal cases involving soldiers.[15]

Though they were reported in less detail, similar 'frays' between soldiers and citizens seem regularly to have occurred in other Irish towns as well. The vice-president of Munster, Sir William Herbert reported to Lord Burghley in June 1588 of the tensions between civilians and soldiers in Munster:

> ... those two bands of footmen that are in this province are grown into quarrel and dislike with sundry of these parts, as lately there hath been a fray between Mr Vice-President's (Thos Norreys) band and the citizens of Cork, and continual jars daily increasing between Sir Edward Denny's band and the townsmen of Youghal, and these jars of discord, howsoever they be salved up for the time, leave scars of discontentment behind them unfit for this time.[16]

Though many of these incidents arose in the heat of the moment, others were calculated and stage-managed to remind the authorities of the limits to townspeople's forbearance. Disorders in Galway in July 1580, which were probably related to the need to equip and support extra troops at the height of the Desmond rebellion, just as the Baltinglass revolt was breaking out in Leinster, were followed by further demonstrations that were not violent but were nonetheless designed to be provocative. Sir Nicholas Malby decried 'the bravery used by them after the fury appeased in marching up and down the streets with sound of drum, with spiteful speeches of their conquest against the English soldiers, terming them and all the rest no better than English churls'. He argued that a fine be imposed on the citizens and put towards the building of a stronghold 'without which the governor and English shall ever be in danger of those odious people upon every drunkard's quarrel'.[17] It is unlikely that anything came of this. It was more often the case that officials were forced to take notice of the grievances expressed on such occasions, and to step back from provocative policies. For example, the disturbances in Limerick in 1599 led to some efforts on the part of the Irish council to limit the numbers cessed on the town, especially those from the troublesome native Irish companies led by Thomond.[18]

On occasion, companies of soldiers themselves showed familiarity with the conventions of protest and some appreciation of the advantages of formal peaceful (if armed) public demonstrations over violent confrontation. For example, the mutiny in May 1590 of the band led by the president of Munster, Thomas Norreys (already mentioned in the context of disturbances in Cork), was initially carried out in an orderly way. Seventy-six soldiers made their way from Limerick to Dublin 'without officer or Ensigne', arriving on 28 May (Ascension Thursday) 'armed and weaponed' and 'with drum and fife' to the gates of Dublin Castle 'and possessed the whole length of the bridg with a martiall warde'. The members of the Irish council who had been attending a meeting of the Court of Castle Chamber were obliged to pass by the soldiers on their exit, and to accede to requests for Sir Edward Waterhouse to present a petition on their behalf. The formally worded petition complained that they had 'remayned without victualling ... and have not of long time had their paye', that their credit was used up and that they were unable 'to endure without reliefs any longer'.

They claimed that they had not been paid in five months, and that the old bands were being neglected, while new bands that had recently been formed were being paid monthly. The situation escalated the following day, when the soldiers rejected offers made to them and attempted to pester members of the council who were on their way on horseback to Christchurch cathedral. As Lord Deputy Fitzwilliam passed the soldiers pressed forward:

> … and besought his Lo[rdship] to have consideration of them, and to be good unto them, with sundry such like words. His Lo. turning his horse about unto them, said, 'What is he that speaks?' They at an instant answered, 'All, all, all!' Whereupon his Lo., as I think, replied to himself only, 'Very well, I will think on you', or some such like speeches, and passed on, being by this time past the armed men about the middest of the bridge.

However, 'one of the shot' demanded money, at which the deputy lost his temper and 'turned his horse upon him, calling him baggage, mutinous knave'. In his attempt to hold back the horse, the soldier raised his gun and the deputy, thinking himself threatened, drew his rapier and called on his retinue to disarm the soldiers, to which they acceded peacefully – in any case, the bridge was so thronged that the soldiers would not have been able to use their weapons. (Sir George Carew noted indignantly that some of the confiscated weapons were stolen in the fracas.) Despite his fury about the incident, Fitzwilliam ended his report to London on a conciliatory note, acknowledging that the soldiers had some cause for complaint given that 'they see some that were but latelie their boies in better condicon then [*sic*] themselves'. Though the perpetrators were imprisoned for a time, they were subsequently pardoned.[19]

In some cases of crowd actions by soldiers, they may have been acting less on their own initiative than on the suggestion or orders of their commanding officers, or at least in the knowledge that their activities would be unlikely to be punished. In September 1628 Richard Rothe, mayor of Kilkenny, described to the Earl of Ormond how that town's mayor of the bullring and former captain of the watch, John Seix, had been taken in for questioning, and imprisoned in the dungeon of the castle of Richard Preston, Earl of Desmond. By some means he was 'made stark drunk', and at eleven in the evening he was brought out by some of the soldiers in Preston's company and 'mounted upon one of the said earl's chief horses, having one of his honour's foot cloths under him'.[20] From the castle he was brought through the town:

> ... having two of either side to bear him up: many torches lighted before him and most of his Majesty's soldiers under his lordship's command being armed and marching before the said Seix with the drum of that company through the city street with matches burning until they came to my house where, being denied entrance [they] left the said Seix prostrate upon the street and discharged two great volleys of shot ... to the great terror of his Majesty's subjects dwelling within this city.

The reason given for the mistreatment of Seix was that, as an officeholder charged with regulating the conduct of the young men of the town and punishing those who frequented brothels and engaged in other sexual misdeeds, he had 'apprehended one for adultery who was a dependant of one of the said Earl of Desmond's servants, and ... committed the said adulterer to prison for his offence by way of punishment'. Whether or not Preston was ultimately behind the humiliation of Seix and the implicit insult to Mayor Rothe, this incident drew attention to the conflicting claims to jurisdiction over an urban area by the corporation, the army and the local magnate. Preston, the recently created earl, sought to take the Earl of Ormond's place as overlord in the Kilkenny area. He had increased pressure on the people of Kilkenny by various actions, including placing cannon on the battlements of his castle 'all bent towards this his Majesty's City of Kilkenny to the great terror of his Majesty's subjects'. Rothe's claim that Seix's ordeal had made other 'officers of the city … terrified in doing of their duty by punishing of offences' may have been exaggerated, but nonetheless it indicates the pressure citizens were under during a period of what David Edwards calls 'crown assault' on Catholic landholding and office-holding.[21]

There are parallels between this case and the disturbances engaged in by the troops of Richard Bingham, the colourful and ruthless president of Connacht, in 1589. When Thomas Jones, bishop of Meath, John Garvey, bishop of Kilmore, Sir Robert Dillon, Sir Nicholas White and others were appointed as commissioners and dispatched to Galway to agree a pacification between Bingham and the O'Flahertys, Burkes and other Connacht lords, the president was reluctant to co-operate. When two of the Burkes and a member of the O'Malley family came to Galway for negotiations, six soldiers, including two recognised as being part of Bingham's company, assaulted the house of Alderman Roebuck French in which the Irish delegates and commissioners were staying, throwing stones at the windows and trying to break down the door. Ten other soldiers stood by to assist the attackers, and the occupants of the house armed themselves to repel any attempt to enter, but none was made. When the commissioners complained, 'Sir Richard excused the soldiers, saying in all likelihood they were soldiers lately come to the town … which sought for lodgings'.

A few days later the commissioners ventured forth from Galway to meet other of the Burkes, including William Burke, the Blind Abbot, claimant to the title of MacWilliam Burke, who had refused to come into the town for fear of their lives. While waiting at St Francis' Abbey for a boat to Newcastle, where the meeting was to take place:

> There came into the Abbey two of Sir Richard's household men, and one of Sir George Bingham's men. Two of them were apparelled in women's mantels and caps, and the third in a black gown. They passed through the abbey into the cloister, we being in the upper part of the chancel. I, the Bishop of Meath, said, Let us go and tarry no longer, for I see they do begin to mock us already. So soon as we were in the boat they three, accompanied by others, came into the chancel, and there challenging to themselves the names of Her Majesty's Commissioners, one said: I am the Bishop of Meath; another said, I am the Bishop of Kilmore; and another said, I am Sir Robt Dillon; and so of the rest. He that challenged the name of the Bishop of Meath began on this wise, saying, Now speaks the Bishop of Meath. You are they which have put out those men into rebellion against Her Majesty, to spoil the country and to hurt the subjects. How are you able to answer this? Another of themselves rose up, and with a low courtesy began to say, I trust your Lordship shall be better informed. To the like effect a descant was made of the other four Commissioners.[22] The three first mentioned actors then in that disguised sort went through the streets of Galway, saying thus: Room for the Queen's Commissioners. I am the Bishop of Meath, said one; another said, I am the Justice Dillon, reverence for the Queen's Commissioners, etc.[23]

Such acts of mockery were particularly provocative since they were directed at men conscious of their dignity as senior clerics and gentlemen and, more importantly, as representatives of the queen herself.

Similar reasons explain why a series of disturbances in Limerick in May 1636 ended up in the Court of Castle Chamber and drew thousands of pounds of fines upon their protagonists. Edmund Sexton, a former mayor and one of the few native Protestants still persisting in that faith in the city, was on his deathbed, and several Protestant clerics who attempted to visit him were energetically impeded by members of his family and neighbours who were themselves Catholics and were determined that he would die in that faith. When ministers did manage to enter the house they were abused, threatened and impeded with 'such an outcrie and Clamor' that they were obliged to desist. Over the next few days when several ministers and the bishop of Limerick himself attempted to visit Sexton's chamber, they were either shut out or, when they managed to enter the house, were impeded in their prayers – even during communion – by noise and were vigorously abused by Sexton's children and wife Joan. On a number of occasions the 'Irish Crye' was raised, bringing large numbers of people to surround the house and intimidate and abuse the clergymen. After Sexton died (as a Catholic, his family claimed), Joan Sexton and Edmund Sexton the younger were convicted of 'high impiety and inhumanity' and fined £5,000 apiece in the Court of Castle Chamber; Joan's daughter Mary was fined £1,000. They were also to be imprisoned, to apologise to the bishop and ministers, to be pilloried in Limerick during the assizes, and to repent of their offences publicly in the Court of Castle Chamber and Four Courts in Dublin. It is unlikely that the fines were ever paid, though some of the other penalties may have been carried out.[24]

The fate of the Sextons is a sign of how confessional allegiance had increasingly made certain Catholics vulnerable to discrimination and prosecution because of their religious stance. Access to formal political structures was also greatly restricted from the later sixteenth century. As attempts intensified to secure the appointment of amenable (and, if possible, Protestant) governors and officials in both Dublin Castle and in the towns, the agents of the state increasingly intervened in election and appointment processes, and in other internal matters. This inevitably led to protests, as was the case during the elections to the Irish Parliament of 1613, discussed elsewhere by Stephen Carroll, when riots broke out in a number of constituencies when attempts were made to ensure the return of Protestant candidates. While some of the disorder was attributed, as in Dublin, to 'the ruder part of the citizens', more detailed accounts demonstrate that it was the freeholders, free citizens and gentlemen of constituencies, and their servants, who became most involved in disturbances, seeking not merely to elect the candidates they favoured, but also to defend their basic right to vote.[25]

Challenges to the moral authority of Ireland's governors were also very evident, on a smaller but still significant scale, on occasions of the capture and execution of those defined as criminals. The state papers make regular reference to the violent rescue of prisoners in Irish towns, particularly priests and members of religious orders. For example, in 1596 a Jesuit captured by the bishop of Limerick was rescued, 'the whole town for the most part rising and taking the prisoner perforce as he was going to jail'.[26] Though the St Stephen's Day riot in Dublin in 1629, dealt with by Mark Empey, was in part provoked by wider political issues, including the cessing of soldiers on Dublin, its immediate cause was the raiding of the Franciscan chapel at Cook Street, and women, youths and country people acted assertively to free some friars who had been seized. Executions likewise might precipitate protests, ranging from 'murmerings', gestures of sympathy towards those condemned, to outright demonstrations, both on the part of the condemned and the audience. The citizens of Galway showed their disapproval in 1589 of the killing, on the orders of Lord Deputy Fitzwilliam, of Armada survivors – whose lives had previously been spared – by ensuring they received spiritual support and proper burials. The Augustinian friars of the town 'who served them as chaplains exhorted them to meet the death struggle bravely', and 'the matrons of Galway piously prepared winding sheets [shrouds] for the bodies'.[27] The best-recorded examples are the cases of those who were perceived to be martyrs for the Catholic faith, such as Bishop Conor O'Devany and Patrick O'Loughran, killed in 1612 for high treason. The citizens of Dublin lined the route, loudly lamenting as the clerics passed, stormed the gallows to gather relics from their bodies and spent the night in 'heathenish howling' and attending masses at the execution site.[28]

On many of these occasions it is clear that religious grievances fed (but were not the sole cause of) tensions between government officials and townspeople. Religious feeling might ignite conflict at other times of heightened emotion as well. For example, a number of reports of riots at funerals survive from the early seventeenth century, especially at times when Protestant ministers sought to take over the funerals of Catholic women.[29]

There was room also in Ireland's towns for rather more straightforward cases of riot when groups sought to defend their economic and personal interests. In May 1641 groups of women were involved in food riots in Belfast (problems of restricted food supplies, compounded by the necessity of victualling Wentworth's Irish army, also caused conflict elsewhere in April and May that year).[30] Special interest groups and corporate bodies such as members of town corporations and trade guilds might act in concert to preserve their rights, privileges and property. In Youghal in 1616, the Company of Butchers 'disturbing the markets and taking away the victuals of foreign butchers [i.e. those not possessing the freedom of the town] resorting hither, were for their misdemeanour many of them committed to the marshall's [prison]; the ringleaders were fined, and paid their several fines before they were discharged'.[31] That year a group of aldermen, merchants and 'Dyvers other of the Inhabitantes' of Limerick, led by their mayor, William Hally, were accused of plotting to entangle Edmund Sexton (he whose tumultuous deathbed has been mentioned) in lawsuits over his possession of 'the late Abbey or Monestery Called St Maryhouse'. The abbey had been granted to Sexton's grandfather, also called Edmund Sexton, following the dissolution of the monasteries in the 1540s, but the corporation had long claimed it, and the matter must have become more urgent when Sexton started building there. On 4 August 1615, the conspirators 'armed in warlike and hostile manner with swords, head peeces, gunnes, staves and other weapons offensive and defensive' had gone to the site and driven away carpenters working there, returning four days later to 'dispoyle, breake and plucke downe to the ground the mayne tymber of the house the said Edmund Sexten [*sic*] had then lately sett uppe and erected upon the said tenements'.[32] It is a scene reminiscent of English enclosure riots, where the privatisation of communal resources often provoked robust defiance.[33] Sexton was a determined adversary, and the case ended up in the Court of Castle Chamber, the mayor being fined £20 and eighteen others £10 each.

However, the butchers of Youghal were prosecuted within their own town, and it is unlikely that their fines were unusually high, or that they were imprisoned for very long. In a town the size of Youghal, those charged with dealing with them would also have been their friends, neighbours and customers. Before the crown started on a more determined course to check their powers in the seventeenth century, the citizens of Ireland's towns were generally protected from serious repercussions by the special legal status conferred by their charters, even on occasions of more serious disturbances. The judicial powers accorded to the mayors or sovereigns of corporate towns, and other officials, allowed them considerable leeway in arresting and releasing alleged malefactors, and it is clear that they often exercised their rights in a manner that prioritised and protected their own interests and those of their colleagues.

One report from the late 1590s claimed that 'The mayors are justices of peace, but they never apprehend or commit any traitors, though many in their times have been committed by others; but their service consisteth in bailing, in enlarging, and rescuing prisoners.'[34] It was alleged that their special privileges allowed considerable room for stonewalling, evasion and partiality, with the result that, rather than attracting punishment, certain kinds of urban crowd actions – and even murders – were ignored or even colluded in by town authorities. The killing of soldiers in Limerick during the 1599 riots was effectively condoned by the mayor: the coroner's court over which he presided failed to find anyone guilty of murder. If a mayor or sovereign refused to exercise his judicial powers over the free citizens of a town and their families, they were effectively immune from prosecution, unless a plaintiff had the wherewithal to pursue a case in the Court of Castle Chamber. Increasingly, however, clashes arose between town officials and the garrisons housed within their walls, as attempts to exempt soldiers from civil law and subject them instead to martial law threatened the mayors' authority.[35]

Their anomalous legal position was clearly exploited by soldiers, especially those not of officer status, to excuse or explain riotous actions. Military men could to some extent claim to be outside the law, since they were subject to the orders of their captain, and could demand the right to be tried according to martial rather than civil law. Their frequent involvement in disturbances must thus be attributed not only to the fact that they had weapons and knew what to do with them, but also to hard-headed calculations about the likely repercussions. Likewise, when seventy-six men, or when corporate bodies such as members of corporations or trade guilds, acted in concert to defend their interests they effectively spread, and at the same time minimised, the potential consequences to individuals.

John Walter's comments on the concern of early modern crowds with 'how to have a riot and not get done for it' are pertinent here. His article on 'Faces in the crowd' reminds us that early modern crowds were socially diverse. The involvement of members of the highest echelons of town society in protest reminds us also that crowds were not necessarily solely made up of members of the lower orders. The mayor and aldermen of Limerick were prominent participants in the riots of 1599 and the attack on Edmund Sexton's property in 1615, and the election riots of 1612 involved the gentlemen, landowners and free citizens who sought to defend their rights to vote.

Walter also points out that crowds comprised both men and women, and the early modern crowd was often youthful.[36] For example, youths and women were prominently involved in the 1629 St Stephen's Day riot, and in Limerick in 1636 Edmund Sexton's wife, his youngest son and two of his daughters were the prime movers in the riots over his soul and his dying body. There was a tactical element to their activities, since women and young people could easily justify their actions by stressing their vulnerability and innocence: mistreatment of them went against the duty of those in power to protect the weak and helpless, and drawing attention to this brought shame on the perpetrators. Moreover, since in law they were technically subject to their fathers, masters or husbands they were less likely to be prosecuted than men.[37]

As Mark Harrison has commented, 'there is a theatrical element in almost every large gathering of people'.[38] In Ireland, as elsewhere in Europe, we see the theatrical and tactical exploitation of space, symbol and ritual, of special times and meaningful gestures, by protesting crowds. Above all, such crowds exhibited a strong sense of space and place: the aim was to draw attention to grievances, so the more prominent the place of protest, the wider the audience and the more effectively that aim was fulfilled. The fact that even the largest of Ireland's towns and cities were relatively small focused protest into certain areas and ensured it was noticed by most of the inhabitants. In Galway in 1589, for example, Bingham's cross-dressed soldiers initially made their point to the peace commissioners as they waited for a boat in St Francis' Abbey, outside the walls, but then repeated their demonstrations in the streets of the city. An audience also helped to minimise the repercussions for those involved. Once there were witnesses for their actions, it would be more difficult for officials to retaliate, to shirk responsibility for dealing with grievances or to trump up charges in retrospect. Norreys' mutinous company brought their petition in person right to the gates of Dublin Castle, the greatest symbol of crown authority in Ireland. By gathering at the gate they ensured that the councillors would eventually have to deal with their requests. In the butchers' riot in Youghal in 1616, the participants targeted their competitors in the market place, rather than waylaying them outside the town: punishment was therefore inevitable, but the aim of challenging the interlopers and differentiating them from themselves was achieved. In Kilkenny in 1628 the unfortunate John Seix was conveyed through the centre of the town to the mayor's house, and despite the late hour 'many torches' were lit to illuminate the proceedings.

In certain riots, the participants can be seen to discriminate between potential sites of confrontation. Donald Horowitz talks of crowds being 'risk-averse', choosing locations for protest that reduced the danger to participants.[39] In Limerick in 1599, displeasure with the soldiers cessed on the city was publicly displayed when they were attacked in residential streets and then in St Mary's cathedral, but the fact that the citizens avoided conflict at the dilapidated fortress of King John's Castle, called 'the queen's castle', made the point that they were not challenging the person of the monarch but the abuses of those who claimed to act in her name.[40] Fittingly, the public spaces of towns were used also to disseminate warnings to those who might consider disturbing the peace. In Youghal in 1624, 'Several proclamations from the Lord Deputy and Council of Ireland in regard of riots and unlawful assemblies were read in the most noted parts of the town': the procedure was probably replicated in other major towns.[41]

Riot and revel were interlinked. There was a large degree of cross-pollination between traditional festive customs and popular protest. The use in the 1599 Limerick riot of a game as an excuse for riot is familiar from England, where rioters might use football matches or other games as a cover for the assembly of crowds with more illegal intent. If it resembled any of its later namesakes, the game of 'fox to hole' in which the boys of Limerick were engaged would have been a rowdy one, in which it would have been easy to cause or manufacture offence.[42] That games could easily lead to confrontations is seen by an ordinance in Clonmel in 1640 'to prevent severall abuses frequently committed at the footebale': once the portreeve of the town had signalled the end of the game, anyone continuing to play 'shalbe comitted and punished as a breaker of the peace and a violater of the laws of the kingdome'.[43]

It is also clear that, as elsewhere, Irish rioters 'often drew on rituals already familiar to many from the festive calendar to rally protestors'.[44] The soldiers who dressed in clerical and women's clothing in protests against the activities of the peace commissioners in Galway in 1589 reflected the element of cross-dressing and disguise that was common in popular festivities on holidays like Halloween and Christmas. The activities of Preston's troops in Kilkenny in 1628, when they brought a drunken John Seix through the town riding on the Earl of Desmond's chief horse, which was dressed with the earl's own richly embroidered 'foot-cloth', drew many of its elements from English skimmington traditions. Skimmingtons, also called rough music, ridings or riding the stang, were crowd actions usually designed to punish and shame those responsible for domestic violence, adultery, cuckoldry or scolding, usually involving the forcible public 'riding' of the victim on a mule, broom handle or cowlstaff (used for carrying heavy loads over the shoulders).[45] They were also used against officials charged with wrongful prosecutions (as Seix was in this case, since he had apprehended an alleged adulterer) or inadequate decision-making and, it seems, against soldiers 'whose behavior ... endangered relations with the civil populace'.[46] In an inversion of the standard procedure, rather than being carried on a miserable mount, Seix was brought on a richly appointed thoroughbred. The implication was that Seix had usurped the earl's authority, and being deposited prostrate in the street returned him to his rightful station. The insult also targeted the mayor, who was powerless to prevent this mistreatment of one of his officials, to protect the townspeople from the fright they experienced at being woken by the noise of drums and shooting or to punish the perpetrators. Mockery and laughter are often overlooked elements of crowd actions. We assume riot and protest to be a serious business, but it was often more effective to undermine targets by the use of scorn and derision than to subject them to violence.

Certain times of the year might likewise allow crowds a degree of festive licence that left room for the expression of grievances. The most obvious case of this is the 1629 St Stephen's Day riot, but it is possible to point to other occasions as well. For example, it may not be a coincidence that Norreys' troops mutinied and proceeded to Dublin in Rogation week in 1590, arriving to present their petition on Ascension Thursday.[47] The authorities badly misjudged the timing of the execution of O'Devany and O'Loughran, carrying it out on 1 February 1612, St Bridget's Day and the eve of the important Marian festival of Candlemas, used by the citizens as an excuse to prolong the demonstrations and masses said on that occasion.[48] That the 1599 Limerick riot occurred on the day after St Martin's Day, the feast day associated with young men, may also be significant.[49] From the examples cited above, it seems that the summer months, especially May, were the most likely times for crowd actions to occur. This was the campaigning season for troops, and could be a time when food shortages began to bite as stores began to run low in advance of the new harvest. But the festivities of May, Rogation tide, Corpus Christi, Midsummer and Lúnasa may also have provided the carnivalesque intervals and imaginative resources that prompted and facilitated protest.[50]

Noise was a standard element. Shouting, clapping, music and shooting are all noted as being used during Irish crowd actions. A drum and fife announced the 1590 mutineers, Preston's soldiers in 1628 had their drummer precede them and finished proceedings with a volley of shot, and the citizens of Galway in 1580 marched through the streets to the sound of drums, loudly excoriating the 'English churls' in their midst. Bell-ringing may also have featured. Some British and Irish towns kept a bell that might be sounded in times of crisis to warn the citizens – Dublin housed one such bell in the tholsel, and during the election riots of 1612 attempts were made to ring 'the alarum', but it was under lock and key.[51] Noise registered protest and drew attention. Sound could fill and, metaphorically, take over a space; it could unite performers and hearers in a common action; and it could intimidate people or evoke emotions like indignation or sorrow. However, certain elements of the soundscape of Irish protests were quite unusual.

Two key vocal acts or performances seem to have been extremely important: 'raising the cry' and keening. In the case of the 1599 Limerick riot in St Mary's, hundreds of armed men arrived promptly when the cry was raised; in the disturbances at the house of Edmund Sexton in 1636, the raising of the cry immediately brought reinforcements ready and willing to intervene on the side of the Sexton family. The Castle Chamber proceedings even give some detail on the manner of the raising of the cry: at one point 'Joane Sexton went upp into an upper roome of the said howse and putt her hands out of a window and clapped her hands, and raised the Irish Crye', leading to the arrival of so many people that soldiers needed to be called to disperse them. The performance thus involved both the noise of the cry and the gesture of clapping the hands.[52] In the medieval period in Britain, the whole community had been obliged to turn out to attempt to apprehend malefactors once the 'hue and cry' was raised. However, though the tradition of hue and cry has been little studied for the early modern period, it seems that in most areas of England at least, communities were no longer expected to participate in such hunts and the cry gradually fell into disuse. Some Irish towns, however, renewed the obligation to answer the cry in the sixteenth century – in 1505 Galway corporation passed an ordinance that 'every man that answerith not the crye or skrimishe[53] at every of the town gates, at the beginning, with his feansabull [defensive] weapon, to pay and forfayte xii*d*'.[54]

What Barnaby Rich dismissively called 'the Irish Hubbub' was still alive and well over 100 years later: he sneered at the frequency with which the Irish raised the cry, even 'upon … sleight occasions', and also at the fact that 'as these Hubbubs are thus raised in cases of anger and discontent, so they use to give the Hubbub againe in matters of sport and merriment'. Fynes Moryson recorded that the Irish 'are by nature very Clamorous, upon every small occasion raysing the hobou (that is a dolefull outcrye) which they take one from anothers mouthe till they putt the whole towne in tumult'. Edmund Spenser seems to have seen the hubbub as being so removed from hue and cry that he believed that 'the manner of raysinge their Crye in their conflictes, and at other troblesome tymes of uprore' was a remnant of the Scythian origins of the Irish.[55] The cry had the potential to create consternation and escalate minor incidents into major ones. For example, one of the charges against Charles Egerton, constable of Carrickfergus Castle, who with several of the warders had assaulted Captain Rice Mannfyelde on 18 August 1596, was that as a result 'a great tumult and outcrye was raised in the saide towne of Carrigfergus', and the intervention of the townspeople could have caused 'great peril to all her maties Guarrison theire' except that the town's mayor and 'some well affected' had calmed the situation.[56]

Spenser distinguished the Irish hubbub from the 'other soarts of cryes, allso used among the Irishe … as their lamentacons at their burialles, with dispairefull outcryes, and imoderate waylinges', so seemingly the two sounds were different to one another.[57] Seventeenth-century writers noted that funeral keening, like raising the cry, was both a physical and a vocal performance. Keening women accompanied the lament with gestures such as the loosening and tearing of the hair and clothing, the clapping and raising of the hands, the embracing of the dying or dead person, and even the drinking of their blood. Anthropologists and folklorists who have looked at ritual laments in Ireland and in other parts of Europe, especially Greece, have commented on their role not only in expressing sorrow for the dead but as an outlet for protest that was particularly important for women – a 'weapon of the weak'. Laments might chastise the deceased person for dying and leaving his wife and family behind, or might even berate him for his mistreatment of them during life.[58] In the case of those condemned to death, the keen might be used to protest at the authorities as well as to mourn the fate of the victim. The importance of ritual lament to Irish protest is clear when Rich talks of the citizens of Dublin watching the progress of Bishop O'Devany to execution crying 'as if Saint Patricke himself had bin going to the gallowes' and then spending 'the fore part of the night in heathenish howling': that latter in particular must have been especially intimidating as the Protestants of the city lay in their beds. A Catholic account of the execution confirmed that 'when he was mounting the scaffold, the people raised a terrible wail, and shed copious tears, and uttered such tender laments that even the executioners were softened'.[59] But the mix of protest with mourning seems to be evident at other executions as well and is likely to have been part of the reason for a scene witnessed by William Brereton in 1636, when he watched a condemned man being led back to the castle in Wexford following the Assizes: 'the women and some other following making lamentation, sometimes so violent as though they were distracted, sometimes as it were in a kind of tune singing; one of them ('twas said) was his wife'.[60]

Brereton's chance note of this spectacle reminds us again of the difficulties of divining the true extent of protest in early modern Ireland, and understanding its meaning. We can be so caught up in the activities of British governors, Old English elites and Irish nobles that we sometimes miss the voices of the ordinary people of Ireland, natives and newcomers, as they negotiated their places in a changing society. The authorities in Ireland gave them more credit, believing they did have strong opinions and might act to defend their rights. We see in many cases that protest had some impact, especially when used in combination with other resistance tactics such as petitioning, lobbying and non-cooperation. As in England, the authorities were often forced to treat popular grievances seriously. Protest, especially protest with the threat or use of violence, reminded those in charge that some element of consent was needed in return for acquiescence to their rule. By distinguishing 'faces in the crowd', by attending to the use of space, time, ritual and gesture, and by listening as their voices express opinions, rather than closing our ears to a meaningless hubbub, we can get closer to the experiences of the ordinary inhabitants of early modern Ireland.

2

THE DUBLIN PARLIAMENTARY ELECTIONS, 1613[1]

STEPHEN CARROLL

Reflecting upon the parliamentary elections of 1613, the Protestant commentator William Farmer declared that:

> … many hollow-hearted papists were produced for knights of the shire and burgesses of the parliament, and amongst all other[s] many of the citizens of Dublin, who were always accounted the patrons of loyalty … and paragons of obedience to the kings of England, were now found to be possessed with other spirits.[2]

Farmer questioned the loyalty of Irishmen because of their choice of Catholic candidates for Parliament, but he cited the citizens of Dublin in particular, as they had remained loyal subjects until 1613, when they instigated a tumult in the tholsel court of the city council. The fracas arose from a number of grievances, which reached tipping point in the tense atmosphere prior to Parliament. Catholics on Dublin city council had experienced the silencing of their political voice, a challenge to their religious beliefs and the loss of customs privileges. They saw a new Protestant elite taking on responsibilities traditionally reserved for them. This alienation pushed them into alliance with an emerging Catholic interest in the country as a whole. This chapter will analyse their actions to show how Catholics on the council expressed their political consciousness in a period of transformation.

English monarchs, since the conquest of 1171, had bestowed privileges on Dublin through charters and parliamentary acts, granting it certain trade exemptions and a measure of self-governance. Throughout periods of expansion and contraction, the port towns had largely remained loyal to the crown, protecting the colony from the Gaelic Irish within and foreign intrigue without. The wars of the late Elizabethan period attested Dublin's loyalty to the English administration. The city council used its revenue to defend the city from rebels, maintaining a watch by night and day. At night there was a standing watch of twenty at the gates and on the walls, and a running watch of twenty in the town. Short-term loans from Dublin merchants to the government offset delays in shipping treasure from London or in raising cess (tax).[3]

In April and May 1603, following the death of Elizabeth and the conclusion of the Nine Years' War, a number of hitherto loyal Leinster and Munster towns asserted their corporate independence and liberty of conscience by rising up in arms and openly celebrating mass. Dublin had remained aloof in this cause, yet the new administration of Sir Arthur Chichester focused on the city for a revival of the Reformation in Ireland. In targeting the Catholic clergy and the city's elite, Chichester hoped to bring Dublin and, in turn, all Ireland to conformity in religion. To Chichester, Dublin was 'the lantern of this whole kingdom, & in this matter the only place whereon the eyes and expectation of all the rest are earnestly fastened'.[4] The city council came under scrutiny from November 1604 as Chichester insisted the leading officers of the city take the oath of supremacy to the king – an oath, so leading Jesuits insisted, that a Catholic ought not to take.[5] This ensured that subsequent mayors, recorders and leading sheriffs would be conforming Protestant men. The following November twenty-two wealthy citizens, many aldermen among them, were issued with letters or mandates calling on them to attend Protestant worship.[6] Failure to obey these missives resulted in heavy fines and imprisonment. The unenthusiastic response to this policy by the English privy council brought an end to the sending of mandates in summer 1607, yet this provocation caused lasting resentment among the elite.[7]

On 4 July 1605 a proclamation ordered all clergy deriving their authority from Rome to leave the country by 10 December that year. The proclamation outlined the perceived threat the clergy posed: they 'not only seduce our people there to embrace their superstitious Ceremonies, but do maliciously endeavor to alienate the hearts of our Subjects from Us, by insinuating and breeding a distaste in them, both of our Religion and civil government'.[8] Priests, and Jesuits especially, were viewed as fomenters of rebellion, a permanent link between Ireland and Spain. This link led to periodic rumours of invasion, particularly following the Flight of the Earls to the continent in 1607.[9] In February 1612 the Dublin government, acting on directions from London urging the exemplary punishment of clergy, executed two Catholic clerics on charges of treason.[10] The execution of Bishop Conor O'Devany and Fr Patrick O'Loughran proved to be a huge public event in the city, with the streets thronged with people. Among the crowd were said to be the wives and relatives of leading citizens. Both Protestant and Catholic commentators noted the huge numbers present at the execution site, from which people took away countless relics.[11] The two clergymen were subsequently venerated as martyrs, strengthening the resolve of the Catholic populace and creating further tension between them and Dublin Castle just before Parliament convened.

The merchants of Dublin found it was not just their religious beliefs that London was challenging, but also their trading privileges, as the Dublin and London governments sought to maximise crown revenues in Ireland. Following the financially crippling Nine Years' War, the government targeted port cities and began moves to end their customs exemptions. In 1608 Dublin lost the right to keep the great and petty customs of the city in negotiations between their agents, Richard Bolton and Robert Ball, and the king's judges at Serjeants Inn in London. Their right to poundage was upheld by an Act of Parliament of 1500 that exempted the freemen of Dublin, Drogheda and Waterford from this duty.[12] However, the collection of poundage was to form the basis of a customs farm that was being auctioned off in London court circles. The crown stood to profit greatly from this auction, thereby pushing the Dublin government to more forceful measures. In October 1611 the crown used the great seal of Ireland to create a customs payment comparable to poundage in Dublin, Drogheda and Waterford, thereby by-passing the statutory exemption of freemen outlined in 1500. Without the assent of merchants from these cities, the new tax was likely to face resistance in the courts, so an Act of Parliament would be needed.[13]

In his study of the 1585–6 Parliament, Victor Treadwell has shown that opposition to cess brought about a 'principled political opposition' divided along confessional lines.[14] The course pursued by Chichester – manipulating city politics, enforcing religious conformity and removing economic privileges – ensured consolidation of grievances, creating a distinct opposition interest group. On 20 November 1610 the lord deputy called the leading lords, knights and gentlemen to Dublin and announced his intention to call a parliament the following year. By 4 December the city council of Dublin had set up a subcommittee to 'consider what is meet to be provided in Parliament for the good of the city'.[15] Its four Catholic aldermen, four Protestant aldermen and Protestant mayor would find common ground on a number of points, but the confessional divide must have caused some dissension in the council. Correspondence in the lead-up to the elections shows the fractured nature of society in Ireland. On 14 April 1613 Chichester wrote that the 'contrary faction are now in consultation daily, with their Lawyers Jesuits and Seminary Priests' working out how to 'make their party Strong and to give impediments unto the designs in hand … suspecting some hard Laws to be conceived and carried against them by the greater Number of Voices' on the government side.[16] The Catholic elite in Dublin had close experience of the 'designs' of Chichester's government, to oppose which they needed a majority of voices in the Commons.

The government employed various tactics in the two years prior to Parliament to ensure they had 'the greater Number of Voices'. During Sir George Carew's visit to Ireland in 1611 he drafted a report on the 'Motives of importance for holding a parliament in Ireland' in which he bluntly spelled out ways to ensure a Protestant majority in the Commons.[17] Bríd McGrath divides these measures into three categories: controlling the selection of mayors and sheriffs (who acted as returning officers), arranging for the return of specific government supporters and the creation of new boroughs.[18] In his report, Carew compiled a list of every county, town and borough and the likely returns for each. For the city of Dublin he expected the return of two Protestants, the recorder (Sir Richard Bolton) and an unnamed alderman. As the offices of sheriff, recorder and mayor all had to subscribe to the oath of supremacy, Carew doubtless thought they would use their influence in the elections.

A look at the abstracts of bills intended for the Parliament confirms the fears of Catholics at that time, as they contained measures to repeal the 1500 statute exempting freemen from poundage and banishing priests. Another bill 'authorising Commissioners to give the oath of Allegiance unto all the subjects of Ireland' had the potential to become a penal measure to restrict Catholics' access to political office.[19] Six Catholic lords from the Pale petitioned the king in November 1612 about their fears, which broadly represented the feelings of Catholic elites at the time. They protested against the lack of consultation on bills for the coming Parliament and expressed their fear that a majority Protestant assembly would pass 'extreme penal laws' against them. They also condemned 'the deposing of so many magistrates in the cities and boroughs of this kingdom, for not swearing the oath of supremacy in spiritual and ecclesiastical causes'.[20] This defence of the rights of cities and boroughs shows a unity of purpose among Catholics prior to Parliament, forging links that would be used in later conflicts between the Catholic 'party' and the Dublin government.

With a gulf emerging between government supporters and a 'contrary faction', the securing of a majority of voices in Parliament became crucial. The field of electoral politics in this period was far from an exact science, however, as there was no definitive set of rules or precedents to follow. Both Irish and English returning officers followed local practice, which differed from county to county, town to town and borough to borough. Returning officers followed the precedent prevailing in the area, yet also had to be mindful of the influence of a powerful local lord or member of the elite who could be expected to exert his influence to secure the return of members for Parliament. The influence of the elite had a considerable impact on the choice of those returned, as the principle of a majority of voices securing an election did not necessarily apply. For instance, in two election disputes – Worcestershire in 1605 and Yorkshire in 1625 – the 'quality' of the voters for each candidate was examined rather than which side carried the majority.[21] At Helston the majority was deemed to be whichever side the mayor was on.[22] Majority rule predicated that each voice counted equally, yet this principle violated the social norms by which people lived at the time by according equal power to a gent and a shirtless man.[23] In studying English procedure, Mark Kishlansky notes the rarity of contests before 1640, arguing that when they did emerge 'contests grew from conflict within the elite'.[24] In Ireland this could be more appropriately be termed 'conflicts between the elites' because the elections in 1569 and 1585 witnessed what Treadwell terms a 'country party' emerging to challenge candidates put forward by the Dublin government.[25]

Under these difficult circumstances the sheriffs of Dublin held the election on 20 April 1613 in the tholsel court. It passed off without incident, as the sheriffs made indentures for two Catholic aldermen, Francis Taylor and Thomas Allen, with no details of whether there had been any rival candidates or a poll. Upon hearing the result, the Protestant mayor, Sir James Carroll, declared the returns to be unlawful because the election had been held while he was out of the city, at the county election at Kilmainham. Whether or not the mayor of Dublin had authority in this regard is a question worth investigating, with a variety of explanations emerging from the records. A petition delivered to the king from Catholic agents in May 1613 shows they regarded the sheriffs as the rightful returning officers.[26] The solicitor-general of Ireland, Sir Robert Jacob, reported that the sheriffs had usurped the mayor's right to hold the election, adding oddly that the sheriffs attempted to hold an election on 19 April, for which the mayor reproved them.[27] William Farmer wrote that the mayor and sheriffs received the warrant for the election,[28] whereas the commissioners' report of November 1613 recorded that the sheriffs received the warrant on 1 April and next day granted this authority to the mayor.[29] The issue raises questions over the perceived authority of the mayor in the eyes of the aldermen. Sir James Carroll had been elected as an alderman only weeks before he rose to the mayoralty in place of his father, Alderman Thomas Carroll, who would not take the oath of supremacy.[30] The position of mayor traditionally fell to the most senior alderman yet to serve, a custom severely disrupted by the policies of Chichester's government. Sir James Carroll's willingness to conform, and his close alliance to the lord deputy, had brought him wealth, recognition and power, yet this may have alienated him from the Catholic aldermen.[31] The sheriffs John Francton and Edmond Cullon were both Protestants, but their acceptance of the results of the first election showed that they had closer ties to the Catholic-dominated city council than to their Protestant mayor.

In his description of the election, Jacob called Francis Taylor and Thomas Allen 'two of the most Spanish and seditious Schismatics in all the city'. He ascribed their return in part to the 'Counsel of [William] Talbott & [Sir Patrick] Barnewall the Lawyers', and saw this election as part of a desire among Catholics to choose 'men long since agreed upon & appointed by the priests for those places, which indeed are for the most part the very firebrands of sedition, the most open and apparent enemies to the state, and the principal opposers against the present government'.[32] Yet Francis Taylor remained a loyal citizen and possessed the ideal attributes for a representative of the city: he had not been prosecuted for recusancy, had been treasurer and attorney-general of the city and had served as mayor. His absence from mandates proceedings may owe much to the conformity of his son, James Taylor, who served as sheriff in 1605–6. Thomas Allen was sheriff in 1608–9 and had close ties to leading Dublin families, a well-connected man probably chosen for his religious conviction.[33]

Having voided the returns of 20 April, Mayor Carroll called for a fresh election to be held at the tholsel court at four o'clock on the morning of 21 April. Elections at the time were normally held between eight and nine in the morning, though some held in 1613 deviated slightly from this prescription.[34] The calling of snap elections, delaying tactics and the movement of venue were all means used by returning officers to favour their preferred candidates. The Catholic members of the city council may have pressed the sheriffs into holding the election in the mayor's absence to secure their candidates. The unusual time did not deter the aldermen and free citizens, who attended the tholsel court in numbers. Considering that the majority of free citizens likely to attend were Catholic, who would once again find in favour of their candidates, the mayor invited all the male inhabitants of the city to the tholsel court to take part in the election. It can be assumed that Mayor Carroll invited men that he knew would represent his political and religious convictions. Inviting un-free men into the tholsel court to take part in the election caused outrage among the sheriffs and aldermen, who 'commanded all those that were not freemen to depart'.[35] The Catholic agents' petition of May 1613 to the king described the presence of 'diverse men that were not free of the city with [their] serving men'.[36] By contrast, Farmer's commentary on the dispute described the division as one between 'English' (meaning English Protestant) and 'Irish' (meaning Irish Catholic), neglecting to mention the debate over free and un-free members of the city. In presenting the dispute as solely religious in nature, Farmer misrepresented its origins.[37]

Mayor Carroll made use here of the uncertainty of electoral

politics, as the franchise of Dublin was not clearly defined. The aldermen and sheriffs felt that only those who were freemen of the city could choose candidates for Parliament, whereas the mayor defended his right to extend this privilege to all inhabitants. The freemen believed the mayor, by opening up the franchise, had violated their privileges. In taking the civic oath, they had accepted a trade-off between a freeman's onerous tasks and his right to certain exemptions and self-governance.[38] The freemen in the tholsel court reacted angrily to this supposed infringement of their ancient liberties. Farmer reported that 'those of the recusant faction would not suffer any Englishman or any other to speak but such as they knew to be recusants', and 'being the greatest number, quickly thrust all the English men with violence out of the doors'.[39]

Jacob reported that the sheriffs and aldermen debated with the mayor over the presence of un-free men within the tholsel and threatened to remove them from the election. They then 'required the mayor to either be silent and suffer them to proceed as they would, or else presently to depart'. Upon his refusal to do so 'the whole house of the conspirators fell in an uproar, some of the Aldermen shaking their fists at the mayor reviling and threatening him ... crying pull out those Protestants by the ears'. In this mêlée a cry went out to 'ring the Tholsel bell, and gather the young men and apprentices together, that they may pluck them out by the ears'.[40] It was said that a former sheriff, Nicholas Stevens, 'would have rung the alarum with the tholsel bell if he could have found the key'.[41] The ringing of bells in the early modern period had different connotations depending on context, yet ringing the tholsel bell at four in the morning surely signified a call to arms. During the Nine Years' War the city council organised the defence of the city walls, with an 'alarum or sudden cry' being the call for each ward to arm itself and repair to its assigned post.[42] Jacob reported that the ringing of the tholsel bell was 'never done but of purpose to draw the people in Arms, when there [was] any sudden commotion or Insurrection in the City'.[43]

This 'great tumult and mutiny' lasted 'for the space of a quarter of an Hour' whereupon, having failed to ring the tholsel bell, the crowd 'made such a loud confused Noise, that drove great numbers of people about the House, ready to put in execution whatsoever should be directed unto them by those of their faction'.[44] Attention focused on the mayor: some 'offered to lay hand upon the Kings sword that was before the mayor but the mayor in this hurly burly took the sword in his own hand and went to the Lord Deputy to complain'.[45] The sword represented the mayor's authority, both martial and civic, as bestowed on him by the lord deputy. Attempting to wrest the sword from the mayor was a symbolic challenge to his authority, but also a physical threat to his means of defence. Though largely decorative, the king's sword had been used by Mayor Thomas Barbie in 1531 to quell a riot between soldiers and apprentices.[46]

Were the events of 21 April 1613 a 'riotous assembly'? Those writing at the time variously described them as a 'tumult',[47] a 'tumultuous outrage',[48] a 'great tumult and mutiny'[49] or a 'tumultuous and rebellious disorder'.[50] The term 'riot' has long carried direct legal connotations, of course. In Ireland's first Riot Act, that of 1787, an action could be punished as riot only if twelve or more people refused to disperse within an hour of the reading of a passage from the Riot Act by a magistrate, or a crown or other local official.[51] For the purposes of this study, a handbook written for Irish justices of the peace in 1638 is an ideal guide to answer this query. The author, Sir Richard Bolton, was a principal actor in the tumult, served as recorder for the city council and was returned as one of the city's two representatives in Parliament the following month. Using handbooks written by English legal experts for English justices of the peace and based on his own knowledge of the Irish legal system, Bolton provided definitions and procedures to be followed by commissioners of the peace. In defining a riot, Bolton stressed the need for the existence of prior intent for an act to be considered unlawful, whereas if 'diverse [people], being lawfully assembled, shall quarrel or fall out upon the sudden without any former intent, this is no riot, but a sudden Affray'.[52] The citizens at the tholsel court met lawfully, without intent to commit unlawful acts, so in Bolton's terms the outbreak ought to have been defined as a 'sudden affray', rather than a riot.

Although this affray spilled over into violence against the un-free members of the crowd, the level of force employed was low and the assaults were symbolic gestures rather than causing physical harm or destruction of property. In removing the un-free from the assembly place, the crowd was defending its privilege as freemen to meet and return its own candidates to Parliament, physically excluding those with no stake in the running of the city council. In calling for the ringing of the tholsel bell, the citizens sought to draw attention to the violation of their ancient privileges, intending to rally the city to their cause. Finally, the attempted confiscation of the mayoral sword represented a desire to remove the regalia of power bestowed on the mayor by the lord deputy. The fact that the mayor 'gave forth of the House, and then went to the lord deputy to advertise him of this tumultuous and rebellious disorder' further shows the loss of authority of the mayor, who fled his tholsel court to seek protection from his patron, Lord Deputy Chichester.[53]

In the aftermath of this disorder, Chichester 'sent for the Ringleaders of this unlawfull assembly, & openly explaining the matter, bound over the sheriffs to answer their misdemeanors in the Star chamber', owing to their 'choosing the burgesses before the mayor came home'. Afterwards '6 or 7' aldermen were committed to the castle and '12 or 14 others were afterwards committed to other prisons'. For his attempt to ring the tholsel bell Nicholas Stevens received exemplary punishment, being committed to the castle with the aldermen and 'threatened to be executed by Martial Law as a Traitor'. The petition of the Catholic agents criticises the harsh treatment of Stevens 'who was continually kept in fetters & at length warning was sent to him to provide himself for death'. According to Jacob, the accused 'were delivered of their imprisonment within 5 or 6 days after, and are now as Jolly as ever they were'.[54]

Six days after the failed second election at the tholsel court, a third and final election was held at Hoggen Green to the east of the city, outside the city walls. It is likely that the prisoners were kept six days rather than five so that the election could be held while the leading aldermen were in prison. Moving the election from the tholsel building clearly showed that the lord deputy distrusted the city council's ability to hold an election; an outdoor site, away from the cramped tholsel court, presumably ensured a more settled election contest with less chance for disorder. The Catholic 'party' present 'ceased not still to uphold and maintain their former election of Alderman Taylor, and Alderman Allen', whereas the Protestant 'party' chose Richard Bolton and Richard Barry. Each freeman called out their preferred candidates in a process called the 'voice'. Uncertain which party held the majority, the mayor 'willed them to sever themselves' in a process known as the 'view'. The Catholic petitioners later complained that the mayor failed to use the 'poll' as a final means of deciding the election, even though, in their eyes, 'the far greater number appeared to be for Taylor and Allen'.[55] A commissioners' report of November 1613 found that the mayor ordered the two sides to divide and upon seeing the two separated found for Bolton and Barry, without needing to conduct a poll. The report found that the two sheriffs and thirteen others believed Bolton and Barry carried the majority, while fifteen others, among them aldermen, deposed that in their opinion Taylor and Allen held a majority.[56] The position of the two sheriffs in this final election is interesting, as they found for Bolton and Barry. Both had received a 'heavy check' following their return of Taylor and Allen in the first election, and had sided with the aldermen in the call to remove the un-free members from the tholsel court.[57] Neither Jacob nor Farmer cited Richard Barry by name in their accounts, possibly owing to his relatively low status among the aldermen. Sir Richard Bolton, however, had represented the city in the customs negotiations and held the role of recorder, a position that had produced an MP for the city in the four previous parliaments.[58]

The rise to prominence of men like Richard Bolton, Richard Barry and Sir James Carroll shows the threat that the Catholic elite faced following the Nine Years' War, as their loyalty continued to be questioned by the Dublin government. The privileges that the city had enjoyed were rapidly being taken away, with the city council in 1613 being led by a rising Protestant elite, previously exempt freemen paying customs duties to English courtiers and their liberty of conscience being challenged, where before the authorities had tacitly tolerated Catholicism. Chichester's government created a division along confessional lines, with the Catholic elite in Dublin increasingly finding common cause with the Catholic lords of the Pale and other port towns. In a short period of time the Catholic elite in Dublin had been transformed from 'patrons of loyalty' and 'paragons of obedience' to members of a 'contrary faction', with the tumult in the tholsel epitomising their increased radicalisation.

3

'WE ARE NOT YET SAFE, FOR THEY THREATEN US WITH MORE VIOLENCE'

A study of the Cook Street riot, 1629[1]

MARK EMPEY

On St Stephen's Day 1629, the Protestant archbishop of Dublin, Lancelot Bulkeley, with the support of some of the city's officials, stormed a Franciscan chapel in Cook Street. The raid was quickly marred by violent scenes. As the authorities tried to arrest the celebrant of the mass, they were overwhelmed by members of the congregation who retaliated by hurling stones and clubs, eventually forcing the archbishop and his entourage to take refuge in a nearby house on Skinners' Row.

The riot at Cook Street provides a rare insight into sectarian tensions in Dublin in the 1620s. The source of the pent-up frustration of the Protestant government officials was the royal policy enforcing relaxation of measures against Catholics. But, though detailed accounts of the skirmish from both sides reveal this underlying communal hostility, the attack itself was as much politically motivated as it was religiously inspired. In this chapter

I identify the various forces at work in the disturbance and explore the ways that religious division fuelled the descent into disorder. To what extent was the freedom granted to Catholics, as evidenced by the large attendance at the mass in Cook Street, a contributory factor? How far did successive administrations, specifically the joint governors, Lords Justices Cork and Loftus and then Lord Deputy Wentworth, try to derive political capital from the conflict? And what were the implications of the riot for the Irish mission during the Counter-Reformation? These are important questions not just for our understanding of the impact of the Cook Street riot, but also to gain a valuable insight into life in early seventeenth-century Ireland.

The deputyship of Henry Cary, 1st Viscount Falkland, from 1622 to 1629, was fraught with difficulties. For the most part, external forces dictated the course of his governmental agenda, not least his treatment of Irish Catholics. King James' marriage negotiations with Spain, and then with France, ultimately triggered a war against the two Catholic super-powers of Europe. As foreign relations deteriorated, the position of Ireland and Irish Catholics inevitably became a source of intense debate in Whitehall.[2] That the kingdom was predominantly Catholic and seemingly closely allied with England's enemies naturally caused considerable alarm, as did Ireland's strategic importance – Spain's attempted invasion at Kinsale in 1601 was a constant reminder of the crown's vulnerability.[3] The focus of Falkland's administration, therefore, was to secure the country's defence while refraining from any outward persecution of Catholics.

As one might expect, the Catholic church sought to capitalise on this opportunity. The hierarchy was restored in 1618, and nineteen bishops were appointed over the following eleven years.[4] The numbers of priests and regular clergy were no less striking.

As early as 1623 the Catholic archbishop of Dublin, Eugene Matthews, confidently asserted that there were 800 secular priests, 200 Franciscans, forty Jesuits, over twenty Dominicans, four or five Capuchins and 'a few' Cistercians and Augustinians.[5] That there were reportedly so many regular and secular clergy in Ireland is interesting, given that the hierarchy was restored at such a late stage in Counter-Reformation Europe. It indicates how far the Irish rejected the Church of Ireland, but conversely it also shows how receptive they were to Catholicism and the Irish mission. In 1623, for example, some of the leading citizens in Drogheda wrote to Rome requesting more 'excellent religious of the same *familia reformata*, like the two whom it has already sent, Fathers Michael Miles and Joseph Everard'.[6]

The early success rapidly gathered momentum: in 1628 the superior of the Carmelites in Dublin declared that residents 'attend at the chapels and frequent the sacraments … each week they flock in such crowds to the sacraments of penance and the holy eucharist, that scarcely is it possible for the priests to meet their demands'.[7] The Bishop of Ferns, John Roche, claimed that he found 'our holy religion flourishing' in Meath. In his own diocese, he added, there were over thirty priests attending about seventy parishes.[8] Catholic resurgence was no less visible to Protestants. In Cavan, the Bishop of Kilmore, William Bedell, lamented that the vast majority in his diocese were recusants. Attempts to convert them were hampered not only by the resident Catholic bishop, but also by the greater number of priests, which he estimated to be double the Protestant equivalent.[9] An official at Dublin Castle bemoaned the fact that there were fourteen mass houses in the capital catered for by the religious orders, while there were eighty Jesuits 'who have their altars adorned with images and other idolatrous popish trash as fully as in Rome if not more'.[10]

The fortunes of the Irish mission took a different direction in April 1629, when King Charles agreed a peace treaty with France while negotiations with Spain were in train. This prompted a dramatic shift in government policy in Ireland, and Falkland issued a royal declaration banishing Jesuits and friars. The lord deputy had broadcast the same decree five years earlier, only for it to be undermined by England's marriage alliance with France.[11] In 1629, though, circumstances had notably changed in favour of the Irish administration. Charles had ended his search for a bride and, crucially, had withstood pressure to grant full toleration to Catholics. Besides, the European powers were weary of war and welcomed an end to hostilities. The Irish privy council immediately responded to this turn of events by sending a strongly worded petition to Whitehall, seeking to curtail the influence of friars and clergy, and requesting permission 'to restrain their arrogance, coerce their jurisdiction, diminish their numbers, deaden their attempts, and make known their practices'.[12] Consequently, on 1 April the lord deputy outlawed the exercise of ecclesiastical authority derived from Rome and commanded the dissolution of religious houses.[13]

Within days of his announcement, Falkland reported back to London that 'there is hardly a Papist left in Dublin, and all their houses are locked up with the locks hanging on the doors'.[14] It was transparently an attempt to deflect attention away from the criticism he was getting from his enemies at court. The reality was that Catholics paid little attention to the decree. In Drogheda, Falkland later revealed, the proclamation was first read out in public by a 'drunken soldier' and then by his inebriated sergeant who allegedly re-enacted the instructions 'to seem like a May-game'.[15] There were no indications that the religious were unduly alarmed by the government's actions either. In correspondence to their superiors they barely acknowledged the new measures.

Essentially, the Irish mission resorted to its tried and tested policy of going underground until the storm abated. The front doors of the mass houses may have been closed but, as Archbishop Ussher was informed, the congregation simply entered from side passages to attend 'their superstitious service there, as if there were no command to the contrary'.[16]

Falkland's recall in the summer of 1629 was inevitable.[17] His failure to reassert the government's authority, and in particular to curb the activities of the Catholic clergy, lost him the confidence of the king and the Protestant ruling elite in Ireland. To remedy this, and indeed restore the credibility of Dublin Castle, Charles looked to more hardened Protestant figures in Adam Loftus, Viscount Loftus of Ely, and Sir Richard Boyle, Earl of Cork. Free from the constraints that had hampered Falkland's administration, the two lords justices were given every encouragement by the crown to implement an aggressive religious programme.[18]

Loftus and Cork were quick to exploit these advantages. On 13 December 1629 the Capuchin friar, Francis Nugent, informed Propaganda Fide that Loftus had warned Catholics in Dublin not to open schools or provide housing for mass if they wanted to avoid the government's wrath. Senior Catholic ecclesiastics were certainly perturbed by the changing climate. Archbishop Thomas Fleming summoned the secular and regular clergy in the hope of negotiating a temporary cessation to their public ceremonies.[19] His efforts were in vain. Writing to the king's secretary on 22 December, Cork asserted: 'the Jesuits and friars tested our strength by trying to return to the houses from which they were dispersed by the proclamation; but they find us quite firm'.[20] Sure enough, the general of the Irish army was ordered to lodge a company of soldiers in every walled town.[21] This was not just to protect the Protestant New English; it was also a warning shot to the friars and priests. Yet this strategy was neither successful nor essentially different from the measures that brought about Falkland's downfall. If anything, it demonstrated the limits of the new government's power and their lack of imagination in tackling Catholicism.

It was perhaps ironic that the conduct of Thomas Babe, superior of the Franciscan order, triggered events that paved the way for the administration to check the progress of the Irish mission. On Christmas night, Babe reportedly 'made som[e] little speech unto the people'. This was brought to the attention of the authorities whereupon 'they holding it for an affront & contempt caus[e]d the first irruption'.[22] A council meeting was called the next morning to consider an appropriate response. What ensued was a frank discussion about the significant inroads made by friars, Jesuits and priests in the capital. The Irish council was informed that Dublin had up to ten mass houses with a resident head or governor protected by powerful members of the Catholic laity, notably the Dowager Countess of Kildare and also the Earls of Westmeath and Fingal, and Viscounts Gormanstown and Dillon.[23] The councillors could hardly have been ignorant of this, but they all agreed that something must be done about the Franciscans. After all, the authority of the lords justices and council was at stake. Under the directions of Loftus and Cork, therefore, Archbishop Bulkeley and the Mayor of Dublin, Christopher Forster, supported by Captain Carey and his soldiers, were ordered to ransack the Franciscan chapel in Cook Street.[24] They had further assistance from Nathaniel Catelyn, recorder of the city, Aldermen Johns and Kelly, and Sheriff Foster. The intention was to apprehend the friars and cause extensive damage.

There are numerous accounts of the riot from both sides of the religious divide and they make fascinating reading, if only to highlight the underlying sectarian tensions which had been largely suppressed in the delicate political circumstances. 'On ther comming in the pepell were in aubproare', an eyewitness declared, 'the Maior had the pickterr pulled down and the Lord Archbishop pulled down the pulpett; the sowlders and the peopell weare by the heres one with another, and the pickteres were all brocken and defaased, and they toke within five sutts of vestments and one chales'.[25] But as the officials attempted to arrest the two presiding friars, the irate congregation, mainly women and children, retaliated. Leading the charge was an unnamed 'widow Nugent' who was singled out for specific praise in the Catholic reports. She was credited with raising the cry to help the friars and apparently flung herself on the soldiers. Soon her fellow parishioners joined in and the skirmish quickly spiralled out of control: 'they strick [strike], they shoulder, they catch, they scratch, thump & tread underfoot whom soever they lay hands on'.[26] Outnumbered and seeking respite, Bulkeley and his colleagues fled the chapel only to be confronted by a large group of pilgrims who had come to visit St Stephen's Well and celebrate the saint's feast day. In their efforts to escape, the angry mob pursued them 'casting stones and the durt of the kenel' until they found refuge in a house on Skinner's Row.[27] It was not only the authorities' pride that suffered; it was reported that 'One of ye souldiers was so tumbled, tossed, concalcated in the mire, that he hardly escaped death'.[28]

The violent scenes induced senior Protestants to send a stream of letters to Whitehall. Sir Thomas Dutton argued that 'had not the Justices and others come from church for the rescue it would have been a bloody business'.[29] The general of the Irish army, Charles Wilmot, petitioned for more soldiers and gunpowder for fear of more unrest.[30] In this highly charged situation the lords justices and council deliberated on the proper course of action. They immediately ordered a curfew. Two days later, all the Catholic aldermen were ordered to come before the council table and explain their reasons for not coming to the aid of the authorities. In effect, it was a show trial. One embittered alderman revealed: 'my brother James, Mr Torner, Mr Edward, and Robert Arthur, and Mr Russell of Lecale were committed to the Castell'. Only he and Walter Usher escaped punishment. It was a similar story the next day: Aldermen Gooding, Mapas and Stephens were examined and then imprisoned. On the third day, the widow Nugent from Wine Tavern Street was incarcerated for her role in the disturbance along 'with many others', including all the constables of Cook Street, Corn Market and High Street, after which the proceedings concluded.[31] They were soon released after successfully petitioning for liberty by promising loyalty to the crown. But the hefty bail, set at £1,000, served as a reminder that the government was determined to keep up pressure on the Catholic community.

It would be easy to conclude that the sentences handed down on the Catholic aldermen and citizens were part of the lords justices' religious agenda. To some extent that was true. Writing to Viscount Dorchester, Cork stressed the need for greater commitment to reforming the kingdom 'infected as this is with like convents and the dregs of popish frenzy'.[32] Yet it is obvious from the reports on the riot that cess (a form of local tax) played a key part. Only days before, the mayor and citizens of Dublin refused to provide 'lodging, fire and candle light' for the fifty soldiers protecting Loftus and Cork.[33] The disagreement originated in an order the city council had passed at Easter declaring they would no longer foot the bill for soldiers: future payments were to be regarded as loans. Tensions were further exacerbated during the lead up to Christmas, when the aldermen arranged to send an agent to England to protest against the taxation. But before the agent left, Loftus and Cork met Forster in a desperate attempt to find a last-minute solution. After careful consideration, they concluded that only the orchestration of some form of civil unrest would convince the crown of the need for the soldiers. This in turn would compel the mayor and aldermen to discontinue their opposition.[34] As a Catholic bystander noted, the disorder was concocted at the council table, where 'it was done of purpose to draw the sowlders on the City; for we stod out that we wolde not give the sowlder lodging or fire and candel-light, and now we have 2 companies both forssessed on us'.[35]

For all the lords justices' shady dealings, there is no indication that either the king or his ministers were aware of the part Cork and Loftus played in the uprising. Cork's close friendship with the king's secretary, Viscount Dorchester, meant that he controlled what information was relayed to Charles. The riot was therefore portrayed as a papist rebellion and a serious threat to national security. Cork's direct line to Whitehall was highly significant. First, it provided him with a platform to justify the measures that were implemented immediately after the conflict.[36] These measures could also be presented as the basis of an effective religious strategy in the medium term. Second, and crucially, it gave him the opportunity to make a bid for the deputyship, a position he had long coveted.[37] In Cork's eyes, successfully managing the aftermath of the Cook Street riot could usefully demonstrate his ability to govern Ireland as viceroy.[38]

The government's response was swift and decisive. Having convicted the Catholic aldermen, the lords justices shifted their attention to mass houses in the city. On 5 January 1630 they commanded the aldermen on bail to attend the mayor and sheriffs at the Franciscan chapel and seize it for the king's use. From there, the group proceeded to the houses belonging to the Dominicans, Carmelites and Capuchins (ten houses altogether) with similar intent.[39] This process continued over the next few days. Forster, who was 'well guarded w[i]th souldiers', sequestered the large Jesuit mass house at Back Lane on 7 January, and on the following day the authorities confiscated the nunnery at Newgate.[40] But the ejection of the priests and friars from their houses was merely the beginning. After the English privy council endorsed the lords justices' actions, the latter sought to exploit the episode for all its political worth.[41] Thus, at the end of February city officials were instructed 'to pull downe to the ground the Franciscan howses in the Cookstreete because there formerly the s[ai]d mayor & archb[isho]p of Dublin had received an affront & disgrace by the baser sort of papists'.[42] Furthermore, the mass houses in Bridge Street and Back Lane were transformed into places of correction or business. Trinity College was the prime beneficiary. Fifty students took up residence in Back Lane where Archbishop Ussher delivered lectures and held public catechisings that were attended by the Dublin gentry every Tuesday.[43] Similarly around eighteen scholars attended the chapel in Bridge Street for prayers twice a day. As a passing shot at the friars, priests and wider Catholic community, the room was aptly named St Stephen's Hall.[44]

The government's clampdown on friaries, convents and mass houses was not confined to Dublin. Similar scenes were enacted in Cork, Limerick and Galway. On 15 January the president of Munster, William St Leger, informed the lords justices that he had raided four chapels in Cork used by the Franciscans, Dominicans and Augustinians.[45] This was greeted with considerable alarm among all sectors of the Irish mission. Having learned of the seizure of mass houses in Dublin and Cork, Bishop Roche lamented how 'ye like ordre is sent to Limrike, and we know not how farre it will extend'.[46] The Franciscan William Farrily likewise remarked in a letter to his colleague Hugh de Burgo in Madrid that 'at

Corcke ther was the like and as I suppose through the kingdom, so that I do not remember to by [*sic*] in so trobled a case sithenc my remembrance'.[47] The chorus of lamentation was echoed by Valentine Browne, Franciscan guardian of Galway: 'so great is the persecution we are subjected to … that there was none so grievous since the commencement of the oppression of the Catholic religion in this kingdom'.[48] The actions of Dublin Castle had a significant impact in the early months of 1630. Even in Whitehall there was talk that the priests, Jesuits, friars and nuns were 'so hunted and imprisoned there, as they are rare to be found'.[49] In reality this was nothing more than court gossip: the government did not have the resources to complete such a task, which was rarely, if ever, achieved. In autumn 1630, for example, St Leger arrested the Franciscan Eugene Field in Cork. But this was intended to serve as a reminder to the friars and priests not to return to preaching public services, rather than signalling a new spell of persecution.[50]

It was a mark of the relative success of the lords justices that Thomas White, vicar-general of the archbishop of Dublin, and Thomas Strange (*alias* Strong) were sent to London in May as agents for the secular and regular Catholic clergy. Upon arrival, they were instructed to attend the court of Queen Henrietta Maria and present a memorial designed to induce her husband to grant freedom of conscience to his subjects in Ireland. Yet, as Strange noted, the petition had no effect; worse still, there was no indication that the king's stance would shift in favour of Catholics. Furthermore, when they appealed to the ambassadors of France and Spain, who were negotiating a peace settlement, they were promptly rebuffed. Indeed, the peace treaties were viewed as the final blow. 'Experience has taught us,' Strange glumly stated, 'that after every treaty of peace with Spain we have but seen the Catholics of Ireland more persecuted.'[51]

But Charles' rejection of their appeal was not just influenced by the more pressing issue of securing peace. The agents also had to contend with unfounded rumours reaching the court.[52] 'Our adversaries are using certaine diligences for to fill His Majestie's eares,' Rothe complained, 'that Catholicke churchmen be of over great charges to the land, and therefore they procure to know all their names, dwellings, benefactors, almes or stipend, which is for to make a great noise of it to our disadvantage.'[53] The bishop pointed to a recent assize where one judge was heard saying that the priests collected more than £200,000 a year – a sum so exaggerated, Roche added, that not even £2,000 would have been a realistic estimate in the poverty-stricken towns and countryside. 'The truth is,' he declared, 'that the Catholicks have subject to complaine of the Protestant clergy by means of their extortions in that their officialities or Bishops' courts be more chargeable to the land then [sic] would the maintenance of an armie be.'[54]

Political circumstances certainly played a crucial role in Charles' decision to ignore all pleas from the Catholic clergy and their agents. At the same time, however, the success of Dublin Castle's intrusive measures was instrumental in effecting a dramatic shift in policy. Whereas the administration's attempts to curb Catholicism had failed miserably in the past, the disorder provided Loftus and Cork with a prime opportunity to begin a vigorous and intrusive religious campaign with the full backing of the crown, which hitherto had not been forthcoming. Such was the significance of the episode that the administration used it as a scaremongering tactic whenever friars and priests were perceived to be overstepping the mark. This was especially the case as financial pressures began to dominate the government agenda. By the second half of 1630, measures against the religious occurred only intermittently, in contrast to the regular raids in the spring.[55]

To hold Catholic activities in check, Loftus and Cork needed only to renew sectarian tensions by reminding their fellow Protestants of the recent disorder. In November, Strange complained that none of the laity would rent a house to the Franciscans for fear of being reported to the administration. The Capuchins faced similar problems. Their superior, Father Barnabas, revealed in April 1631 that they still could not preach in the cities and had to go to the countryside to avoid being caught.[56]

Despite his aggressive religious policy, Cork failed to secure the deputyship. Instead, that honour fell in January 1632 to Sir Thomas Wentworth, who had made a name for himself as the king's representative for the northern territories in England. Although the urgent need for subsidies to pay the Irish army and fund the administration was Wentworth's priority, it did not prevent him from exploiting opportunities for other actions. Prying into the affairs of the Catholic church was one such activity.[57] He played a key role from the outset in stoking hostilities between secular and regular clergy, but his cross-examination of the Carmelite friar, Stephen Browne, is of particular interest.[58]

Browne had been in the government's sights since the Cook Street riot. As the Carmelite friary was close to the Franciscan chapel, he was a key witness to the skirmish and was strongly suspected by the lords justices of provoking the pilgrims into attacking the officials.[59] There was not enough evidence to charge him, but then Loftus and Cork heard of accusations that he was involved in the exorcism of a twelve-year-old girl.[60] He was arrested and imprisoned without trial for a year. The conspicuous failure to convict clearly suggests that this was the authorities' retaliation for his role in the disturbance. But Browne's release meant that it was a pyrrhic victory for the government. Wentworth sought to immediately remedy this, however. Shocked by the 'infinite swarmes of friers' in Dublin when he arrived in 1633, the lord deputy responded by hauling Browne before the Court of Castle Chamber.[61] The friar therefore served as the symbolic victim.

The details of the case against Browne are thin, but what is known encapsulates the ruthless efficiency of Wentworth's deputyship. Whereas the previous administration could not find sufficient evidence to convict Browne, the lord deputy only needed a couple of days. In the course of the proceedings, the chief baron of the exchequer, Richard Bolton, accused the friar of luring Protestants away from their religion and allegiance to the king. Where Bolton focused on the exorcism, the allegations were linked to the events at Cook Street. The council predictably ruled in favour of the chief baron and on 11 February 1635 Browne was censured, fined £3,000 and ordered to be pilloried 'as an impostor and sorcerer' in a square in Dublin.[62] To compound matters, the friar was subsequently imprisoned for failing to pay the excessive fine. The severity of the punishment is an indication of how much political capital Wentworth and his colleagues expected to derive from the trial. Writing to the king's secretary, John Coke, the lord deputy proclaimed that the sentence caused 'a kind of pannick terrour affrighting them [the religious orders] as if certainly there were a p[re]sent change of religion intended in soe much as the Jesuits have allready shutt up their oratory … for feare of a suddain persecution [and] a Benedictin frier hath done the like on ye other side' of Dublin.[63] His comments, especially in light of the judgement against Browne, show that Wentworth had the events of Cook Street firmly in mind when he summoned the friar to court. Browne's conviction was a very public demonstration of the lord deputy's authority: he refused to countenance the openness with which the religious orders had previously conducted themselves. Browne's fate was a stern warning to the numerous friars in the kingdom who continued to defy the government.

Wentworth's relentless pursuit of the young Carmelite reinforced the significance that Cook Street had for many Protestants in 1629. Where the lords justices were instrumental in stirring up the underlying sectarian tensions, Wentworth's revival of the controversy six years later ensured that such apprehensions were embedded in the minds of the New English community for decades to come. He used the Browne case for his own advantage without consideration of the future ramifications. The raid on the Franciscan chapel in Cook Street in 1662 is a case in point. With the Restoration, the Franciscans returned to Dublin and settled in Cook Street once more. Their political position had substantially improved with their advocacy of the Remonstrance of loyalty to Charles II. This gave them leeway when they were re-establishing themselves in the city. Despite this, on St Stephen's Day the procurator of the chapel, Father Peter Walsh, was interrupted by a company of soldiers 'with naked swords' as he officiated at mass. A scuffle between the soldiers and congregation ensued. One report noted 'the altars rifled, the priests carried prisoners to Newgate, and many hurt both men and women grievously, and some slashed and wounded sorely, even to the great endangering of their lives.'[64] The parallels with the 1629 riot are striking. Sectarianism was clearly endemic in the capital. Moreover, the soldiers' intolerance of the Franciscans celebrating the mass stood in marked contrast, if not actual defiance, of royal toleration. The fact that the chapel was raided on St Stephen's Day was hardly coincidental. The message was unambiguous: nothing had changed – *plus ça change, plus c'est la même chose*. Even though Protestants were politically more secure than at any time in the past, they showed the same knee-jerk defensiveness that was so apparent in 1629.

More exactly, events showed just how much the riot had affected relations between Catholic and Protestant.

The significance of the Cook Street riot in 1629 is not diminished by the fact that it was an isolated incident. On the contrary, it is precisely because the outburst was unique at the time that it demands attention. That Ireland simultaneously enjoyed a rare period of sustained peace and stability serves only to highlight its importance. Not since 1496 had Cook Street been the focus of unwelcome attention when the unfortunate Jenico Marks, mayor of Dublin, was killed while endeavouring to quell 'a riot of citizens'.[65] The disturbance in 1629, on the other hand, reveals the extent of subliminal sectarianism in the capital, which was kept under wraps. The prolonged spell of toleration commanded by the crown certainly exacerbated underlying tensions. As priests and friars openly celebrated the mass without fear of government persecution during the 1620s, Protestant opinion hardened incrementally. This was apparent when Loftus and Cork were promoted to take charge of the administration. Their religious outlook undoubtedly aggravated tensions in Dublin. This, in tandem with a shared political interest in penalising Catholics, precipitated a conflict that inevitably deepened the sectarian divisions of an already polarised community.

Wentworth's decision to revive memories of the riot was a conscious attempt to tap into this Protestant psyche. By publicly examining Browne, the lord deputy intended to exploit New English anxieties as a means of contesting the visible presence of regular clergy. In so doing, he ensured that the uprising on St Stephen's Day lived long in the memories of a continually apprehensive Protestant population. The upshot of this was that hostilities between the two religious groups were never far from the surface, as the raid on the Franciscan chapel in 1662 clearly demonstrated.

4

THE 1830S TITHE RIOTS

NOREEN HIGGINS-McHUGH

The 1830s tithe war is dominated in popular memory by the numerous tithe riots, particularly at Carrickshock, County Kilkenny and Rathcormac, County Cork, although such violence formed only a small part of all tithe agitation. The tithe war began in Graiguenamanagh (commonly called Graig), County Kilkenny in November 1830. Over the next two months in that county an undercurrent of violence characterised the riotous assemblies of hurlers, who came together to demand that the Anglican parochial clergy reduce their tithe rates. While the authorities moved quickly to suppress these assemblies in January 1831, tithe resistance began to mutate into demands for tithe abolition. Within months both parts of the movement adopted passive resistance, constitutional agitation, intimidation and violence.

The first fatal confrontation between the peasantry and the military and police parties occurred at a tithe sale at Newtownbarry, County Wexford in June 1831. Other riots followed across Munster, Leinster and Ulster, which were labelled 'tithe slaughters' by the popular liberal press. About eighty country people were killed and nearly 200 wounded in these affrays. The infamous 'battle of Carrickshock', County Kilkenny in December 1831, proved to be the exception to the general pattern of tithe affrays, since more police were killed than peasantry there. After the notorious Rathcormac tithe riot on 18 December 1834, when twelve people were killed and forty-five more injured, the automatic assigning of military and police escorts for tithe duties was suspended. This change in policy by the Dublin Castle authorities meant there were fewer tithe riots in the remaining years of the tithe war, which ended with the passing of the 1838 Rent-charge Act.

The word 'tithe' derives from the word 'tenth'. The concept of tithes is first mentioned in the Old Testament when one-tenth of the crops were set aside annually to support the Levite tribe who served in the Jewish Temple.[1] Although tithing was unknown in the early Christian church, a forerunner of the tithe system existed by the fourth century. This was a common fund of voluntary offerings and land revenues set up to support the poor and those clergy unable to support themselves.[2] The Synod of Tours in 567 and the Council of Macon in 585 authorised tithe payments to Roman Catholic clergy.[3] In 1274, Pope Gregory X decreed that tithe payment was to be compulsory throughout western Europe.[4] The sixteenth-century Reformation transferred both church property and tithes to the newly established Anglican Church in Britain and Ireland. However, as the vast majority of Irish people remained stubbornly Roman Catholic, they had to support the parochial clergy of the state church – through the payment of tithes and other taxes – as well as their own clergy. By the eighteenth century, the setting aside of tithe crops in the fields had evolved into a money payment, and tithes were only levied on the main tillage crops such as barley, flax, oats and wheat.[5] An anomaly in the Irish tithe system was the tithing of the potato crop throughout Munster and south Leinster. Potato tithe was unknown in the northern half of the country except for parts of Counties Donegal and Derry.[6] As the Irish Parliament exempted grassland from tithe payment by passing two resolutions on 18 March 1735, it meant that the poorer sections of Irish society – the tenant farmers, cottiers and labourers – paid the greater part of the tithe burden.[7]

By the late eighteenth and early nineteenth centuries, tithe violence had become an integral part of agrarian disturbances, including the Rightboys' protest, 1785–7, the Connacht Trashers' protest, 1806–7[8] and the Rockite disturbances of 1821–4.[9] These last were economic in origin, as agricultural prices had fallen by more than half after the Napoleonic wars. Prices for wheat and oats fell from £23 7s. and £12 14s. per hundredweight in 1812 to £7 14s. and £4 19s. by 1823.[10] Milch cows and dry cattle commanded half their previous prices of 14 to 16 guineas and £9 to £12.[11] As this agricultural depression combined with poor harvests, land occupiers found it 'impossible to pay rent or the tithes'.[12]

Riots against the tithe occurred near Askeaton, County Limerick on 15 August 1821, leading to the deaths of one member of the Limerick Peace Preservation force and two of the peasantry. As rumours multiplied that one man had been buried alive, Stipendiary Magistrate Major Going was assassinated in revenge exactly two months later on 15 October 1821.[13] A number of violent clashes occurred between Rockites and the armed forces in late January 1822, at Millstreet, Dunmanway and Kanturk, County Cork, resulting in the deaths of nearly fifty Rockites.[14] In July 1823, thirteen members of the peasantry and five of the police escort protecting tithe proctors died at another tithe riot at Castlehaven, near Skibbereen, County Cork. The clash occurred as the peasantry attempted to rescue distrained cattle for arrears due to Rev. Morrit of Skibbereen.[15] It later emerged that the tithe warrants for distraining had been signed by local magistrates in Morrit's glebehouse, contrary to the law.[16] The Rockite protests were eventually suppressed under the 1822 Insurrection Act, which proclaimed eight counties. More than 1,500 Munster men were brought to trial, leading to 200 convictions and transportations.[17]

To quell further agitation, three Tithe Composition Acts were passed in the 1820s. The first, in 1823, compounded the parish tithe amount, which was based on the average tithes paid from November 1814 to November 1821.[18] Having agreed the total tithe, the sum due from each landholder according to the quantity and quality of their land was allotted.[19] The 1824 Tithe Act allowed for revisions of the tithe amount every seventh year in a twenty-one year period.[20] The 1827 Composition Act allowed for appeals against applotments at the quarter sessions or they could be referred to the privy council.[21] However, the failure to make composition compulsory led to a two-tier system of compounded and non-compounded parishes as large graziers voted *en bloc* to prevent composition in their parish so they could enjoy continued tithe exemption.[22] In contrast, tithe composition 'was universally popular with the lower orders' as it distributed the tithe burden onto grazing lands.[23] By March 1830, some 60 per cent of parishes in Ireland had compounded their tithes.[24] Nationally, average tithe composition was 1s. 6d. to 2/– per Irish acre, whereas tithe in non-compounded parishes was 10/– per acre for wheat and potatoes and 8/– for barley and oats.[25] There was also increasing antagonism between Anglican clergy and the Catholic majority because the clergy had actively campaigned against granting Catholic emancipation in 1829. This heightened tensions around the tithe issue.

The tithe war began in November 1830 when a parish priest, Fr Martin Doyle, refused to pay tithes on a second farm of 40 acres that he had rented in Graiguenamanagh, on the Kilkenny–Carlow border. The union [group of parishes] had been compounded for £1,000, a figure set by the Anglican Bishop of Ferns and Leighlin, who considered the original agreed amount of £720 to be too low.[26] Long-established custom dictated that priests did not pay tithe on holdings surrounding their parochial houses, and Doyle believed this courtesy should extend to his second farm. Therefore he refused to pay tithe composition to the heartily disliked Anglican curate, Rev. Luke McDonald, who was running the union since the rector, Rev. Alcock, was old and in poor health.[27] Doyle organised a number of parish meetings in Graig courthouse in October and November 1830 to discuss 'measures to prevent the further payment of tithe rent in the parish'.[28] As a result, the parishioners demanded a reduction in the tithe composition and sent petitions outlining their demands to the Anglican Bishop of Leighlin and Ferns[29] and to Rev. Alcock.[30]

When further meetings in Graig were prohibited, Fr Doyle held meetings under the guise of hurling matches. He advised his parishioners to avoid open, possibly violent confrontation with the authorities on the issue, advocating tithe evasion instead.[31] A common parish fund, based on a levy of a penny per acre, was set up to relieve financial suffering incurred by tithe distraint and legal costs.[32]

In December and January assemblies of tenant farmers and labourers met, again under the guise of hurling matches, at various places in County Kilkenny, including Ballyhale (27 December), Gowran (28 December), Inistioge (31 December and 7 January), Bennettsbridge (30 December and 3 January), Dysart Bridge, near Castlecomer (1 January), and Graig itself (2 and 7 January). The practice of cutting down ash plants from some landlords' plantations to make hurleys, despite the penalty of transportation, caused these assemblies to be nicknamed 'the hurlers'. They sent deputations to a number of rectors to demand a reduction in their tithes, and notices were posted throughout the county threatening violence on those who continued to pay tithe. Similar meetings took place in the neighbouring counties at Old Leighlin, County Carlow (26 December), Ballywilliam, near New Ross, County Wexford (26 December) and in Queen's County.[33] Over 2,000 people attended the Old Leighlin meeting, where an orange-and-green flag was unfurled.[34]

On 27 December 1830 the hurlers visited Rev. Hans Hamilton of Knocktopher union. On seeing the mob gathered on his front lawn outside the vicarage, Hamilton's initial reaction was to believe that his end had come. He refused to talk to their spokesman, a Carmelite friar from Knocktopher village, but he agreed to meet a deputation on 3 January 1831. When he received the twelve 'very respectable farmers' in the hall of his vicarage, also present were the inspector-general of police for Leinster, Sir John Harvey, Major Browne and other magistrates. While acknowledging that Hamilton had been one of the better resident gentry during his thirty-five years in the union, the deputation still demanded a reduction – even as little as 5 per cent of the £1,750 tithe composition would satisfy them – but Hamilton refused on the grounds that the tithe amount was as low as he could make it. He suggested a 10 per cent reduction if he were spared the expense of collection. The deputation, knowing Hamilton would gain by this, since his agent received a 12 per cent fee, rejected his offer. They also rejected his comment that they would soon be objecting to rent, answering that they got value for their rent but none for tithe.[35]

On the same day, another meeting of 3,000 hurlers took place at Bennettsbridge, Burnchurch union, County Kilkenny. While the people waited behind in the village, Patrick Blanchfield of Clara and his neighbour Anthony Byrne led a deputation of six farmers to the local rectory to ask Rev. Dr Butler to reduce his £2,000 tithes.[36] After forty-five minutes, half of the crowd went to the rectory.[37] Fearing for his life, the rector addressed the mob from an upstairs window alongside his two sons, William and John, as the mob made threatening remarks in Irish.[38] Butler's declaration that the law prevented him from reducing his tithe composition was received with derision. Blanchfield then proposed that the mob pass a resolution not to pay tithes to any rector unless compelled by law, which was received with great cheering before the people departed *en masse*.[39]

On 6 January 1831, another deputation went to Rev. Stephenson of Callan. On 18 January the hurlers visited three more rectors, Rev. Kearney of Kilkenny city, Rev. Park of Inistioge and Rev. Darley of Kells. All refused to lower tithes, pointing out that the Composition Acts only allowed revisions every seven years. As frustration grew, notices were posted up across the county advising a general refusal to pay tithes.[40] As the hurlers' meetings breached the peace under the 1787 Riot Act, the chief secretary, Lord Edward Stanley, circularised the local magistrates to suppress the meetings early in January 1831.[41] This was followed by Daniel O'Connell's open letter of 3 January 1831 to the Kilkenny hurlers in *The Kilkenny Journal* and the *Freeman's Journal*, advising them to refrain from holding meetings that breached the law.[42] As the hurlers' movement faded away, Bishop Doyle of Leighlin warned the newly appointed lord lieutenant, the Marquis of Anglesey, that 'the strength of feeling in the country' on the tithe issue would not be easily extinguished.[43]

Within weeks, tithe agitation mutated into passive resistance, which did not breach the law but effectively disabled the tithe system. Such tactics were pioneered in Graig union to prevent the tithe bailiffs distraining their cattle for their tithe arrears between March and May 1831.[44] Another variation on passive resistance against tithes was initiated by O'Connellite supporter Patrick Lalor (1781–1856) of Tenakill, Queen's County.[45] Though he allowed his twenty-five sheep to be distrained for tithe arrears, he ensured that there were no bidders at the subsequent Mountrath tithe sale on 10 March 1831, except for the rector's agent, Mr Brough.[46] These tactics borrowed heavily from the example of the Quakers, who did not pay tithe or any ecclesiastical dues as a matter of conscience,[47] allowing their property to be distrained without offering resistance.[48] As passive resistance spread like wildfire through Munster and south Leinster in 1831–2, tithe collection became 'utterly impossible'.[49] Although local O'Connellites and the Catholic clergy succeeded in channelling much tithe anger into political agitation, there was continuing violence and intimidation against all those involved in the tithe system, culminating in a number of fatal confrontations between the peasantry and the military and police escorting tithe agents.

Although isolated tithe riots had occurred in County Antrim with the loss of four or five lives in 1819 and at Skibbereen, County Cork with the loss of thirteen lives in July 1823, such affrays were more numerous during the 1830s tithe war.[50] This was due to the common practice of assigning a police or military party to escort tithe agents on tithe duties from 1831 onwards.[51] Although the police were forbidden under the 1827 Petty Sessions Act to assist in serving tithe processes or distraining property for tithe arrears except in cases of forcible resistance, the public considered them to be 'virtually collectors'.[52] Moreover, the succession of tithe affrays in that decade destroyed any goodwill between police and people, reinforcing popular determination to resist tithe payment and increased political pressure to find a solution.[53]

The first tithe riot was at Newtownbarry (now Bunclody), County Wexford on 18 June 1831. It was notable for being the first and only time when the yeomanry (a predominantly Protestant force) were used to quell tithe agitation. Three heifers, distrained for tithes due to Rev. McClintock of Newtownbarry, strayed from the main market area before the tithe sale.[54] Although they were rounded up and placed in the pound by the police, as the cattle were being brought back to the market place, a menacing mob began stoning the police and the yeomanry.[55] The yeomanry retaliated by shooting dead fourteen people, including a pregnant woman named Mary Mahony, and wounding between twenty-five and forty others. One yeoman, William Rogan from Kilbride, was shot dead by the mob.[56] The subsequent inquest failed to arrive at any verdict owing to 'the bitterness of party spirit' between Catholics and Protestants.[57] However, the incident put an end to use of the yeomanry to quell tithe agitation and led to their eventual demise as a force.

The Leugh tithe affray, near Thurles, County Tipperary, set the pattern for later tithe affrays. The process-server Billy Fleming and his twenty-nine-strong police escort were surrounded by a mob in Leugh townland on 5 October 1831.[58] The crowd began stoning the police, demanding that Fleming be handed over to them so they could destroy the tithe decrees. The police opened fire and shot one local girl, Catherine Maher, dead and wounded two or three more. The process-server was also wounded in the affray. Although attempts were made to charge the police with wilful murder at Catherine Maher's inquest, the police were absolved from all blame because they were deemed to have fired in self-defence, since two shots had previously been fired from within the mob.[59] Similar tithe riots occurred at Athbo, County Tyrone on 7 August 1832,[60] Carrigeen in the south of County Kilkenny on 8 October 1832,[61] Dunmaine parish, near Carrickmacross, County Cavan in early December 1832,[62] Knucknaglass, Desert parish, County Cork on 12 March 1833[63] and Keady, County Armagh, on 1 December 1834.[64] In each case, large mobs of people vainly attempted to prevent tithe evaluation or the serving of tithe processes or distraining for tithe arrears. In every case the accompanying magistrate attempted to coax the mob to disperse. Failing that measure, he then read the Riot Act to disperse them while ordering the armed escort to prime their guns. Sometimes warning shots were fired over the heads of the crowd in a last effort to disperse them before the guns were turned on them. Invariably, the subsequent inquests justified the police or military action on the grounds of self-defence.

The Doneraile area of County Cork had the most tithe affrays during the tithe war. On 5 September 1832, four local men and fifteen others were wounded in a tithe riot in Wallstown parish during an attempted tithe valuation.[65] The tithe affray at Knucknaglass, Desert parish, County Cork on 12 March 1833 ended in a man named Quinlan being shot dead, and fifteen to twenty people injured, four or five of them very seriously. Four others were arrested.[66] Two country people were killed and five or six were wounded at another tithe riot near Dunmanway as a tithe party attempted to distrain for arrears due to Rev. Kennyin in late November 1832.[67] The Thernagree affray, six miles from Kanturk, on the night of 6 January 1833, resulted in the deaths of three local men, Saville, Meade and Leary.[68] On 30 April 1834, three men were shot dead and several injured at Feohanagh, Monegea parish, Newcastlewest, County Limerick, where a crowd of men and women had stoned the police and their military escort in a vain attempt to rescue their cattle and other property distrained for arrears due to Rev. Locke of Newcastle.[69] Chief police magistrate Thomas Vokes was also struck several times with stones.[70] After this affray, the *Freeman's Journal* commented 'there is only one way of tranquillising the country in this respect, and that way is by an honest and utter abolition of tithes – no half-measures will do'.[71]

There were two exceptions to this general pattern – of more country people than police or soldiers dying in tithe affrays – and both were popularly seen as significant victories in the tithe war.[72] The first was the infamous 'battle of Carrickshock', near Knocktopher, County Kilkenny on 14 December 1831.[73] Chief Constable Gibbons and thirty-eight mounted policemen had accompanied the agent, Butler, as he served tithe processes for arrears due to Rev. Hamilton of Knocktopher. Tithe resistance had continued in the union despite the failed attempt by the Kilkenny hurlers to compel Hamilton to reduce his tithes nearly a year earlier. After Butler had pushed a latitat (writ) under the door of the house of Dick Walsh (known as Dick Waterford), Gibbons and his men found the road blocked by a mob of 1,000 to 2,000, armed with sticks, mallets, scythes and billhooks, shouting 'the process-server or blood'.[74] Although told to give up Butler to ensure his own safety, Gibbons' refusal meant that he and his men paid with their lives.[75] The affray lasted forty minutes and left sixteen men dead: twelve policemen, the process-server and three local men, Treacy, Power and Phelan. The Hamiltons left that night for Kilkenny city and travelled on to London, never returning to Knocktopher. The rector died eight years later in England.[76] The *Freeman's Journal* commented that Carrickshock added 'to the many melancholy proofs already afforded of the incompatibility of the tithe system in Ireland with order and good government'.[77] A comparable incident occurred at Bealnavallen, near Doolin, County Clare on 4 April 1831, when five policemen were killed by the Terry Alts,[78] who were attempting to rescue one of their men named McInerney.[79]

The impact of Carrickshock was considerable. Whereas twelve constables had been killed in the four years between 1826 and 1830, the same number had been killed at Carrickshock in one day. The 'victory' was celebrated in many ballads in both Irish and English, especially as the government failed to get any convictions for the killing of the policemen, despite holding four trials in Kilkenny city in 1832. Ultra-Protestants blamed the acquittals on intimidation of the jury.[80] The following year Kilkenny was the first county proclaimed under the Coercion Act, which effectively imposed martial law.[81] Not surprisingly, many felt that Carrickshock was a big factor in the county being proclaimed.[82]

The Dublin Castle executive changed its policy on tithe collection after the huge public outcry that followed the Rathcormac and Keady tithe affrays in December 1834. Rev. J. S. Blacker of Keady, County Armagh, was granted a police force of twenty-nine men to protect his tithe drivers distraining for £25 tithe arrears on 1 December 1834. He accompanied the distraining party in his role as magistrate.[83] Only four townlands in the parish owed two years' tithe arrears to Blacker; in the other townlands the local landlords had undertaken to pay tithes under the 1832 Tithe Composition Act.[84] About sixty people gathered with pitchforks, bludgeons and a gun as one cow was seized and four or five processes delivered. As the police attempted to seize the gun and arrest its owner, a shower of stones fell on them and two police were knocked to the ground. Almost immediately, their colleagues opened fire despite the absence of any order to do so, and it was later noted that Blacker made no attempt to stop the police firing.[85] Ultimately, three peasants were shot dead and five police badly wounded.[86] Chief Constable Hill told the subsequent investigation at Armagh that another group of 300 to 500 persons had been converging on the nearby hills to join the mob.[87]

The infamous Rathcormac tithe affray in County Cork on 18 December 1834 resulted in twelve deaths of the peasantry and forty-five wounded. Major Walter Tithe, with two companies of the 29th Regiment and a dozen 4th Royal Irish Dragoons had met up with the distraining party at Bartlemy Cross, outside Rathcormac.[88] With them were three local magistrates, Captain Bagley, Archdeacon Ryder and Captain Collis. The latter two gentlemen were owed tithe arrears that had become due on 1 November.[89] A crowd of 200 to 250 people armed with sticks, stones and spades attacked the distraining party with a hail of stones at Bartlemy Cross, before retreating up a bótharín to the Widow Ryan's haggard, which had been barricaded with rocks, logs and carts.[90] The distraining party and military escort followed them.

Archdeacon Ryder stopped on the way to the Widow Ryan's house to make her neighbour, William McAuliffe, swear on the Bible that he would pay his tithe arrears of £4. Meanwhile, the mob prevented the soldiers entering the haggard for forty-five minutes as they 'fought eagerly with spades, sticks and stones'. Repeated calls were made to the Widow Ryan 'to pay the demand and put an end to the strife' and they were followed by readings of the Riot Act.[91] Despite repeated attempts, the soldiers failed to charge through the barricade as the mob drove them back. Some soldiers were severely wounded by the swinging sticks and the stone missiles, and some had their bayonets bent.[92] Seeing that the soldiers could not break through and the people refused to disperse, Major Walter gave the fatal order to fire. Nine men were killed instantly and forty-five others were wounded, three of whom died later. After the firing had stopped, the Widow

Ryan came out of her house and paid her tithe, and all resistance ceased.[93]

The events at Rathcormac sparked much interest in Britain and a sermon on the affray by a Unitarian minister, Mr Harris of Glasgow, was printed eleven times in five months.[94] Daniel O'Connell lamented the loss of life at Rathcormac, 'committed in the name, and for the support, of religion'.[95] O'Connell also held that the deaths at Rathcormac 'did in point of Law amount to murder' as the distraining party were 'guilty of a double trespass': firstly, they had forced open the gate on the private bótharín leading to the Widow Ryan's house, which meant that she, with her servants and assistants, was within her legal rights to resist the trespassers, and secondly, her haggard conformed to the description of an enclosure that under the law could not be forced open for the purpose of distraining.[96] As O'Connell's legal opinion was published two days before the inquest verdict, it was not surprising that it charged Ryder, Bagley and Collis with wilful murder for their part in the affray.[97] The Rathcormac inquest did indeed find against the three magistrates, but all legal proceedings against them were dropped in May 1835.[98]

The ministers in Peel's minority Tory government were just as appalled as the previous Whig government had been by the presence of Anglican clergy at the above tithe riots. The new Irish secretary, Sir Henry Hardinge, regretted 'the extreme impropriety of any magistrate, and more particularly a clergyman' distraining for his own tithe arrears, though he noted the Rev. Blacker's plea that he had been forced to attend the distraining party at Keady because two other magistrates had declined to come. Hardinge wrote to Henry Goulburn, the home secretary, about the Keady affray:

… that there was no doubt that every collision with the people of the country in enforcing the law interposes an additional obstacle to the prospect of a future favourable settlement of the question of tithe.[99]

Subsequently, Blacker was told by the Irish under-secretary, Sir William Gossett, that the government disapproved of clerical magistrates distraining for their own tithe arrears, owing to the conflict of interest. Then Dublin Castle issued instructions to all magistrates that no tithe owner who was also a magistrate could grant a military escort for tithe duties or 'take a part in enforcing its payment, or personally appear on the occasion of its levy'.[100] Thomas Drummond brought in further changes shortly after he became under-secretary in July 1835, allowing military or police escorts for tithe duties only in cases where there were actual breaches of the peace.[101] A memorandum to all magistrates on 26 October 1835 decreed that no police escort could be employed 'for the recovery of tithes or in the levy of rent by distress except in the cases where two or more magistrates describing the extent of that resistance' submitted an affidavit to the Dublin Castle authorities.[102]

Drummond refused a police presence for a tithe sale for Rev. W. Beresford of Ballincally, County Galway, but the sale went off peacefully.[103] He also refused police assistance for tithe collection for Rev. Maxwell of Inishowen, County Donegal, despite the fact that Maxwell had paid the tithe composition of his tenants-at-will under the 1832 Act in his other role as landlord. Surprisingly, Drummond also refused Rev. M. Beresford's request on 10 August 1836 for police assistance to execute writs of rebellion in Inniscara parish, two miles from Ballincollig, County Cork.[104] A tithe riot had already occurred in that parish earlier that year, on 7 January, resulting in the deaths of two of the peasantry with a third fatally wounded.[105] However, Drummond's policy bore fruit because the last recorded riot of the tithe war was the Dunkerrin affray in King's County on 21 October 1836. This mêlée resulted in two deaths, one of a man called Hogan, assistant to Proctor Philip Ryan of Nenagh. In July 1837, the ensuing trial ended in acquittals as it could not be proved that the Dunkerrin men had struck Hogan, but only that they had been among the crowd. They were later convicted on a lesser charge of unlawful assembly.[106]

The tithe war saw a sea change in attitude by the authorities in the handling of violence and riotous assemblies. In the early years of the agitation, the Dublin Castle authorities were determined to enforce the law and granted police and military escorts as a matter of course to those collecting tithe arrears. This led to numerous riots, and eventually such escorts were severely restricted under the reforming policies of Under-Secretary Thomas Drummond. This removed one of the more provocative aspects of the tithe system until the partial resolution of the vexed question of Irish tithes with the 1838 Rent-charge Act.

5

THE GREAT PROTESTANT MEETING OF DUNGANNON, 1834

DARAGH CURRAN

The period between the 1830s and 1840s has been described as 'the age of crowds' and the mass meetings of Daniel O'Connell have been well examined and documented.[1] Less attention has been paid to Protestant meetings from the same period which, though not as big as O'Connell's monster meetings, were of great significance to the Protestant community. The meeting that took place in Dungannon on 19 December 1834 was one of a series of great Protestant gatherings in Ulster that year, others attracting 75,000 people to Hillsborough in October, 30,000 to Cavan a month later, and 20,000 to Enniskillen in late December, if crowd reports are to be believed.[2] These meetings were called to unite Protestants of all sects, as it was perceived that 'their privileges were in peril',[3] to show their support for the king and for maintenance of the Protestant ascendancy.

Because of changes in society and in the economy in the early nineteenth century, many Protestants felt threatened by (what they saw as) the erosion of what they considered their rightful position of superiority over Catholics. The collapse of the linen industry after the Napoleonic wars, coupled with technological advances in manufacturing, signalled a great change for the numerous weavers, many of whom were pushed downwards into the poverty-stricken cottier class. An expanding population increased competition for land, competition heightened by a trend for landlords and their agents to eliminate the practice of land subdivision on leases being inherited. Many landlords also sought to impose modern agricultural methods, such as enclosure, farm consolidation and crop rotation, to make their land more productive. These 'improvements' were not always welcomed by a tenantry who often considered them detrimental to their way of life. It is commonplace to read of the effect of these changes on the Catholic population, but such changes affected many Protestants too, especially in Ulster, and added to anxiety within this community. Despite this, little agitation occurred. The gentry of Tyrone retained the loyalty of their Protestant tenantry and could count on their support when mass mobilisation, such as the Dungannon meeting, was required.

For many Protestants, the series of political reforms carried out by the Liberal government in the 1830s proved to be more contentious than local land issues. The granting of Catholic emancipation in 1829 led to a rise in sectarian clashes as angry Orangemen reacted with violence to this threat to the Protestant ascendancy; changes in the educational structure promised to lead to a non-denominational system of schooling; the Church Temporalities Act reduced the number of bishops of the Established Church and created a body of commissioners who now controlled much church income. Protestants perceived the changes as part of a government policy which would lead to disestablishment of the Church of Ireland if allowed to go unchecked. Reforms led to more centralised control over law and order, and this lessened the power of that cornerstone of rural society, the local magistrate, usually a Protestant middle gentry figure, often sympathetic to breaches of the law by Orangemen. The government-enforced disbandment of the yeomanry in 1834 was a further aggravation because it denied Protestants the security provided by what was essentially a local defence force controlled by the gentry, many of them Orangemen.

By the mid-1830s, the latest concession being sought by Catholics – led by Daniel O'Connell, a figure who could mobilise the masses – was repeal of the Act of Union. In the words of one Presbyterian clergyman, Henry Cooke, repeal was just a discreet word for 'Romish ascendancy and Protestant extermination'.[4] The idea of repeal and the leadership of O'Connell caused much fear and anxiety among a Protestant population that was becoming increasingly unnerved as they saw their superior position over Catholics being undermined. One welcome champion of the Protestant cause was the king, William IV, who, dissatisfied with the liberal policies of the Melbourne government, dismissed several members of the cabinet in November 1834, thereby provoking a general election in January 1835. It was in anticipation of this election and in appreciation of the actions of their monarch that the Dungannon meeting was called by the gentry in Tyrone one month before the election.

The meeting was initially planned for 'the gentry, clergy, and freeholders of the county of Tyrone'.[5] No mention was made of the lower classes of society, who made up a large part of the Orange Order in the county. Indeed, it is highly unlikely that the Earl of Caledon, lord lieutenant of the county, would have allowed the meeting, still less supported it, had he thought the Orange masses were to be present. He had said, 'I do not anticipate anything but unanimity as regards to the avowed purpose of the meeting, and I hope it will not be made a handle for any party feeling'.[6] On these assumptions, Caledon gave permission for the meeting to be held and did not seek any extra police or soldiers, later stating that 'when I considered that the meeting was convened at the desire of persons of the highest respectability and weight in the county, I thought it would be unbecoming in me to require a military force or an increase of the constabulary'.[7]

Caledon, while supporting the Conservative cause, was moderate in his views; he did not subscribe to the ultra-conservative stance of the Orange Order, shared by much of Tyrone's gentry, including many of those who called the meeting. They were determined to secure the Protestant position of ascendancy by mobilising the Orange Order if parliamentary procedure failed to satisfy their demands. The result was what the *Londonderry Journal* later called a 'struggle between sedate conservatism and conservatism run mad'. In December 1834, the moderates and ultra-conservatives were prepared to unite for the meeting. However, the following month's election would see a bitter battle between twenty-two-year-old Lord James Alexander, son of the Earl of Caledon, and twenty-one-year-old Lord Claud Hamilton, brother of one of the biggest landowners in Tyrone and Donegal, the Marquess of Abercorn.[8]

The choice of Dungannon was geographically curious. The county town of Tyrone was and is Omagh, much more central than Dungannon, which is in the east of the county. In 1829 Omagh had hosted a meeting organised by the Tyrone Brunswick Clubs, which had attracted 20,000 people to voice their opposition to Catholic emancipation.[9] Dungannon was far from convenient for the Marquess of Abercorn and his tenantry, who faced an almost 100-mile round trip from Strabane on roads described as 'shameful' by government commissioner Jonathan Binns.[10] *Ordnance Survey Memoirs* stated that the roads around Dungannon were 'not kept in good order' and 'all are in bad repair', making the journey yet more difficult for the crowds that flocked to the town.[11] The MP for Dungannon was Lord Northland, a member of the powerful Knox family, but he lived in Brussels, did not support the Orange Order and was not involved in organising the meeting, so he did not influence the choice of meeting place.

The most likely reason for choosing Dungannon was its historical importance to Protestants. By holding monster meetings at venues like Clontarf and Castlebar, Daniel O'Connell delved into events of historical and nationalist import to stoke up emotion and popular support. The historical significance of Dungannon was much less, but the organisers of the meeting may have had a similar idea to O'Connell, because the town had hosted the volunteer convention of 1782, a meeting of Presbyterians and other Protestants that had forced the government into granting major concessions, including Grattan's Parliament. The motives of Protestants in 1834 were very different from those of their more liberal predecessors, but by invoking the spirit of 1782 the organisers obviously hoped to appeal to popular memory by choosing the location of a previous triumph. The difficulties of getting there do not appear to have affected the size of the crowd that attended.

In the mid-1830s, County Tyrone had 1,447 freeholders, that is, those with sufficient property to qualify to vote.[12] If we add the gentry and clergymen for whom the meeting was supposedly convened, there should have been roughly 5,000 people at the meeting whereas, according to newspaper reports, 75,000 people attended.[13] Even allowing for biased reporting, this figure is way above the police estimate of 3,000.[14] The meeting was staged in the confined area of the great square of the town, in contrast to the large open spaces used by O'Connellite meetings, and this also tends to cast doubt on the crowd size. The square itself measured

156 yards by 43 yards, an area surely incapable of holding a crowd as large as 75,000 along with their horses and carts, banners and drums.[15] Furthermore, the town itself stood on high ground with the approaches, particularly from the south, being described as 'very steep and difficult'.[16] Just four streets led to the square, which again leads to a question mark over the numbers. It can be seen that the conservative press grossly overestimated the crowd size, a common occurrence since meeting organisers depended heavily on propaganda to further their cause. Gary Owens points out that crowd estimates in this period need to be scaled down considerably and that clearly applies in this case.[17] Nonetheless, the crowd was much larger than Caledon expected. Where did they come from, and why?

According to the chief of police in Ulster, Sir Frederick Stoven, the initial announcement would not have deterred Catholics from attending the meeting had they chosen to do so.[18] The factor that turned what Caledon envisaged as a meeting of the highest classes in Tyrone into a party meeting of the plebeian rabble was the circulation of a notice throughout the county in the days preceding the event:

Protestants of Tyrone, will you desert your King? No; 'you will die first'. The King as becomes a son of GEORGE the third, has spurned from his council the men who would have overturned the most valued institutions of your country, and would have led your monarch to a violation of his coronation oath. Your sovereign has done his duty, will you ABANDON yours? If you will not; if you will support your King as honestly as he has supported you; if you will maintain the LIBERTIES which your FATHERS purchased with their blood, you will be found at the GREAT PROTESTANT MEETING to be held in DUNGANNON, on FRIDAY 19th instant at 12 o'clock, and your cry will be 'The King and Constitution; The Altar and the throne'.[19]

Stoven later reported that sixteen emissaries had distributed hundreds of these notices the night after the meeting had been convened; they gave a new character to the meeting, so that Caledon was 'completely deceived' according to Stoven.[20] It is not known who distributed the notices or who was behind the idea of bringing the lower classes on board, but the way some of the county's elite entered the square in Dungannon provided evidence that many of them must have played a part in getting the mob there.

Owens asserts that 'processions lent colour to every public occasion; no great event was considered complete without one' and Dungannon did not disappoint in this regard.[21] The Omagh meeting of 1829 had seen Beltrim landowner Alexander Cole Hamilton arrive at the meeting on horseback at the head of 400 of his tenantry,[22] and this precedent was very much imitated at Dungannon in 1834. In what appear to have been well-choreographed grand entries to the square, 'local Orange lodges appeared first, next came the tenantry of Mr Pettigrew, and Squire Mountray, followed by Orange lodges from Aughnacloy, Carnteel, and Emyvale. Then came the Ballygawley "Boys" led by Captain Crossley and Sir Hugh Stewart. Moy and Killyman came next led by Joseph Greer.' Stoven later recalled that:

> … all morning large quantities of people had been coming in from all directions, particularly from the Ballygawley side, a great many horsemen. I heard one large procession of 50 to 60 horsemen, who were said to be Mr Murdrie's tenants, and then I heard drums coming … I saw three separate Orange processions with two flags each,

very large flags, like the ensigns of a regiment, drums and fifes, and playing 'Protestant Boys', and all those sort of tunes.[23]

Ladies waving their handkerchiefs from windows added to the colour of the occasion, while the most spectacular entrance was reserved for Abercorn and Lord Claud Hamilton who rode in mounted on white horses 'splendidly decorated with orange and purple' followed by 1,061 of their tenantry on horseback, a procession said to have 'occupied upwards of two miles'.[24] It is obvious that the tenants, who came from as far away as Strabane or Emyvale, did not merely turn up of their own accord on the morning of the meeting. They had to be organised, mobilised and transported to the venue, something that required advanced planning by the gentry with whom they entered the square.

The liberal newspaper *The Londonderry Journal and Tyrone Advertiser* was of the opinion that tenants had been forced to attend the meeting and, in a passage worth quoting at length, was scathing in its criticism of their landlords:

We have had several communications regarding the means which were taken to *persuade* the Marquis of Abercorn's tenantry to attend the meeting. We have no pleasure in speaking harshly of this young nobleman; but certainly, we do not calumniate him when we say, that there are few, indeed of his tenantry, who would go an inch out of his way to serve him, if they could avoid it; and yet he collected about 1,000 of them, as his retinue, at this county meeting, where they were compelled to listen to and applaud sentiments which most of them cordially abhor. The truth is, circulars were distributed among them requesting their attendance; and as nearly the whole of them are tenants-at-will, disobedience was out of the question ... We learn that the tenantry were *paraded* at Baron's Court on

Thursday morning; and any *shabby looking*, or *badly mounted*, poor devil got permission to return home; while tickets were given to all *decent* looking tenants, which were given to frank them at the inns at Dungannon and on the road.[25]

If this is true, and the bias of this newspaper must be kept in mind, it would suggest a well-planned mobilisation of Abercorn's tenantry.

The paper had 'little doubt whatever, that the other bodies of tenantry who attended were acted upon by the *same soft persuasions* which so well succeeded with those on the Abercorn estates'.[26] But we have to ask whether it is true that the tenantry was forced to attend. The Orange Order included much of the Protestant lower classes within its ranks, and tenants who were members would certainly not have had to be forced into attending a meeting of this sort. Nor, it may be assumed, would the tenants have been averse to a day spent away from the drudgery of everyday life especially as hospitality in the form of food and drink was provided along the route to the meeting, with the *Strabane Morning Post* reporting that Abercorn's tenantry received 'necessary refreshments' at Omagh and Ballygawley.[27] In addition, what occurred after the meeting would suggest popular Protestant support for its organisers and their aims from an extremely tense crowd indeed. Maura Cronin makes the point that the reason repeal meetings were generally peaceful was the apathy of the crowd and the fact that the main issue in question was of little interest to them.[28] However, the issue in question in Dungannon was of extreme importance to the crowd because they felt that their very way of life was under extreme threat.

The meeting began at midday and was addressed by the Marquess of Abercorn, Earl Belmore, Viscount Corry, the Earl of Caledon and Lord James Alexander, all of them placed on a hustings allegedly capable of holding 700 people, along with the nineteen signatories of the meeting declaration and many other figures from the gentry and the clergy,[29] among them the magistrates A. W. Cole Hamilton, Gilbert King, Charles Irwin, George Lendrum, A. H. Irwin, Rev. J. G. Porter, Thomas Gervois, James Galbraith, Mervyn Stewart, George Vesey, Samuel Vesey, Hind Cryan, George Hill and Edward Litton KC.[30] The language in the speeches could not be considered extreme or inflammatory. Belmore evoked local pride by reminding his audience 'how unnecessary either argument or eloquence must be, to induce the men of Tyrone to come forward in support of their King', while Abercorn called on the assemblage 'not to break the laws but to preserve them; not to invade property but to secure their own; not to intimidate, but to respond to the gracious summons of their sovereign'.[31]

The speeches were well received by the crowd, indeed wildly cheered and applauded, but how attentively they actually listened and whether they could hear what was said is debatable because, according to the police, 'the principal part of [the crowd], contrary to his lordship's expectation, marched in regular procession through the town, and also past the hustings, with scarves, flags, music playing party tunes, and firing shots'.[32] Caledon later complained that 'they [the Orangemen] kept marching backwards and forwards very much to the annoyance of the meeting, and this continued during the time it lasted'.[33] Stoven considered that 'Orangemen bore a most conspicuous and indecorous part' at the meeting. The scale of their presence is indicated by the fact that the police could identify only three of them owing to the quantity of flags and banners, the display of which was of course illegal under the Party Processions Act which forbade party colours in public.[34]

The meeting ended at 3 p.m. without any major incident. However, when the gentry left the platform, one of them, J. C. Stronge, was forced to leave by a back entrance, such was the level of abuse he received from a section of the crowd. Stronge, a magistrate known to be vigorous in enforcing the law and a supporter of Caledon, had ordered the removal of an Orange arch from the town the previous year and had gained the nickname 'Papist' Stronge for his trouble; his presence on stage was not well received.[35] The crowd was further excited by the impromptu action of Lord Claud Hamilton, who allowed himself to be sworn into the Orange Order in a local public house and was then chaired through the town in triumph by the mob, much to the disgust of Caledon. Hamilton's speech from the platform in defence of Protestant rights had been more provocative than that of his brother:

> Let us look back to a time when similar efforts were foiled by the glorious King William – when our ancestors bled and died in defence of the Protestant religion (cheers) and let us prove worthy of the rich boon which they left us, by showing that we are ready to die rather than yield to it.[36]

Following his initiation, Hamilton promptly left the scene, with Abercorn and Sir Hugh Stewart, and proceeded to Stewart's residence at Ballygawley House leaving the excited mob to act as it pleased. Cronin argues that the elite could determine whether mob assemblies ended in violence or not, depending on whether they procrastinated or intervened before matters got out of control and on whether or not they displayed a conciliatory attitude towards the crowd.[37] In this case the actions of Hamilton and the indifference of the magistrates – officials appointed by the government to uphold law and order, who viewed the events from the hustings – very much contributed to the actions of the mob.

Although the meeting had ended, the marching continued until a late hour. As Caledon had not seen the need to bring reinforcements to the town, and because much of the Dungannon police force had attended the monthly market in Moy, there were simply not enough police in the vicinity to deal with the crowd.[38] This left the constabulary relatively powerless, which allowed the mob the freedom to parade and march as they pleased until they finally dispersed at their own leisure. While there was no riot, it was the opinion of the head of the local constabulary, Captain Duff, that 'nothing could possibly be worse than the taunting and irregular conduct of the Orangemen going home, by their continued firing in the streets'.[39] One of the shots fired was aimed at Stoven, who was observing from a high vantage point, missing him by a narrow margin. Stoven, as head of the police in Ulster, was a much despised figure because his job entailed applying the law against Orangemen, a duty he carried out robustly. Captain Duff was regarded in a similar light, judging by a threatening notice placed in the prayer book of his wife the previous Sunday, warning him not to interfere in the rally:

> Sir, as this is the last day to be in this rotten town, I send you this advice, tell Robinson that he and that damned scout Stronge will do very little on Friday at the Protestant meeting; that Duff and Sir F. Stoven had better stay in the house or they may get an Orange ball which may cause them to stay at home on the 12th July. Tell Duff that he and Stronge, that they will not be able to stop the meeting, nor the walking on the 12th; tell them to kiss my ... and suck my ... I remain yours, Dodd, Amen.[40]

The fact that certain individuals entered a place of worship, of which they were possibly members, and had the audacity to place this note inside a lady's prayer book, shows that the perpetrators were willing to ignore the norms of respect and decency of upper-class society, which suggests lower-class involvement. As the note was placed five days before the meeting, it also suggests that the lower classes were already briefed about it and fully intended to be there. There was always a risk of the lower classes behaving in such a manner, yet the elite who planned the meeting obviously considered they needed to bring the lower classes on board to swell numbers and provide a Protestant show of strength to the government.

This meeting did not result in any serious rioting and it is worth asking why. In many cases where riots occur, a focal point is needed on which the crowd can vent its anger. This crowd comprised Protestants and Presbyterians; no Catholics were present, or at least none willing to announce their presence, and this eliminated one possible flashpoint, as did the fact that the town's Catholic church was in the eastern suburbs, well outside the visible focus of the crowd.[41] One other potential source of contention in Orange circles was absent, and this may also explain why no riot took place. This missing element was the police force which, because of changes in its make-up in the previous years, had become much more centralised and therefore efficient in its dealings with assemblies which broke the law. Many Orangemen loathed the police because of their enforcement of the Party Processions Act, which banned political processions and displays of party colours, and there had been clashes on many occasions. But because the police were not present in great numbers, those who were there kept a low profile. This absence of a force to oppose the law-breaking elements of the crowd removed another possible focus for the crowd's anger.

Nonetheless, though there was no riot, the actions of the mob did form a precedent for trouble at future elections in the county. The Orange Order became a political force locally because it offered those candidates prepared to use its numbers and intimidatory strength the 'muscle' required to secure victory. In the elections the following month, the first election contest in Tyrone in sixty-eight years, Hamilton – with the backing of the Orange mob – defeated Alexander in a bitter campaign between the conservative candidates. The 1839 election, too, saw serious clashes between Hamilton's supporters and those of the Liberal candidate James Alexander Boyle, and the Liberal candidate in the 1841 Dungannon borough election, John Falls, was forced to pull out of the contest after the first day's voting in the interests of his supporters' and his own safety after an Orange mob wrecked the properties and businesses of his supporters.[42]

6

COLLECTIVE ACTION
AND THE POOR LAW

The political mobilisation
of the Irish poor, 1851–78

MEL COUSINS

It is now over three decades since the publication of Clark's seminal article on the political mobilisation of Irish farmers.[1] Yet many aspects of the political mobilisation of different social classes in Ireland remain uninvestigated (or under-investigated). One issue in particular, which has received little study, is the political mobilisation of the Irish poor.[2] I examine one aspect of this issue: collective action by 'poor' people in relation to the operation of the Poor Law in mid-Victorian Ireland, circa 1851 to 1878, the period bounded by the Famine and the Land War.

My interest in this area arose from a study of the Poor Law in Ireland in the nineteenth century. What struck me about the available sources was that none of them allowed me to hear the voice of the 'paupers' themselves or their views on the Poor Law. The sources, whether the official files of the chief secretary's office, the private archives of key politicians or the newspapers of the time, all reflect the views of the governors of the system. One can carry out extensive analysis of the data on the number and type of people availing of indoor and outdoor relief or investigate the material on dietary standards or mortality in workhouses, yet none of this tells one anything directly about how people in workhouses or on outdoor relief themselves felt about the operation of the Poor Law. However, incidents of collective action by the poor in relation to the Poor Law do allow us to get some insights into their views.

It is of course difficult to define the term 'poor' strictly. In nineteenth-century Ireland, much of the population could be considered poor. In this chapter, I use a narrower sense of the term, specifically to mean the pauper classes: those eligible for or potentially eligible for poor relief under the Irish Poor Law acts. The term 'political mobilisation' is also not unproblematic when applied to examples of collective action by the poor in relation to the operation of the Poor Law. Collective action may be defined as 'any goal-directed activity jointly pursued by two or more individuals'.[3] Political mobilisation may be defined as 'the actors' attempts to influence the existing distribution of power'.[4]

Unlike the situation in England, there was no national system of Poor Laws in Ireland before 1838.[5] Although houses of industry existed in a number of Irish towns and cities, there was no system of outdoor relief in Ireland. Following the introduction of the 1834 Poor Law in England, the British Government decided to introduce a broadly similar system in Ireland, based on a report by Sir George Nicholls, a Poor Law commissioner. The Irish Poor Law was, if anything, a purer version of the 1834 model and was, at least initially, confined solely to indoor relief.[6] Given the absence of any previous Poor Law, there was no equivalent in Ireland of the anti-Poor Law protests seen in England and Wales. Indeed, the initial protests in Ireland during the early 1840s were against the collection of rates.

During the period I am looking at here – from the 1850s to the 1870s – collective action by the poor in relation to the Poor Law tended not to overlap with the violent activities of organisations like the Ribbonmen and Whiteboys. For example, Beames' study of peasant assassinations in Tipperary in the decade after the introduction of the Poor Law does not indicate that any cases were Poor Law related.[7] Nor did collective action by the poor normally involve parliamentary or Poor Law elections. Given the state of the franchise then,[8] very few poor persons had a vote in such elections.[9] Studies to date indicate that, though there was a limited degree of politicisation of Poor Law elections in this period, poor people did not act collectively in the context of these elections.[10] Hoppen's study indicates that poor people were certainly involved in collective action around parliamentary elections, but there is again little indication that this collective action sought to advance any particular view on the Poor Law.[11]

My research in official publications (such as annual reports of the Poor Law commission and local government board), public archives and local newspapers identified two main types of collective action:

- Large-scale protest marches or demonstrations by poor persons (generally not currently receiving poor relief) concerning – in a broad sense – poor relief and often including a march to the local workhouse.
- Small-scale protests by inmates of workhouses including fires, assaults, riots and the like.[12]

Given the incomplete state of the archives it is not possible to say that this chapter offers a representative sample of such collective actions, but it does include all the events of this kind (excluding individual actions) that I have identified. The events are set out in more detail in appendices 1 and 2.

ATTACK ON A POTATOE STORE.

Depiction of a food riot in Ireland, c.1845 © Getty images

There is a perhaps surprising absence of literature specifically on the issue of collective action and poor relief. There is of course an extensive literature on collective action,[13] and particularly on collective action by poor people, for example, food riots.[14] I have not, however, located any study that looks specifically at collective action as it relates to Poor Law institutions. In the Irish context, the literature is even more limited. It is clear that food riots did occur in pre-Poor Law Ireland. Wells discusses the number of food riots during the famine of 1799–1801.[15] Magennis looks at food riots in 1756–7.[16] Kinealy's study indicates that, as one might expect, food riots, attacks on workhouses and soup kitchens, and related violence were common during the Great Famine.[17] However, there appears to have been very little study of such collective action in the post-Famine period.

Looking first at large-scale protests, the events identified here took the form of an assembly and/or march by several hundred persons seeking employment and/or outdoor relief. Four specific events have been identified – in Belfast (1858), Galway (1865),[18] Limerick (1861) and Westport (1863)[19] – and there was considerable commonality among these four events. All took place in or around the period of the agricultural depression of 1859–1864 and all (except Belfast) were in the west of Ireland, which was most severely affected by the depression. All involved an absence of employment and food. In Belfast, Limerick and Galway, the people involved were urban labourers and artisans. In contrast, the Westport demonstration was by rural tenants who had travelled a considerable distance to seek outdoor relief from Westport workhouse. All the demonstrations included a formal approach to the authorities seeking relief: to the Poor Law guardians in Westport and Galway, to the mayor in Limerick. Only in Limerick was there any degree of violence and even here this was very minor, though the response of the authorities in drafting in extra troops indicated their concern that protests might develop further.

Newspaper and other reports are unfortunately vague about those participating. It appears the protestors were predominantly male but this may be a function of the reporting, which may have tended to downplay the participation of women and children. Only in Limerick were there a small number of arrests (all men). In Belfast, Galway and Limerick the leaders of the protest came from the groups affected.[20] In Westport, in contrast, the protest was led by a Roman Catholic curate.

What was the response to the protests? In all cases there was a combination of repression and conciliation by the local authorities. In all cases except Belfast, the police or army forces were significantly reinforced despite the absence of (or very minor nature of) violence. At the same time, however, in all four cases the local authorities attempted to provide employment for the demonstrators and/or to raise charitable relief. One interesting point is the extent to which the local bourgeoisie played multiple roles in local governance. In Limerick, for example, we find the mayor – whom the demonstrators had approached in the course of their march – on the following day sitting as a magistrate on the local bench and sentencing some of the demonstrators to a term in prison.[21] On the same day, the mayor travelled to Dublin and met the lord lieutenant and a number of senior officials to seek finance for public works in Limerick. Given a delay in receiving state support, a number of weeks later we find the Limerick magistrates guaranteeing the cost of public works.

Looking at the aims and objectives of the protest, in general the protestors sought employment and/or outdoor relief. At the time, outdoor relief was very sparingly provided by Irish Poor Law unions. It could only be provided to able-bodied poor on the order of the Poor Law Commission and such an order would only be granted where the workhouse was full or unable to receive inmates due to the existence of contagious disease. In none of these cases was outdoor relief provided; the protestors were instead offered a place in the house (which they generally refused). However, it is clear that the protestors did succeed in advancing their position by their protests, and that public works and charitable donations were provided as a response.

The question of protests in workhouses is clearly linked to the literature on protests in other institutions like gaols[22] and psychiatric institutions.[23] However, though historical accounts of workhouses and similar institutions in the nineteenth century often referred to riots or related issues,[24] with the exception of Green's recent study[25] I have not come across any comparative study of such protests. It is clear that friction between inmates and officials was a common feature of workhouse life in Ireland in the period. How far such friction led to collective action varied greatly in the examples found here. Given that these events are, by definition, smaller in scope, it is more likely that others exist that did not show up in state papers and related documents. On the one hand, there was a long-term pattern of resistance by a large number of young women in the South Dublin Union (workhouse).[26] This resistance went on from 1857 to at least 1862 and consistently involved at least fifty young women in their late teens or early twenties.[27] Their activities varied greatly, from breaking windows or assaulting workhouse officials or other inmates, to setting fire (or attempting to set fire) to the workhouse. Without wishing to overstate this series of events or exaggerate the intentions of its participants, it is arguable that the struggles in the South Dublin Union represent the most sustained opposition to the Poor Law in this period.

At the next level, we find serious but more short-term riots in the South Dublin,[28] Cork, Waterford and Clonmel unions in the early 1860s.[29] The date of the riots is interesting. Again, it is the period of the agricultural depression, but – and this is particularly relevant with the young women in the South Dublin Union – it also corresponds with the coming-of-age of children who had been admitted to the workhouses during the Great Famine, when they may have lost one or both parents. It is also worth noting that these four unions were among the nine largest unions in Ireland;

it appears likely that the size of the workhouse and the difficulty in managing large groups of paupers was a contributing factor to workhouse riots.

Thirdly, we have one-off cases of resistance to specific actions, such as that in Balrothery in 1873.[30] This was a spontaneous response by mothers to a decision by the workhouse officials to take their children away from them, and occurred in a workhouse where contention was otherwise largely absent. This particular example was located purely by chance while going through the minute books of the Balrothery workhouse for a different purpose and it seems likely that many more such occurrences are hidden away in union minute books and local newspaper reports. A dispute in the Belfast workhouse in late 1869 may also be put in this category. Six Catholic men refused to break stones as part of their workhouse duties on the basis that the day in question was a Roman Catholic church holiday. They were charged with insubordinate conduct and sentenced to fourteen days in gaol. Finally, we have a number of one-off incidents such as cases of fire and theft. The specific reasons for these actions are often unclear from the reports and it is not evident whether they are related to broader grievances.

The South Dublin Union case is clearly unique. However, the case of the Waterford Union is perhaps more typical of what may have occurred in a number of unions, only coming to outside attention because a long-term pattern of 'dogged resistance' ultimately crossed the line into violence. The Waterford board in the early 1860s was, to say the least, a fractious one and this may have contributed to trouble in the workhouse. The appointment of a new master, Mr Ryan, in June 1861 appears to have led to an attempt to impose stricter discipline on the inmates. Ryan reported that he had found that about fifteen to twenty able-bodied men and thirty to forty able-bodied women were taking part in 'dogged resistance to those in authority'.[31] This involved shouting at meals, insolent dancing and singing in wards at night, and a disorderly manner in coming into the dining-hall. The involvement of some of the inmates in producing muslin work also appears to have been an issue.[32]

In August 1861, a fight broke out between the assistant master Mr Clery and a number of inmates, and Clery was subsequently convicted of assaulting one of them, Mary Crowley. The Poor Law commission ordered an investigation by the local Poor Law inspector, whose report concluded that Clery had injured the woman when he himself had been attacked, but regretted the use of violence against a female inmate. In September 1861, a discussion at the board of guardians suggested that the workhouse was being 'kept in hot water' by about eight to ten women and four or five men, leading to repeated rows. The chairman directed the master to bring the names of refractory paupers before the board. The following week four 'incorrigible' boys, who were in the habit of going in and out of the workhouse at their pleasure, were brought before the board. They were expelled.

At the end of December 1861, the master was attacked at mass by three young male inmates. Their leader – a John Sullivan – was subsequently charged before the quarter sessions with assault occasioning actual bodily harm. As the reporter of the *Waterford Mail* commented, 'the very spirit of evil seemed to lurk in his half-defiant gaze'.[33] It appears there was a charge against Sullivan – whom several witnesses referred to as a boy – at the time for insubordinate conduct in the workhouse. Sullivan, whose only evidence was to the effect that he wished he had taken the master's life, was sentenced to seven years' penal servitude, afterwards mitigated to three years. He had been convicted already five times for similar offences.

In contrast to the larger-scale actions, the workhouse riots tended to be much more reactive and, with certain exceptions like Balrothery, not to have clearly defined goals. Again in contrast to the larger protests outside the workhouse, the response to small-scale internal riots was almost entirely confined to repression. Almost by definition – because these were much more likely to be reported in the newspapers or commented on – the small-scale riots that are recorded tended to involve violence, including attacks on workhouse officials as in South Dublin, Cork and Waterford. In these cases, the assailants tended to receive significant prison terms. Another response was to move troublemakers to a separate refractory ward, as with the young women in the South Dublin Union. Generally speaking, there is little indication that the workhouse protests led to improvements in the conditions although, as with so many aspects of workhouse life, it is difficult or impossible to know precisely what went on day by day.

From what we do know, the people involved in workhouse riots appear to have been young and able-bodied. Women were very strongly represented in protests, though men were likelier to be involved in violence against the person. One strand of the South Dublin Union resistance appears to have been exclusively female. Reports indicate that women were also involved in the South Dublin riots in 1862, though not in the more serious violence.[34] Similarly, in Cork, even though those ultimately convicted of riot were men, the protests seem to have begun in the female ward where the inmates objected to being given stale Indian meal for breakfast.[35] A number of women were committed to the workhouse cells for offences, and the immediate cause of the riot was an attempt by the male inmates to free these women. In age, the women in the South Dublin riots were in their teens and early twenties; Sullivan, who attacked the master of the Waterford workhouse, was referred to by several witnesses at his trial as a boy; those charged with riotous conduct at Cork workhouse in March 1863 were aged sixteen to twenty-two.[36]

The cases examined here were all found in relevant files in the chief secretary's office, in the archives of key officials at this period (in particular Thomas Larcom, under-secretary 1853–68), in the reports of the Poor Law commission and other relevant parliamentary papers, or in a sampling of local newspapers. A comprehensive study of collective action over the Poor Law would need to examine the minute books of all Irish unions (most of which do have surviving minute books) and all local newspapers (many of which reported meetings of boards of guardians in considerable detail – often in more detail than that contained in the minutes). Such a study might, at a conservative estimate, take twenty years.

What might such a study find? My best guess is that, though similar large protests may well have taken place in other areas, even a comprehensive study would probably not dramatically increase the number of examples. In the case of small-scale protests, the long-standing dispute in the South Dublin Union is exceptional and there is no indication that any similar protest existed elsewhere in this period. As for the smaller-scale riots in Cork and Waterford, it is possible that such riots occurred in other unions or other periods.[37] It is very likely that the sort of 'dogged resistance to authority' reported at Waterford occurred in many other workhouses. Such relatively minor protests would not be likely to feature in any of the sources examined here – even the minute books – until there was an outbreak of violence.[38] Likewise, one-off events like the protests in Balrothery and Belfast probably occurred in many other places.

In the period from the Famine to the Land War, it is clear that there was a high degree of collective activity, including riots of various kinds. In addition to collective action related to the Fenian movement, there were three main kinds of crowd activity:

- religious marches and riots, including sectarian riots in Belfast[39] and the Gavazzi riots;[40]
- electoral activity and riots related to parliamentary elections;[41]
- political protests and riots.

There were other significant riots that may or may not have had a political motivation. For example, shortly after the Cork workhouse riot, a much more extensive riot took place in Cork city after the celebrations of the Prince of Wales' wedding.[42] At times, there was also some collective activity by labourers in relation to conditions of employment, though this appears to have been limited in extent.[43] Even if the events identified in this chapter understate the numbers that probably occurred, it appears that large-scale collective activity in relation to the Poor Law made up only a very small proportion of total collective activity in Ireland at the time. Unfortunately, though there are isolated references to riots in prisons and other institutions, it is impossible to compare the extent of such riots with those in workhouses.

It is difficult to make any comparison with the earlier period. In the years from 1838 to 1846, the main collective activity in relation to the Poor Law, albeit not by the poor, appears to have been resistance to paying rates.[44] Collective activity by the poor was common during the Great Famine, but circumstances then were so exceptional that it cannot reasonably be compared to the post-Famine period in any meaningful way. In the Land War period, there was a dramatic increase in collective activity, particularly in relation to land agitation.[45] In the decade from

1879 on, as Feingold has shown, the Irish tenantry engaged in a struggle to take control of the Poor Law boards of guardians from the landlords, and they succeeded to a significant extent in doing so.[46] However, my researches do not indicate that the Land War and subsequent period saw any significant increase in collective activity by the poor themselves. Of course the tenantry fighting for control of the Poor Law institutions were less well-off than the landlords, but they were not generally poor. My researches have located a number of demonstrations and marches similar to the large-scale protests described here.[47] In addition, there appear to have been extensive labour disputes about wages and conditions of employment on public relief works in the west of Ireland in 1891. Finally I have found instances of labourers' protests against a board of guardians' activities (or inactivity) in the building of labourers' cottages under the Labourers (Ireland) Act 1883.[48]

Clark, in his study of the Land War, identified four main types of activity engaged in by what he calls the challenging collectivity.[49] These were open-air meetings or public demonstrations, the boycott, assistance to tenants and violence. As we have seen, large-scale protests against the Poor Law in the period from the Famine to the Land War were all of the first type. The boycott had not yet generally developed as a method of collective activity; by definition the poor did not have the financial resources to assist particular families; and violence was rarely used in collective activity concerning the Poor Law (other than in limited cases in workhouse riots). However, the public demonstrations that Clark describes as a key type of activity during the Land War were very similar to the forms of activity described earlier.[50] Indeed to a large extent they represented the poor person's equivalent of the relief meetings that the bourgeoisie frequently held in disadvantaged areas to raise relief or launch public works. Clark considers it likely that more public meetings were held during the Land War than in any previous political movement in Ireland: from October 1879 until the end of 1880 the constabulary reported an average of forty-six land meetings a month – a striking contrast with the small number of protests identified here.

The protests by workhouse inmates were much more reactive and without clear motives. They were, in general, a reaction to the deliberately restrictive way in which workhouses were run. In contrast to the flexible response to protest without, the response to protest within was almost always repressive, including workhouse punishments, special probationary wards, expulsion and/or refusal of re-admittance, and criminal prosecution and gaol. Overall, it is clear that collective activity by the poor in relation to the Poor Law made up a relatively small proportion of all collective activity in this period.

APPENDIX 1: SHORT DESCRIPTION OF LARGE-SCALE OUTDOOR PROTESTS

In Belfast in April 1858, a 'body of men' approached the *Daily Mercury* newspaper office complaining of 'utter destitution' and claiming that various relief funds had been exhausted or had ceased. A few days later a meeting of the working classes with a 'very large attendance' took place in the Corn Exchange. It was chaired by one Thomas Lloyd, described as a 'tradesman' or 'working man', and addressed by a number of men described as labourers.

Sources: *Daily Mercury, Belfast Newsletter*, April 1858.

In Limerick in January 1861, a crowd estimated at up to 800 or 900 assembled and marched through the city. One of the leaders of the march was described as a shoemaker. The cause of the march was attributed to a lack of employment and food, and the crowd demanded work. The march was, in the main, peaceful, though there was one minor outbreak of violence when a baker's window was broken and some loaves of bread stolen. Those responsible were immediately arrested by the Royal Irish Constabulary. The response to the march was a combination of sixty police reinforcements, prison sentences (of between seven and fourteen days) for those involved in the theft and the establishment of a relief fund and public works.

Sources: *Limerick Reporter*, February 1861; NLI Larcom MS 7783.

In Westport in June 1863, a local Roman Catholic curate led a group of between 200 and 400 'hungry paupers' on a march to the workhouse to seek outdoor relief. The cause of the march was lack of food. Outdoor relief was refused, though relief in the house was offered (but taken up by eighty-five persons only). A relief fund and public works were established.

Sources: *Mayo Constitution* and the *Connacht Patriot and General Advertiser*, June/July 1863.

In Galway in January 1865 an estimated 200 men and boys held a meeting and march around Galway city, including a march to the workhouse. The leaders of the march were described as 'local petty agitators amongst the mechanics' and the cause attributed was lack of employment. The crowd sought work and outdoor relief (which was refused, though relief in the house was offered). In addition to the offer of relief in the house, which was not widely taken up, 400 military were drafted in and a relief fund and public works were established.

Sources: NLI Larcom MS 7609; NAI CSORP/1865/1141; Galway County Archives, Galway union minute book, January 1865.

APPENDIX 2: SHORT DESCRIPTION OF INTERNAL PROTESTS

A. Long-term resistance

The case of the young women in South Dublin workhouse would appear to be in a class of its own; it has been discussed in more detail by Burke and Clark.[51] It lasted from about 1857 to about 1862 and, in total, involved over fifty young women in their late teens or early twenties. The resistance involved fires, riots, destructions of workhouse property and assaults; those participating were sent to gaol on several occasions. The precise causes and the subsequent histories of the women deserve more detailed study.

B. Major riots

I identified a number of serious workhouse riots, including riots in the South Dublin Union in November 1862, in Cork workhouse in March 1863 and in Waterford workhouse in 1862, with low-level resistance eventually leading to assaults.

C. Resistance to specific events

Examples include resistance by women to an attempt to take their children away from them and place them in a separate ward, in the Balrothery Union in March 1873, leading to minor assaults on the officials involved; and resistance by six Roman Catholic men in Belfast workhouse to being required to work on a Catholic holy day, for which they were sent to gaol for fourteen days.

There can be no doubt that these incidents are indicative of a much wider occurrence of similar events (at least at the lower end of the scale of seriousness). Robins, for example, in his book on pauper children cites a number of incidents of children assaulting a schoolmistress or attempting to set fire to the workhouse.[52] The focus has been on collective actions and so no account has been taken of one-off or individual assaults and other actions.

7

RECOVERING THE CARGO OF THE *JULIA*

Salvage, law and the killing of 'wreckers' in Conamara in 1873[1]

JOHN CUNNINGHAM

In the early months of 1873, George Bond spent several periods on Lettermullen, an island in the Ceantar na nOileán district of Conamara, in the west of Ireland. A commissioned boatman in the coastguard, he was there to assist a salvage operation. On 11 April 1873, he later deposed, the discovery of a large balk of oak that had been concealed sparked a violent confrontation between local people and the outsiders:

> We proceeded to dig up the timber and erected a shears to get the timber out. It was in a field and oats were sown over the timber. We discovered it by means of tuck sticks and a large crowd was present whose behaviour was very violent. They pulled down the shears, threw stones at us and one man drew out his knife and tried to stab F. Garnier … In spite of all this we took the balk, the crowd saying that if we went into other gardens they would take

our lives. The crowd was armed with spades, pitchforks, stones, etc.[2]

This was by no means the most violent of a series of clashes that took place over a three-month period. In describing these encounters, Bond – and others of the outsiders concerned – represented the Lettermullen islanders as ferocious, volatile and antagonistic to strangers, as 'natives' or 'savages' who could not be reasoned with and were not amenable to ordinary legal process.[3] This was at odds with the impressions formed by other late nineteenth-century visitors to the place. Although the Ceantar na nOileán people were 'probably the poorest and most primitive in Ireland', according to the ethnologist Charles Browne who lived among them in 1897, they displayed kindness, patience and honesty. Moreover, he found them to be welcoming to strangers, even if a language barrier and strong personal and community pride made them seem shy and taciturn at first.[4] That curious and considerate visitors would get a different reception from that accorded to armed enforcers of the law was to be expected, but was serious conflict inevitable from the moment the *Julia* and her unaccompanied cargo of timber was washed up on the island?

If popular fiction and pictures of shipwrecks are a guide, the answer would be in the affirmative, for they depict battles of wit, with hapless officials and strandees facing cunning but imprudent indigenes.[5] Indeed the attitude of the 'civilised' world, in Ireland and elsewhere, to the people of the coastal frontiers was encapsulated in Robert Louis Stevenson's line: 'They will fence their fields with mahogany, and, after a decent interval, sup claret to their porridge.'[6] Underlying Stevenson's condescension lay truth of a sort. The aesthetic sense of subsistence societies was different from that of the literate world, so the luxuries of the latter were not necessarily valued in the former. This understanding, arguably, informed the Merchant Shipping Act of 1854, the relevant legislation in 1873. Its provisions on salvage, which had been promoted by the marine insurers Lloyds, included guidelines for rewarding salvors for their labour and for risks undertaken. The act also provided for the appointment of Receivers of Wreck, who would take charge of wrecked vessels, manage the retrieval of cargo until the owners were traced and divide the proceeds equitably between salvors and owners.[7] Thus, the reward earned by an islander for salvaging mahogany might be used to purchase a greater quantity of more appropriate fencing material.

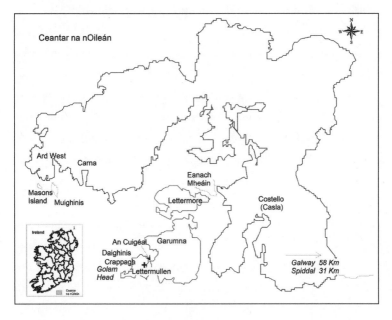

Map of the Ceantar na nOileán area, created by Síubhán Comer.

The salvage provisions of the Merchant Shipping Act may be seen as part of a process of extending the legitimacy of the 'rule of law' to parts of the population that had hitherto held to customary law and had regarded the official legal system as an oppressive or alien force. The rulers of eighteenth-century England, historian E. P. Thompson argued, sought to achieve hegemony by ensuring that, in its operation, the law gave the appearance of neutrality, allowing members of subaltern groups to secure occasional legal victories. With the official law retaining a coercive aspect but allowing for just outcomes, it became rational to engage with it in most circumstances rather than to fight against it.[8] Historians of the Subaltern Studies group have disputed that anything like the 'rule of law' was applied in the British colonial world, and their arguments in this regard have had a resonance among some scholars working on Ireland. Nonetheless, it is clear that, in certain fields of contention at least, the authorities in Ireland resorted more often to appeasement than to repression when faced with rebellious groups or crowds.[9]

In a classic article, Douglas Hay showed that, even where they co-operated with salvage law, communities around the coasts of Britain and Ireland continued to hold to customary notions. People from poorer households in particular, were dependent on what the sea might bring for their furniture and for occasional indulgences, so, in the aftermath of a shipwreck, they naturally tended to prioritise their own real wants over the claims of those who were manifestly less needy.[10] It was not that coastal communities lacked morality in the matter, rather that where customary law clashed with the 'rule of law' at moments of crisis and distress, there was potential for grave misunderstandings. Arguably, such misunderstandings contributed to the negative depictions of islanders in mainstream culture.

Shipwrecks were frequent in the second half of the nineteenth century, although the total varied widely from one year to the next. In the admittedly adverse conditions of 1859, it was estimated that one in 175 voyages by British ships engaged in overseas trade ended in total or partial shipwreck. During the third quarter of the nineteenth century, there were generally more than a hundred wrecks annually around the coast of Ireland, but only a small percentage fetched up on the western seaboard.[11] That salvaged materials were important to the lives and economies of island and coastal communities in Ireland is indicated by folk memories surrounding the bountiful yields of particular wrecks. Since most shipwrecks occurred away from inhabited places, however, it was relatively unusual for abandoned cargoes to arrive intact and ready for salvage. Rather, they yielded up their treasures over a wide area and over an extended period, so the garnering did not generate much conflict.[12] Of course, whenever a cargo was deposited close to shore, there was the potential for a dispute involving two or more of the interested parties – rival groups of finders, the owners, the insurers and the forces of order.

Each case was different, and the available details are usually scanty and unreliable; but the tragic events surrounding the salvage of the *Julia* generated extensive evidence – including depositions from Irish-speaking witnesses. Testimony relating to events at Lettermullen was gathered for and presented at a coroner's inquest, a manslaughter trial, a Board of Trade inquiry and an internal admiralty inquiry, and it was commented on in the press. With such plentiful primary sources, we can draw conclusions about issues on which no judgements were made at the various hearings of the 1870s. The details of the case should be regarded as illustrative rather than representative, but they shed light on a number of interesting questions: the extent to which a coastal population was prepared to operate the law on salvage; the way that the full 'majesty of the law' was experienced by an isolated community in Ireland in the 1870s; the attitudes towards each other of a coastal population and a body of public officials; and the attitude of *petit-bourgeois* anglophone Ireland, generally, towards an Irish-speaking community.

For the people of south Conamara, the tragedy of the *Julia* began on the night of Thursday, 2 January 1873, when the barque-rigged sailing ship of 974 tons was dashed against Golam Head, just off Lettermullen. The Liverpool-bound vessel was derelict, having been abandoned by her crew during an Atlantic storm, and that part of her cargo of Quebec-grown timber that had been stored on deck was already washed away.[13] But the rest of her cargo was a welcome bounty for the mostly impoverished inhabitants of the treeless district. According to an inventory, the cargo consisted of 109 pieces of oak, 50 pieces of elm, 240 pieces of white pine, 715 pieces of square white pine, 1,827 deals and 6,467 pipe staves. Some of the pieces of 'square timber' were substantial: there were enormous balks of coffin oak, for example, 22 inches (0.56 m) square by 75 feet (23 m) long, valued at £7 10s. each, equivalent to five months' wages for a fully employed agricultural labourer.[14] News spread quickly and within days a large number of people had arrived to stake their claim. There were 'strangers' from near-by island and mainland communities hoping to salvage a balk or two, and there were officials seeking to protect the entire cargo on behalf of the owners – whoever they might turn out to be.

The first public official arrived on 4 January. This was William Farraday, a coastguard officer based on the mainland at Casla, ten miles away. Accompanied by two policemen and two subordinate coastguards, his immediate concern was to save the cargo before it was washed out to sea and he employed a number of islanders to help him. Frederick St Clair Ruthven, a police sub-inspector based in Spiddal, twelve miles further east than Casla, learned of the wreck on 4 January. On the following morning, which was 'wet and wild', he set out along with several underlings. It was dark when they reached Lettermullen, having crossed by currach from Carraroe to Garumna, and walked the five or six miles from there, pausing to cross the Cuigéal, a narrow but treacherous strait between the islands of Garumna and Lettermullen. Approaching Golam Head, they met 'several parties' carrying pieces of rigging and other salvaged material; arriving there, they found that the vessel had separated into three sections more than a hundred yards from one another. St Clair Ruthven took charge of nine men, police and coastguards, and set a guard on the timber. At first he allowed islanders to take small pieces for firewood, but he withdrew this concession when he considered it was being exploited.[15]

The coastguards and policemen found shelter close by the wreck in an abandoned cottage, which served as their barracks for the next few months. One of them said: 'It would be impossible to describe the inconvenience of the shanty, and the misery of spending the night in it. The accommodation was shared by a cow and a calf, two pigs, and sundry cocks and hens, which laid their eggs in the room in which we slept.' The senior men did not remain long in the shanty – St Clair Ruthven, for example, found 'digs' with Fr Nagle, the island priest.[16]

If the officers found the shanty lacking in creature comforts, they were little worse off than their near neighbours, many of whom also shared accommodation with animals.

According to a report on the area prepared for the Congested Districts Board in the 1890s: 'The houses of the poorest are of rubble stone work, set dry and plastered thickly inside. The rafters are of bog deal ... The simplest form of interior plan is one general living-room, with fireplace against one end wall.'[17] Charles Browne reported that 'tempered cow-dung' was used to plaster the interiors of the poorer houses, whose floors were 'usually of bare rock, or large stones, the spaces between being filled up with mortar or beaten clay'. Furnishings were meagre too, due largely to the lack of timber. Browne's descriptions – 'a rough table, perhaps a rude dresser knocked together from a few boards' – indicate that they were fashioned from driftwood and maritime wreckage.[18] A generation later, a medical doctor told a government inquiry: 'So long as the population is allowed to stay in Lettermore and Lettermullen, you will have nothing but misery and poverty. Their economic means are practically nothing.'[19]

Despite their attested inhospitability, the islands had a substantial and growing population. Not yet affected by emigration, Lettermullen's 787 craggy acres supported 383 people in 1851 and 626 in 1881.[20] That it could support so many was a source of puzzlement, even after the islands were linked by bridges to the mainland in 1897.[21] Survival on what one islander described as a 'bit of a rock that a dog wouldn't look at, where the pigs die and the spuds die' meant exploiting every resource of land, shore and sea. Charles Browne wrote that the community was 'one of fishermen and kelp-burners, who till a little land and keep a few cattle and sheep', but it was more than that, for poitín-making, turf-cutting and salvage were further elements of household economies.[22] There were highly regarded boat-builders, a number of shop- and síbín-keepers, and a prominent family of middlemen and merchant shopkeepers, the McDonoghs – based on the small island of Crappagh but dealing throughout the district.[23]

Charles Browne was a rigid social Darwinist – given to measuring heads and categorising people according to an 'index of nigrescence' – but he was a sympathetic observer, and his report of life on the islands of Ceantar na nOileán and on the 'psychology' of their people was quite comprehensive. The Lettermullen people, in particular, were 'shrewd and intelligent', and had other positive qualities. For one visitor to Ceantar na nOileán, however, the disposition of the people was a source of mixed blessings:

> An almost perfect community of goods exists on the island ... This is a happy state of things from a moral standpoint, but, taken economically, it is sad, as indicative that each man knows not the day or the hour when he himself may have to fall back on the charity of his neighbour.[24]

Farms were rented jointly by several families, in rundale, with commonage for their animals.[25] The typical family cultivated an acre of potatoes and an acre of oats or barley, crops that were fertilised by 'black weed' brought from the shore. As there were no wheeled vehicles on the islands and few beasts of burden, the weed was carried in baskets, a task which fell to the women. Women evidently performed a large portion of the labour – they also carried home the turf and joined in the field-work. Sheep-shearing, milking, butter-making and the care of fowl were all regarded as women's work.[26] For almost all the economic activities of the men, a boat of some sort was required and a variety of them were built on the islands. A *bád iomaire*, a sturdy rowing boat, was used for heavy loads; also widely used was a large currach, fitted with a sail when conditions were suitable. Of the purpose-built sailing vessels in use, the *púcán* and *gleoiteog* were used for fishing, while hookers were used in the turf trade and by shopkeepers bringing merchandise to and from Galway.[27]

There was a school on Lettermullen, with 120 boys and girls on the roll, but average attendance was about a third of that. Apart from the poorly paid teacher, the Catholic priest was the only figure of outside authority. There was, complained one official, no 'public building on which cautionary notices could be placed except the chapel'.[28] That building in 1873 was 'a small, rude, structure of the most primitive style ... perhaps the oldest of its kind in Connemara ... [with] neither belfry nor cross, nor any architectural ornamentation to mark it out as a house of worship'. For want of a bell, a 'small flag flying from a pole' summoned the congregation to mass.[29] The island had not always been quite so neglected by the outside world: there had been a coastguard station there and others nearby at Lettermore and Muighinis until the early 1860s, and the landlord family, the Comerfords, had a house there, which they occupied until the early 1860s.[30] If contact with outsiders was the reason English was more widely understood on Lettermullen than in neighbouring communities, as one observer suggested, it may also have given the islanders a better understanding of the mores of the outside world.[31]

Some hours after the arrival of Inspector St Clair Ruthven on 4 January, Denis Duvally, acting Receiver of Wreck, landed on Lettermullen. Duvally, an Irish-speaking Galway-based career customs officer, was accompanied by a friend, Michael Connolly. After an uncomfortable night in the shanty – it being too late to find lodgings – Duvally spent the following morning 'enumerating' timber. In the afternoon, he recovered twenty substantial pieces buried under freshly dug earth. The same day, he addressed the people in Irish, explaining the law on salvage. On 6 January, he employed three gangs of salvors, who would be entitled to a share of the value of timber they rolled above the high-water mark – ranging from two-thirds of items worth £3 to one-third of items worth over £5. Duvally was satisfied that twenty large balks were salvaged on the first day, but next day two more coastguard officers,

John Clarke Drew and Richard Jago, arrived and questioned these arrangements.[32]

Lieutenant Drew, an inspecting commander of the coastguard, left Galway on a steam tender on learning of the wreck. Facing a storm, he returned to Galway, and hired a horse and car to take him to Casla. There, adverse weather detained him for two days, and then forced him to take a circuitous route to Lettermullen. On his way, he counted fifty boats towing timber 'in different directions'. When he eventually arrived on 7 January, accompanied by Jago of the Bearna coastguard station, both had formed poor opinions of the salvage operation.[33]

Next day Duvally changed his system, probably in response to their criticism. Despite inconsistencies between the testimonies of Duvally and his friend Michael Connolly, it is clear that Connolly was appointed salvor at that point. Initially, for several days he acted as joint salvor along with the local people; then, he became sole salvor, and the status of the islanders changed from that of salvors on a percentage to that of day labourers. According to Connolly, he paid each man 3s. 6d. a day and also provided a daily barrel of whiskey, because 'it was wet and stormy and they had to go waist deep in the sea'. If the wage was good – three times the agricultural labourers' rate – the working conditions around Golam Head in January were truly appalling.

The change was made because it made things 'easier for the Customs', according to Duvally, or because the local people could not understand the salvage principle, according to Connolly. In either case, the new arrangements benefited Connolly, and possibly Duvally. They certainly marked an important change in the relationship between local people and the newcomers.[34] In the circumstances it is understandable why there might have been resentment. Having agreed to work under the 1854 Act, local people now saw the rules changed to benefit outsiders – and fewer local people benefited at all. With twenty to thirty people employed each day, only a quarter of Lettermullen households were legitimately sharing in the bounty. And that does not take account of the sense of entitlement among the people of Garumna.[35]

As soon as it became calm enough, timber had been towed away by men in currachs. This activity now intensified, especially at night; there was an air of excitement as groups of men, many from Garumna and elsewhere, gathered around shops and *sibíns*. Wherever he saw a crowd, Duvally urged them (in both languages, perhaps indicating lack of fluency in Irish) to disperse. He also asked Fr Nagle to 'caution his parishioners against plunder'. At mass on Sunday 12 January, Duvally was pleased with the sermon in Irish on the seventh commandment – the timber has owners, the priest told his flock; taking it was theft.[36]

The islanders were not the only ones needing to be reminded of the commandment. That same weekend the Bearna coastguard officer, Jago, accused Michael Connolly of salvaging already-salvaged timber and advised him that he would not be paid for his work. An agreement was brokered that meant Connolly would be paid for the work already done, provided he ceased to act as salvor and continued only as an auxiliary coastguard. It seems his friend Duvally's authority was diminishing, since Connolly was dismissed from that post too after nine days. Lieutenant Drew took the role of salvor.[37] To complicate things further, there was a concurrent dispute for custody of the *Julia* between Duvally and Captain Lodge of the insurers, Lloyd's, who arrived on 9 January. This went on for two weeks and was resolved only when the Receiver of Wreck instructed Duvally officially to defer to the insurer's representative.

The combined force of coastguard and police reached twenty,

but even this was inadequate as news of the abundant timber spread. At a time of year when there was little work to detain them at home, much of the population of neighbouring islands and the nearby mainland descended on Lettermullen – one report estimated there were 800 men on the island on a particular day.[38]

The coastguards and policemen devoted their days to retrieving buried balks and spent the nights guarding what had been retrieved or resting in the shanty. Famished and lacking sleep, they sought warmth and solace in whiskey – both local and legal kinds. Although only one man, a police sergeant, was reported for drunkenness, there are indications that he was not exceptional in this regard.[39]

All the time, local people were subject to annoyances, boats being requisitioned and wires set across the Cúigéil to obstruct currachs. There was continual firing of weapons, moreover, one figure indicating that 300 rounds of ammunition were discharged between 8 January and 8 February. It was claimed that the shots were fired to disturb 'wreckers', but the evidence gives the impression that the occupants of the shanty were trigger-happy. Occasional whiskey-fuelled interrogations of 'suspects' did nothing to mend fraught relationships. Given all this, there was almost an inevitability about the events of 8 February.[40]

That night, the coastguards were more than usually vigilant because they had received intelligence that a major raid on the salvaged timber was planned. When a *bád iomaire* landed at Mulkerrin's Creek long after dark, it attracted their attention. There were nine men in the boat, owned by Stephen Mulkerrin of Ard Thiar, Carna, eight miles away on the mainland. They had come, survivors testified, to collect a boat being built on Lettermullen for Mulkerrin's neighbour, Thomas King. When six of the men went ashore, they immediately came under fire. All scurried away, five towards the boat, one away from it. Five shots rang out as the boat pulled away from the shore. Two of the four oarsmen, Thomas King and Patrick Folan, were hit. King died immediately; Folan survived for an hour. The body of Folan, an only son, was left at his parents' house on Mason's Island. King's corpse was brought to his wife at Ard Thiar.[41]

The incident attracted little public attention, but it was raised in Parliament by Mitchell Henry, a Manchester merchant and Home Rule MP for County Galway since 1871. Henry was an advocate for his poorer constituents and he strove to ensure that justice was done in the Lettermullen case.[42]

Imperatives arising from the 'rule of law' dictated that there were coroner's inquests, before a jury, into the deaths of Folan and King. Opening on Thursday 13 February 1873, five days after the men's deaths, they were protracted affairs, adjourned several times before the delivery of a shock verdict on Tuesday 6 May. Carna was the place chosen for the sittings, because it was the 'most convenient place to Lettermullen where there is a police station and a sort of courthouse'.[43]

The selection of the jurors had fallen to sub-Constable William Doherty, because his senior colleagues at Carna RIC station were gathering evidence on Lettermullen. Doherty conferred with Lieutenant Drew (who had been on Lettermullen on the night of the shootings), and complied with his request to disallow anyone residing on an island near the scene of the shooting and anyone related to either of the deceased.[44] Twelve men were found who seemed to fit Drew's criteria, though their suitability was later questioned. On his arrival in the early afternoon of 13 February, coroner George Cottingham swore in the twelve. The proceedings were observed by representatives of the Board of Trade, the coastguard and Dublin Castle.[45]

The jury's first task was to accompany the coroner to Mason's Island and to Ard Thiar, where the bodies were disinterred and autopsies performed on them by a local doctor. On the resumption in Carna courthouse, Inspector St Clair Ruthven questioned the doctor and several of those who had been present at the scene of the tragedy, whereupon Cottingham adjourned proceedings for three weeks. The inspector reported as follows to his superiors:

> The seven survivors of the boat crew state that they were fired on without warning ... and that they were not near any of the cargo at the time ... None of the witnesses, as far as I am at present aware, identify personally any of the coastguard as having fired, but one gives the names of the coastguards he saw returning from where he saw the shots fired.[46]

The inquest resumed on Wednesday 5 March, but there was little fresh evidence until John Larkin took the stand on Thursday afternoon. Larkin, from the island of Daighinis, was a noted local character, with a reputation as both a courageous, skilful seaman and a tearaway. According to folklore later collected by Seán MacGiollarnáth: 'Fear spóirt agus óil é. Ní raibh daimhseoir ar bith ab fhearr nó é'.[47] Larkin identified two senior coastguards as having fired the fatal shots: Lieutenant Drew, the officer in charge on Lettermullen, and Chief Boatman Jago. There was consternation in the courthouse, and proceedings were adjourned for three weeks. St Clair Ruthven observed that Larkin's testimony was inconsistent with that of other witnesses, and even with his own initial statement.[48]

The sitting on 26 March was brief, because only eleven jurors showed up. According to the crown solicitor, '[Bartley Mulkerrin's] excuse is that he had been at the fair of Roundstone on the day before, drank to be drunk, and forgot all about the inquest – the man is quite illiterate and could not be persuaded of the impropriety of his conduct.' A significant development at the next sitting on 21 April was that Larkin's evidence was supported by John Ridge. The response of the coastguard's solicitor was to seek an adjournment, and to demand that Ridge be charged with perjury.[49] On the last two days of the inquest, 6 and 7 May, the jurors heard further witnesses examined by the coastguards' attorney before retiring to consider the evidence. According to one version of the story, they decided on a verdict of murder, but were dissuaded by the coroner, Cottingham. Ultimately the verdict was delivered in the following terms: 'Thomas King came by his death at Lettermullen on the night of 8 February 1873 by revolver shots inflicted on him by Captain [sic] Drew and Richard George Jago whilst in their own boat. We therefore find them guilty of manslaughter.' A similar verdict was delivered in the case of Folan.[50]

Two weeks after the killings, ownership of the cargo passed to the firm of Cloherty & Semple, which operated a sawmill in Galway. On behalf of the insurers, Captain Lodge accepted £1,050 for a cargo that had cost the previous owners £4,085. The coastguards remained on Lettermullen, protecting the salvaged timber, trying to recover pieces that had been secreted away and awaiting the arrival of cargo vessels from Galway. As for the people of Lettermullen, they were angered by the killing of Patrick Folan and Thomas King, but evidently in no way intimidated.[51] As winter gave way to spring, crops were planted over concealed balks and a spirit of defiance manifested itself in nightly raids and daily confrontations with the coastguard. Boycotted by the island people, and consequently dependent on provisions sent irregularly from the mainland, the coastguards' lives became more difficult.[52]

Between February and late April, Cloherty & Semple recovered almost half of the cargo: 600 of 1,100 balks, but none of the less valuable deals or staves. These, 'being portable', according to Joseph Semple 'were carried away by the natives'.[53] Allowing for what was lost before landfall, it may be estimated that the south Conamara people kept a third of the total. The struggle over this portion ended on 28 April, when another violent confrontation led to withdrawal of the coastguard and acceptance by Cloherty & Semple of the futility of trying to retrieve any more. They decided, instead, to lodge a claim for malicious damages with the county grand jury.[54] Despite his considerable profit, Joseph Semple continued to lobby the authorities, arguing that a firmer stand should have been taken:

> Until the government take up such occurrences on imperial grounds, I am of the opinion that this system of public plunder in those districts in which such wrecks occur will be perpetuated and that the milk-and-water measures generally adopted by the Receiver of Wreck tend in great measure to incite the inhabitants of such districts to those daring and lawless acts. It appears to me that the powers of the Receiver of Wreck are wholly inadequate to repress such tumultuous depredations as took place at Lettermullen, and adverting to the small number of the Coast Guard and the Police available on the occasion, and their want of accommodation and provisions, I am of the opinion that upon such occasions, a vessel of war should be sent to the scene of the wreck.[55]

After the inquest, the coroner issued a warrant for the arrest of Drew and Jago. Drew was dining with his host in Carna, Colonel Forbes, when he was apprehended. The two were taken to Galway gaol, where they spent eight days before being released on bail. Their period in prison, in cells 'intended for the common prisoners' where they were 'subject to the prison rules', they felt very harshly. Drew complained of damage to his reputation: 'There was a run made upon me by my tradesmen which would not have occurred if I had been at liberty.'[56]

After the two regained their freedom, they endeavoured to discredit both the proceedings at Carna and the characters of those involved. Friends and colleagues intervened on their behalf, the most persistent being Captain Bedingfield of the coastguard's vessel HMS *Valiant*. The 'lawless savages' of Lettermullen and Carna, he insisted, should not be allowed to visit 'gross indignities' on dutiful officers or to make a mockery of the legal process. The Carna proceedings would have been 'ludicrous' if the outcome had not been so serious:

> It is admitted that part of the jury were the wreckers engaged in the affray, they were in the coroner's court in their shirtsleeves, each having his shelalah, which they seem to have freely used on the table, and also in poking up the coroner to enforce their opinions. They contradicted the witnesses, and when any evidence was given which they did not like, they howled at them in Irish. Seven of these could not understand English, only two could write their names, and the coroner himself seems to have been quite unable to control them.[57]

These points were addressed by Captain Scully RM, Dublin Castle's observer. Bedingfield exaggerated, he wrote: there was no evidence that any juror was involved in illegal salvage, and while one lame juror supported himself with a blackthorn stick, there were no shillelaghs in the courthouse. They did not attend 'in their shirtsleeves', as alleged, although most were wearing the *báinín*, the 'short jacket ... generally worn by small farmers in that part of the country'. As for their lack of English, this was true, but the coroner had interpreted the testimony for them. Indeed, continued Scully, 'considering that the greater number of them were uneducated, they were well-conducted and appeared to attend to the evidence'.[58]

A key witness at the inquest had been John Larkin, who had been employed by the coastguard until a few days before the shooting. As one of two witnesses claiming to have been able to identify those involved, he could not have been expecting a warm welcome from Drew when he travelled to Galway to claim unpaid wages from his stint assisting the coastguard. Drew's response was to accuse him of being drunk and to have him arrested and locked up for the night. On his release, Larkin was promptly re-arrested and charged with having committed perjury at the inquest, on foot of an affidavit lodged by Drew. It was later alleged that Drew was on intimate terms with the magistrate who heard the case – indeed, that he was dining with him when Larkin called.[59] It was a serious interference with legal process that a man accused of a crime, while on bail, could have the principal witness against him charged with perjury. For that reason, the attorney-general subsequently withdrew the charge. But the eventual outcome of the perjury proceedings did not diminish their intimidatory affect. John Ridge, the other key witness, absconded rather than face prosecution for perjury himself.[60]

On 28 July 1873, during the summer assizes, Drew and Jago faced trial in the crown court for the manslaughter of Thomas King. Chief Justice Monahan, a former MP for the town of Galway, heard the case. The *Tuam Herald* described the scene at the Galway courthouse:

In the grand jury gallery were assembled a fair show of the *elite* of the 'citie' and its vicinity, most of whom seemed interested on the part of the defendants, but in the body of the court appeared the frieze coats, the most enthusiastic portion of the audience. Amongst those stood prominently was a goodly group of blue-coated men, friends and brothers in the craft of the deceased, men whose faces seemed prematurely haggard and careworn from their eternal sea-toil, but whose sense of despotic power and injustice exercised towards them under the pretext of executing government mandates has roused their energetic feelings to the fullest extent, which is vividly depicted on their countenances.[61]

With the Board of Trade solicitor, James O'Dowd, instructing the counsel for the defence, the jury selection took some time. By one account, he challenged all men wearing frieze coats, lest his clients' prospects be adversely affected by any sense of solidarity among the subaltern groups of the county, as had apparently happened at the inquest.[62]

The defence strategy was two-pronged: that the accused were not the men involved; and that, even if they had shot King and Folan, they were legally justified in doing so. In respect of the second, their case was weak, even if there was some ambiguity in the 'Instructions to Receivers of Wreck & Officers of Coastguard' contained in the 1854 Merchant Shipping Act:

They are armed with full powers and may even use force, and they are bound to do so, if they can by no other means prevent plunder, disorder or obstruction to the saving of life and property. But if proper firmness and judgment be shown, it will seldom if ever be necessary to resort to extreme measures, and whilst the law gives indemnity for violence done to others by the receiver or officer of the coastguard and his men in the due discharge of their duty, this indemnity must be considered as not extending to cases where a quarrel ending in violence may have been caused or aggravated by want of temper or misconduct on their part.[63]

To prove that their clients were not present at the time of the killings, the defence relied on a claim that Drew had fallen into the sea earlier, so by that time he was not wearing the distinctive uniform that witnesses used to identify him and, furthermore, that his pistol was out of action due to seawater. The defence also tried to undermine the credibility of witnesses, on the basis of their poor English and their inability to tell the time, focusing in particular on the testimony of John Larkin, who had given different versions of his story. Larkin insisted that he told the truth when under oath, and had dissembled earlier only to secure the wages he was due from the coastguard.[64]

On the second day of proceedings, the trial was halted by the jury, the foreman indicating that they wished to bring in a 'Not guilty' verdict. For their early decision, the jurors were complimented by Justice Monahan, who further remarked: 'I am very glad that two men who have served their country so long & so well were not guilty of the offence with which they were charged. They leave the court without a shadow of a stain on their characters.'[65]

That might have been the end of the matter, but for the interest of Mitchell Henry MP. His lobbying resulted in an inquiry into the affair under the auspices of the Board of Trade, which opened in Galway courthouse in mid-August 1873, three weeks after the conclusion there of the trials of Drew and Jago. Witnesses were again brought from Ceantar na nOileán, but one observer saw the inquiry as a 'bare-faced farce', not least because it was chaired by James O'Dowd, who had represented the accused coastguards a few weeks earlier.[66] No 'man of honour', asserted 'Justitia' in a letter to the *Galway Vindicator*, would have accepted the appointment in such circumstances. The *Vindicator* itself – Galway's main Catholic nationalist paper – had reported the proceedings in matter-of-fact fashion, and its accuracy in this task had been praised by James O'Dowd. But if its coverage was dry and restrained, it did also print Justitia's scathing and passionate critique.[67]

The anonymous correspondent's other major criticism of the inquiry was that its terms of reference precluded it from investigating the issues that were of greatest public interest: the shooting of King and Folan, and the blatant intimidation by a magistrate of a key crown witness, John Larkin. Justitia also questioned O'Dowd's selection of witnesses: asking Drew about the conduct of the Carna jury, he suggested, was like asking a burglar to give a character witness for the policeman that arrested him; calling Henry Warren – a friend of Drew who had enjoyed 'the conviviality of the shanty' during a 'pleasure excursion' – to testify to the exemplary conduct of the coastguard on the island was simply preposterous.[68] However, if James O'Dowd seemed careful to protect his recent clients, Drew and Jago, he did offer the opinion that those charged with protecting a wrecked vessel were not entitled to shoot people merely on the suspicion that they were pilfering parts of the cargo.[69]

By this time, indeed since the end of April, the remainder of the wreck had been left to local people to dispose of, and there is some indication of disagreements over the salvageable material. According to the responsible police inspector, based in Spiddal twenty miles away, a summertime increase in the number of assaults in the district was attributable to 'disputes over plunder taken from the wreck'.[70] There was no hint of such friction, however, in an account from July provided by John Clarke Drew. During his unannounced visit for the purpose of mapping Lettermullen for his defence on the manslaughter charge, Drew claimed to have counted 158 of the large balks and to have noticed great numbers of staves in some houses, as well as numerous open pits from which (he presumed) hidden timber had been recovered. He also saw seven or eight sawpits, apparently recently made, scattered across the island.[71]

Evidently, the sawn timber was put to various uses, and there are still extant structures and items of furniture that popular tradition associates with the *Julia* – including the rafters of the new chapel on Lettermullen, which was built in the late 1880s.[72] Within a few years of the *Julia* episode, there was a permanent police presence on the island, a change no doubt expedited by all the commentary and correspondence about the deplorable lawlessness in the district in the aftermath of the shipwreck.[73]

If the events of 1873 precipitated an era of more intensive policing in Ceantar na nOileán, and consequently greater familiarity with legal processes, they did little to commend the 'rule of law' to the communities concerned. The most recent law on salvage was intended to encourage co-operation between coastal communities, insurers and local representatives of the state, but those responsible for its application on Lettermullen failed to reach the necessary accommodation with the local communities. From that initial failure flowed developments which widened the gulf of misunderstanding between the area's population and the authorities.

The approach of the Receiver of Wreck, Denis Duvally, indicates that he was alert to the potential difficulties. He displayed flexibility in permitting local people to remove inconsequential or smaller items, good judgement in seeking the assistance of the local

Catholic priest and common sense in his willingness to engage with people through the medium of Irish (however haltingly). Taking the trouble to explain the law on salvage, he secured at least some co-operation from a part of the population. If anyone in authority had the capacity to make the compromises necessary to arrange a salvage operation in accordance with the law, while giving something of what they wanted to all those interested, it was he.

However, when challenged by his coastguard colleagues, Duvally made other compromises, which were unfortunately incompatible with the delicate arrangements he had made with the islanders. In reducing the status of local people working with him, from salvors to day labourers, he not only broke a bargain – a serious matter in itself – but he also removed any incentive they had to assist him in protecting what had been salvaged. Moreover, in favouring an associate of his own, Duvally diminished his own standing in the eyes of all parties. At that point individuals who were less sensitive to local circumstances, and less disposed to seek an accommodation with local people, took charge and the salvage operation became a protracted battle of wit and stamina.

It was a battle that took place in terrible conditions – which were much worse for the coastguard and police than for those they described as 'the wreckers'. Quite how bad the conditions were was conveyed by a veteran policeman based in Carraroe, who, five months after spending more than twenty days on Lettermullen, stated: 'I nearly lost my life ... the snow being knee-deep ... I have not yet recovered from the effects of what I suffered.'[74] Even if we can understand why men who were driven to the edge of despair – by an obligation to carry out an impossible task in almost unendurable conditions for an indefinite period of time – should have lost all sense of self-discipline, as they did on the night of 8

February, it is obvious they would have been neither understood nor forgiven by the neighbours and relatives of Thomas King and Patrick Folan. Local feelings found expression at the subsequent coroner's inquest at Carna, and if the people of the area were not aware of the extent of the behind-the-scenes efforts to discredit those proceedings, they were very soon enlightened about what happened to those offering evidence that reflected poorly on the officials sent to protect the wreck.

When the case came to trial, care was taken to ensure that the jury was composed of peers of the defendants rather than peers of those they were accused of killing, and proceedings were duly aborted at a very early stage. The demand for the subsequent public inquiry did not emanate from any of the communities of Conamara – indeed, the parish priest of Carraroe advised the Board of Trade that 'to ensure their attendance here as witnesses, it would be necessary to serve them with summonses'.[75] That demand came, rather, from Mitchell Henry, the constituency MP, and it was a far more circumscribed affair than he had been led to expect.

Apart from Mitchell Henry, the people of Ceantar na nOileán won remarkably little sympathy or public support. From the evidence available, it is my impression that the town of Galway identified with the cause of the accused coastguards rather than that of the fishermen. Few people made any effort to understand the perspective of the hapless 'wreckers' – but, of the two public officials who did, Receiver of Wreck Duvally and Resident Magistrate Scully, it is hardly coincidental that both understood Irish. Otherwise, notwithstanding the efforts of the anonymous letter-writer to the *Galway Vindicator*, and the sympathetic articles in the *Tuam Herald* and *The Nation*, there was nothing like a public campaign on their behalf.

It is conceivable, but by no means likely, that similar events a decade later would have caused greater public controversy. In 1882, an injustice against very near neighbours of the Lettermullen people caused an outcry throughout Ireland, in the wake of the 'battle of Carraroe', an episode of the Land War. However, the militants of the 'battle of Carraroe' – despite being in economic circumstances almost identical to those of the people of Ceantar na nOileán – were perceived very differently. Faced with eviction from their few craggy acres, they were defended as persecuted tenant farmers, and in that capacity could be embraced by the national movement of Parnell and Davitt. There was already a proto-Parnellite political movement in County Galway in 1873, fashioned in the Nolan–Trench by-election campaign of the previous year, but there is no evidence that either its agrarian or clerical constituencies showed much interest in addressing the injustice inflicted on Thomas King, Patrick Folan and their families.[76]

The author acknowledges the assistance of Siúbhan Comer, Páraic Breathnach, Owen MacCarthaigh and Seosamh Ó Cuaig.

8

RIOTS IN LIMERICK, 1820–1900

JOHN McGRATH

A number of large-scale riots occurred in Limerick city between 1820 and 1900. The first series of riots, in 1820, was perpetrated by a pan-trade combination of workmen known generally as 'the United Trades' or sometimes 'The United Trades of Limerick' or occasionally, perhaps in error, the 'Union of Trades'.[1] The rioters, up to 300 men at a time, were targeting non-union workers and any master tradesmen who hired them. In 1828–31, there were a number of large inter-community disturbances apparently sparked by trivial slights and small conflicts between individuals from different communities, these being paralleled by a plethora of smaller conflicts between groups from different areas of the city, in one case resulting in a fatality. A major food riot in the city in 1830 was part of the general subsistence crisis throughout Munster, which caused acute distress among the working-class urban population of Limerick resulting in the sudden widespread eruption of mass attacks on provision stores, mills and any food in transit. Ten years later, in 1840, what began as a protest against forestallers degenerated, despite the initially dignified behaviour of the massive crowd that was demanding work rather than charity, into a massive riot that spread through much of the city.[2] As in 1830, provisions stores were targeted.

Political issues also played their part in rioting in Limerick. In the later 1840s underlying political divisions between Young and Old Ireland were widened when John Mitchel penned an article in the *United Irishman* which was sharply critical of Daniel O'Connell. A highly influential local priest, Fr Richard Baptist O'Brien, had Mitchel's article regarding O'Connell distributed around the city before a planned meeting of the local Irish Confederation leadership. On the day of the meeting a small crowd met in the city to protest against the presence of the Young Irelanders, the crowd swelling by evening time to include what was described as the 'lowest order' of men and women in the city, most of them intoxicated. The crowd quickly turned riotous and set about burning an effigy of John Mitchel before attacking the meeting room of the Confederation and injuring William Smith O'Brien.

A decade later, politics again underlay disturbances. Three parliamentary elections took place in Limerick city in just two years, all hotly contested, if not at the polls then on the streets. The 1859 election culminated in a massive, violent parade through the city that clashed with the constabulary, resulting in two fatalities and a number of injuries. Divisions in nationalist circles led to further rioting in 1869 and 1876 when two major street battles were fought between physical force republicans, led by Fenian John Daly, and constitutionalists. Twenty years later, internal divisions within nationalism in the city again led to rioting when the local working classes were divided along Parnellite and anti-Parnellite lines. Political divisions generally coincided with parochial boundaries, different local communities aligning themselves with opposing political factions, while individuals who differed politically from the community in which they lived were also targeted. These riots started soon after the Parnellite split, and tailed off as the split was beginning to heal.

One final type of riot was that between locals and the military. In 1877 a massive and brutal street battle, preceded by about a month of low-key clashes between a military regiment and civilians in the city and its rural hinterland, erupted in a short space of time in the city centre. Many soldiers were viciously assaulted and the intervention of the constabulary was described as crucial in averting loss of life. Five years later, a trivial incident involving an altercation between military and civilians at the railway station escalated into a massive disturbance in which locals fought the police; extremely violent confrontations between the RIC and the mob caused the constabulary to fire into the crowd, killing several people.

Though riots were often premeditated, they could just as easily be sparked off by nothing more than a trivial slight or altercation. Such was the case in 1828 when the men of the Abbey and King's Island areas clashed, the trigger in this instance being an argument in a public house, which developed into three days of rioting in the area. A few nights later, in an incident which perhaps demonstrates the contagious effect of riots, the Garryowen and Irishtown districts clashed and the resultant mêlée proved too much for the constabulary, who required help from the military.[3] Unlike these riots sparked unexpectedly by individual disagreements, many riots seem to have been preceded by a period when a tense atmosphere prevailed. In these cases the parties were primed for action, monitoring closely the actions of their counterparts. The preamble for violence in such cases was often a perceived encroachment by one party on the other's area. In most cases this was a deliberate tactic to initiate the violence: in the context of the political riot the processional route was all-important and opposing factions would attempt to interrupt each other's routes so as to precipitate a riot. Such was the case in 1858, 1892, 1894 and 1895 when processions over Matthew Bridge and Baal's Bridge were attacked by rioters from St Mary's parish. In all these cases both sides could claim to be the defenders, the marchers claiming to be following a traditional route when attacked, while the parishioners of St Mary's could describe any unwanted marchers entering their parish as interlopers.

In 1876 John Daly's advanced nationalists chose to utilise the strategic location and symbolism of the Daniel O'Connell statue and met the massive Home Rule procession there, a clear example of a premeditated riot.[4] In the case of the 1830 and 1840 food riots the stressed and agitated working classes were monitoring the actions of those they deemed 'forestallers' and when the initial attack occurred in 1830 it took place on another bridge, Thomond Bridge, as a provisions cart was entering St Mary's parish.[5] It is no coincidence that yet another bridge crossing was the trigger of yet another riot, with the bridge effectively serving as a community boundary. The fact that the initial attack on the bridge was followed by an immediate confluence of riotous crowds from the lanes and tenements gives further evidence that the bridge confrontation acted as a trigger to ignite the whole community, which needed little encouragement to revolt *en masse*.

Given the fact that so many riots occurred during this period and often involved hundreds of combatants, the overall death toll of six was perhaps lower than could be expected. All bar one of the fatalities resulted from firearms used by the constabulary, which raises the question of how intense the disturbances were. The principal type of violence was stone-throwing, though a minority wielded bludgeons of one form or another. There were many cases, such as the 1876 riot, where many combatants belonging to one faction were completely overwhelmed and at the mercy of their opponents, and they could have easily been killed if the intent was there. This is not to deny, however, that there was serious violence during that riot, with one Fenian said to have sustained life-threatening injuries, and in other riots many people were described as having jaws broken and teeth knocked out, mainly as a result of stones thrown.[6] In the case of the 1877 riots, the press was unanimous in declaring that the civilian combatants were seeking to kill soldiers, whose lives were saved only by the intervention of the constabulary.[7]

The non-lethal level of violence suggests the possibility that many of the rioters were engaging in a somewhat brutal form of recreation. Many studies have looked at the phenomenon of the urban riot, but few have conceded that many of the combatants were partaking in rough recreation, though this is acknowledged in the case of rural faction fighters.[8] The newspaper reports give some support to the idea of street violence as 'fun' in many of the riots in question. In the twentieth century, mass participation in physical-contact sports, such as Gaelic football, rugby and hurling, may have reduced the amount of street fighting by channelling this energy, most often evident in young men, away from the streets and onto the field of play.[9] Nineteenth-century Limerick was largely devoid of organised sport. Even the Parnellite riots of the 1890s occurred during a particular lull in GAA (Gaelic Athletic Association) activity and before the proliferation of junior rugby clubs that later sprang up in the city.[10]

The recreational aspect of urban rioting has been detailed in the phenomenon of rake rowdyism, particularly in the case of the students of Trinity College Dublin, who often allied themselves with working-class gangs during riots.[11] In Limerick there are occasional instances of rioters who were of a higher social status than the 'normal'. Indeed the food riots, usually taken as an example of purely working-class activism, were joined by many young men of substance who evidently felt thrilled by the excitement of the occasion.[12] The presence of a gang known as the 'Garryowen Boys' during the 1828–31 riots suggests the possibility of rake violence, as they were led by a number of merchants' sons, with one Johnny O'Connell prominent.[13] The Parnellite riots show the greatest evidence of recreational violence. The riotous atmosphere persisted for many weeks at a time and towards the end of each period of rioting the (at least superficially) politically motivated rioters were often joined by the more indiscriminate sort of rioter. In one case the combatants were described as simply being drunken youths fighting for the sake of it and in another case a group of well-heeled revellers in the Ennis Road area tore down the railings of villa residences before 'engaging in pugilistic sport' with the night watch.[14]

It is difficult to establish a definite link between class identity or perceived interclass tension and the origin of any of the riots; the effect of these factors seems to be indirect in most cases. The food riots do give the impression of a massive unified reaction to a subsistence crisis that threatened the lower classes. These classes, defined by their economic vulnerability, appear to have been in communication with each other, particularly in the 1830 riot which began with an extremely sudden eruption of disorder – crowds were described as pouring forth from every lane of the Old Town as soon the first assault on provisions in transit was made. The spate of intercommunal violence that had blighted the 1828–31 period was forgotten in this instance and the city's poor appear to have been united by class – or at least by the desire for food.[15] This exceptionally swift mobilisation of citizens was repeated in

1877 when forty to ninety off-duty members of the 90th Regiment (estimates varied) attacked a group of civilians. Their ability to quickly spread news of the attack to other members of the same class resulted in a rapidly swelling force of locals that quickly overwhelmed the soldiers.[16]

Further details of these incidents demonstrate that the lower orders were often engaged in internal debate on pressing matters, though the authorities were either unaware or dismissive of the agitated state of the populace. Before the food riot of June 1830, there had been a subsistence crisis, high unemployment (especially among the city's weavers, who resorted to emigration) and an inordinately high number of arrests for food theft from March onwards.[17] In 1877 news of an altercation between the soldiers of the 90th and the Catholic clergy of Cratloe parish (11 km/7 miles outside Limerick) a few days before the main riot of 8 April, accompanied by the rumour that the soldiers had stolen a chalice from the church, had primed the lower classes. Tension between the two groups had escalated on Saturday 7 April, resulting in a severe beating of two soldiers. By Sunday news of the soldiers' actions in Cratloe and the assault on them had spread through much of the city's populace so, when the soldiers counter-acted on Sunday, they encountered a large crowd that quickly overcame them. In this case some sort of perceived Catholic identity, rather than class identity, was the unifying agent. In any case, the riots in question serve to show how concerns of the lower classes were not highlighted in the press.[18]

The presence of women was noted in many riots, though in most cases they were not the prime combatants. In the inter-communal riots of 1828 it was noted that 'several females such as did not mingle directly in the fray ... supplied the combatants with stones'. The report went on to note that several women, 'with their aprons full of stones', were taken into custody.[19] Seventy years later, women were also noted as forming a major part of the riotous crowds in several Parnellite riots.[20] Women were most conspicuous in the great food riots of 1830 and, more particularly, 1840. By eleven o'clock on 1 June 1840 the crowd of protestors had swelled to several thousand, two-thirds of whom were women. When the crowd started to attack bakeries and flour mills, women appear to have taken an active part. In the assault on the Catherine Street Public Bakery, the attackers were reported to be mostly women. In this riot, which exhibited clear signs of orchestration, women also seem to have formed part of the leadership, a situation by no means confined to Limerick.[21] Bohstedt qualified this phenomenon, however, by dispelling the myth that women were 'leaders par excellence of food riots'. It is more likely that women took a greater part in food riots than in other disturbances, probably matching male participation on average, and this gives the impression that women were deeply involved.[22]

The presence of women in the riot of 1840 left an impression on many local figures of authority, particularly John Prendergast Vereker, a member of the corporation. At a public meeting after the riot he suggested that the disturbance had little to do with men and that the blame rested almost entirely on women. He saw little that could remedy the demands of '10,000 women and children' who obviously could not all be employed. Though he was shouted down, he was accurate in identifying the role of 'disorderly women' in food riots, reflecting Bohstedt's contention that the pace of industrialisation had left women with a pre-industrial mindset, at odds with that of their male counterparts, leaving them unable to comprehend or cope with the fluctuations of the market – a prime example of how the 'moral economy was qualitatively as well as quantitatively at odds with the market economy'.[23] Whether such a theory can be applied in Limerick is unclear: there is scant evidence there of the male workforce engaging in new work practices and industrialisation; in fact, the only workers in 1840s Limerick who were accustomed to a factory environment were female lace-factory workers who, numbering over 1,000, constituted a very large proportion of the female workforce and quite a large part of the city's entire workforce.[24] Many of the female rioters in 1859 were described as young, and one witness described them as being 'mainly factory girls'.[25]

Following the 1859 election, members of the parliamentary inquiry sought to learn what proportion of the riotous crowd was made up of women, a line of questioning they used with everyone who had directly witnessed the riots. The questioning was partly inspired by the desire to portray the crowd as being composed of non-combatants or, at least, composed of combatants who were not much of a threat – an idea that one constable quickly countered by replying that women could be just as capable of inflicting damage. The questioning also seems to have been inspired by a Victorian fascination with the idea of the Amazonian rioter. The local media in Limerick certainly seemed to share this fascination and reported in detail – with plenty of stock references to Semiramis and Boudica – how one pre-election mob, 300 strong, was led by a woman in 1858. The woman in question, named Clancy, seems to have been active in 1859 as well, and was offering her services as a combatant to the agent of Spaight (the Conservative candidate) in return for financial remuneration. Indeed, one of Spaight's agents actually hired a bodyguard of a dozen or so women during the 1858 election.[26]

Many riots, on the other hand, seem to have had no female participants – for instance, the 1820 United Trades attacks and the 1869 and 1876 advanced nationalist attacks on local constitutionalists. Perhaps not coincidentally, these riots exhibited the highest degree of premeditation and involved combatants drawn from outside the regional/parochial communities. In these cases, solidarity was based on occupational and political allegiance, respectively, two communities of interest that appear, in these specific cases, to have been male only in composition.

The appearance of figures of authority could often crucially affect a riot, serving to either catalyse or soothe the rioters, depending on circumstance. In the 1840 food riot, where rioters exhibited a belief that they were acting rightfully (a belief common to many food rioters), the appearance of city councillors and bank officials temporarily placated the stressed crowd. On the other hand, the constabulary and military often inflamed the crowd and many accounts of riots stress that the stone-throwing increased dramatically when the constabulary appeared. The military were used sparingly, such was their ability to inflame the situation; during periods of prolonged disturbance, such as the Parnellite riots, they were confined to barracks.[27] Situations usually worsened if the constabulary took an offensive rather than defensive approach; eyewitnesses of the 1859 riot described how the violence escalated dramatically when the police arrested a young rioter, after which the police were subjected to such an intense barrage of missiles that they resorted to firing into the crowd.[28]

Open, public and, at times, ostentatious loyalty to the Catholic church and clergy was extremely evident in Limerick throughout this period, giving the impression that the clergy had complete control of the populace. Riots, a crucial means of gauging this assertion, show clearly the extent to which the clergy were able to control the working classes when tensions ran high. The riots engaged in by the United Trades perhaps showed the most blatant disregard for clerical authority and disdain for authority at all levels.[29] Workmen combinations were the closest urban equivalent of the agrarian secret societies and were accorded pariah status by the press, the clergy and the authorities in general, but even round denunciations by the Catholic bishop of the day did not stop the disturbances.[30]

In later riots, disregard for clerical authority was even clearer. John Daly, instigator of two large riots in 1869 and 1876, was predictably condemned by the clergy throughout his Fenian career, and in later years he identified himself as an 'Irish Catholic' rather than 'Roman Catholic'.[31] Tension remained between him and the clergy even after his entry into constitutional politics, marked by his election to the office of mayor.[32] Although a number of factors influenced these two riots and though it is true that not all the Catholic clergy condemned the Fenians explicitly, it is difficult to imagine that the fifty or sixty rioters who attacked the Home Rulers were not completely aware that they were acting contrary to the wishes of the clergy.[33] This is not to suggest that they were all consciously breaking with the church; they were most likely making 'a mental distinction between the Church and the Clergy'.[34]

By the time of the Parnellite riots, many more were making qualified judgements on the role of the clergy in political matters and the maxim 'Religion from Rome and Politics from Home' now adorned banners in public demonstrations.[35] Many of the incidents surrounding the Parnellite riots suggest a deeper schism between sections of local population and the local clergy, accompanied by declining respect for priests and church ceremonies. Redemptorist priests were particularly prone to popular criticism in this period and one, Fr Bannon, was even pejoratively labelled an 'Englishman' for his criticism of Parnellites. Bannon described how the boys' brigade of the Holy Family confraternity, composed of groups from a number of parishes, was constantly disrupted by violent internal disturbances between youths from different parochial units; in one particularly bad riot in 1895, combatants followed an opponent into church to assault him, before a curate intervened.[36] During riots in 1892, the St John's Temperance Rooms were damaged by the overwhelmingly Parnellite parishioners of St John's.[37] Though the Parnellites were keen to portray the anti-Parnellite voters as clerically dominated and ignorant, and there were loud chants of 'clerical dictation' during the 1892 municipal election for Abbey Ward (won by an anti-Parnellite), there is little sign of real clerical political authority.[38] In the anti-Parnellite community of St Mary's parish there is no indication that their political allegiance resulted from clerical pressure; in contrast to 1858–9, there were no city priests involved in election nominations in 1892 or 1895. The only reports of clerical activity were of priests seeking to quell riots.

Many riots, rather than demonstrating adherence to the Catholic clergy generally, instead demonstrate loyalty to individual, charismatic priests. In the 1848 and 1858 riots, mobs exhibited loyalty to some priests and contempt for others, further complicating the issue. Fr John Kenyon, much abused in his lifetime before being eulogised retrospectively by nationalists and republicans, was an extremely divisive figure in Limerick politics. Born in Limerick, he kept in touch with his native city throughout his career and was not afraid of taking part in local politics. He earned the scorn of many in the city when he nominated the Irish Confederation candidate Richard O'Gorman in the election of 1847, when the two O'Connellite candidates were set to be returned unopposed. The fact that the election took place shortly after the death of O'Connell, with his son John O'Connell the main candidate, elicited further contempt.[39] He nevertheless faced down the election mob, won the praise and admiration of many and remained the patron priest of the local Sarsfield Confederation branch. He was opposed by a number of the city clergy, however, particularly Fr Richard Baptist O'Brien who rallied those opposed to the Young Irelanders and was, perhaps unwittingly, instrumental in causing the riot in 1848.[40] The district where he received the most devotion and loyalty was notable for its poverty in the 1830s and its people were exceptionally reliant on charitable donations which were, in the most part, distributed by the Catholic clergy.[41]

Individual Limerick clergy were politically active throughout the 1850s and during the three elections of 1858–9 they escorted voters to the polls, publicly harangued those who differed politically and tended to inflame the passions of the public, which added to the risk of riot.[42] One priest in particular, Fr Moloney, was accused by the Conservative candidate, Spaight, of actively encouraging riot, even of leading a mob and later smiling gleefully when the mob was at its most disorderly.[43] However, in the majority of the riots the role played by the clergy was mainly conciliatory, particularly in the 1877 and 1881 anti-military riots. In the 1877 riot two Jesuit priests played an important role in placating a section of the riotous mob and were instrumental in saving the lives of a small group of soldiers.[44] In 1881 several priests sought to calm the crowds, though with limited success.

Along with the existence of recreational violence, the phenomenon of drink-fuelled violence clouds any satisfactory analysis of the motivation of rioters. In general, alcohol seems to have acted as a catalyst and never appears to have been the principal factor initiating riots. In the case of the 1828–31 riots it certainly seems to have been a major factor, with the riots stemming from a disagreement in a public house. In 1877 a number of small incidents preceding the main riot occurred in and around pubs, and during the main riot the soldiers were reported as being somewhat intoxicated.[45] In the 1848 riot, which was principally political, drink played a major part.

Sectarian tensions also fuelled rioting in Limerick city. A religious riot, as defined by Natalie Zemon Davis, consists of 'any violent action, with words or weapons, undertaken against religious targets by people who were not acting officially and formally as agents of political and ecclesiastical authority'.[46] Limerick's religious demography differed from that of Dublin and, even more so, the urban centres of Ulster, in that it lacked a sizeable Protestant working-class element. There were some non-Catholics among Limerick artisans at this time, but generally they are visible only sporadically as individuals.[47] The one exception to this was a small group of anti-repeal, allegedly Protestant, cordwainers who staged a small demonstration in 1830.[48] Given this religious demographic, we can largely disregard sectarianism as a motivation in rioting, though it must not be ruled out completely. Certainly one riot in particular, the 1877 military *versus* civilian riot, had a strong sectarian component, given that it was sparked by anti-Catholic comments passed by the off-duty members of the 90th regiment stationed in the Castle barracks. Comparisons can be made with the situation in Ulster where pejorative remarks about religious belief could spark intensely violent riots. The fact that the military continued to make anti-Catholic remarks during the fighting magnifies the sectarian element to this riot. However, there were other and more pertinent factors, namely distrust of the outsider, submerged dislike of the military in general and perhaps a nascent sense of nationalism typically manifesting itself through violence against the army.

The 1858–9 election riots also displayed a sectarian under-current. During the second 1858 election the majority of the local Catholic clergy supported the Protestant Conservative James Spaight, though the bishop tentatively supported the Catholic Liberal, John Ball. The Catholic press did not hide its concern over the support for Spaight, commenting that 'Protestant constituents do not accept Catholic candidates' and, while acknowledging the patriotism of individual Protestants like Tom Steele, declaring that the electors of Limerick were entitled to one or two representatives of their own faith.[49] The sectarian dimension of the election is clear in the pattern of attacks on polling booths. According to James McMahon, a solicitor, there were several polling booths, but the courthouse booth, set aside for freemen voters (many, though not all, of whom were Protestant and/or Conservative), seems to have been the only one attacked. McMahon himself, who voted and campaigned for Spaight, was subject to sectarian abuse, being called a souper and a blue-gut – terms reserved for converts from Catholicism to Protestantism – while one voter called him 'a black orange Protestant' and threatened that 'all his kind would be run into the Shannon'.[50]

Some rioting was linked to occupational identity. As in other Irish towns and cities the Limerick trades had, since the early eighteenth century, been organised in guilds that, despite mutual rivalries, saw themselves as parts of one skilled artisan community.[51] In Limerick the greatest examples of rioting inspired by occupational allegiance were the 1820 United Trades riots, which differed significantly from all other riots in two ways: an apparent absence of alcohol and the violence being limited to specific targets, with little wanton destruction or recreational violence. The trade riots shared many similarities with the agrarian Rockite insurrection rocking the county at the time; indeed, early trade combinations have often been compared to agrarian agitators, because they both temporarily united rival groups in a common resistance to unwelcome economic change.[52] Like many agrarian agitators, the United Trades sought to make their law the law of the land, seeking to control the local labour market and eradicate unaffiliated workers (referred to in this period as 'colts'). Like the agrarian groups the United Trades present clear evidence that a section of the populace could and did organise themselves while excluding the 'political' class, clergy and other figures of authority, and could mobilise in crowds that numbered in the hundreds. In the case of the United Trades of the early 1820s there is evidence of a central governing structure, unlike the agrarian groups, who were often like a many-headed hydra with countless Captain Rocks and Captain Fear-noughts existing simultaneously. Both the agrarian groups, particularly those pre-1790, and the United Trades were largely retrogressive rather than radical, aiming to recreate some half-imagined utopia of yesterday that had been eradicated by new economic practices. Thus the Limerick United Trades specifically aimed to re-establish aspects of the guilds that had fallen into disuse, and in this way they saw themselves as upholders rather than breakers of the law. Their riotous activities, therefore, as well as attacking unaffiliated workers and their employers, also targeted anyone who did not financially contribute to the organisation and certain individuals who dealt in goods that were deemed foreign (in many cases goods manufactured in Bandon were deemed foreign).[53]

Territorialism was also a factor in fomenting riot. In Limerick most of those involved in rioting came from working-class communities in certain parts of the city, particularly enclaves where rural immigrants clustered in the parishes of St Mary, St John and St Munchin, Boherbouy and Carey's Road. These areas were populated by rural immigrants arriving from the 1770s onwards and it is certainly possible that their community identity sprang from families sharing a similar place of origin in the rural hinterland. My great-great-grandfather came to Limerick City as an infant from the Cappamore area of County Limerick in

1847 with his two aunts and settled in what was, according to oral testimony, a sort of shanty town in the Blackboy Turnpike area, where the road from Cappamore entered the city.[54] There the family most likely lived with other immigrants from the same region as themselves, thus helping to mould the bonds of this new urban community. In a similar way the Boherbouy–Carey's Road area may have originally been defined by people from rural west Limerick, while St Munchin's and St Mary's were receiving areas for those from Clare.[55]

Physical barriers, in particular the Abbey and Shannon rivers, also helped to define communities, notably in the case of St Mary's parish, on an island formed by the Shannon and Abbey rivers, where a strong sense of community identity existed well into the twentieth century. St John's and St Mary's, broadly synonymous with Englishtown and Irishtown, were collectively known as the Oldtown by the mid-nineteenth century. They had become almost exclusively working-class communities by the 1820s as the wealthier inhabitants were siphoned off to the prosperous Newtown, which acted as a barrier of sorts between the Oldtown and the working-class community that grew up around the Boherbouy suburb.

The political involvement of the population was already considerable before 1820, but further developed during the Catholic emancipation campaign in the first few incarnations of the Catholic Association. The marching route generally included Nelson Street, Wickham Street, High Street, Mungret Street, Broad Street, Mary Street, Nicholas Street and Castle Street, thus linking the three principal working-class areas. George Street, axis of the prosperous Newtown, was used less frequently. For the most part these overwhelmingly Catholic areas were politically united, but whenever this unity was shattered then the divisions between communities became apparent, and the instances of mass violence allow the observer to calculate exactly how many communities there were and what communal ties were most important. Regional attachment was certainly a factor in forming these communities, two of which – St John's and St Mary's – were roughly defined by parish boundaries. The river acted as a clear and unequivocal boundary between them, and it is not surprising that the two bridges were scenes of a number of riots.

A study of rioting in Limerick suggests that local identity sometimes fused with occupational identity and sometimes competed with it. One occupation that attracted particularly intense loyalty and served to bind communities together was fishing, and the loyalties inspired by this shared occupation became linked with political and local rivalries. This is evident in the Parnellite riots, particularly in the clashes between rival bands during those riots. Marching bands were the totemic fronts for communities by the 1890s – a phenomenon that was not confined to Limerick.[56] St Mary's Band represented the parish of that name, reported as being overwhelmingly anti-Parnellite in 1892 but fractured politically by 1894–5. This parish split produced two rival bands, the St Mary's Band (anti-Parnellite) and the No. 9 Band (Parnellite), which frequently clashed in the street riots of the following years. A social analysis of band membership suggests at first glance that the two bands were very similar in social composition, consisting primarily of unskilled workers along with some fishermen. The political split alone does not, however, fully explain how two bands grew from one: an equally important factor was that the bands drew their support from opposite sides of the island parish of St Mary's and, though both communities contained many fishing families, they belonged to different fishing cultures. The Crosby Row fishermen faced onto the main branch of the Shannon and fished downriver, whereas the Abbey fishermen faced onto the branch of the

Shannon known as the Abbey River and they fished upriver. The differences did not stop there for, when the fishing season finished, the Abbey fishermen mainly worked as casual labourers in bacon factories, whereas the Crosby Row fishermen usually worked as dock labourers. They occupied the same social class but had limited opportunities to socialise with one another apart from at church; the Parnellite riots gave them added cause for division, with the two communities choosing different sides politically.

For most of the nineteenth century, Limerick city's population was between 40,000 and 50,000, with an electorate that rose from 1,500 to 4,000.[57] This, along with the absence of a secret ballot until the early 1870s, meant that mass assembly was a vital means of coercing or influencing voters. Candidates for election paid lip service to voters' independence, but most realised that control of the mob was a very powerful tool to ensure political domination. For instance, Thomas Spring Rice in the 1820s was privately opposed to engaging the masses in elections, but his political campaign was often aided by the crowd.[58] A large political meeting in 1828 featured an extremely large and intimidating crowd, most of whom seemed to be tenants of Rice's political allies. The 1830 election saw another pro-Rice mob – most of them workers on the Wellesley Bridge project, who had been purposely released for the day by their employers, the Bridge Commissioners (allies of Rice) – who congregated in the vicinity of some of the polling booths.[59]

The repeal interest enjoyed the support of a potentially threatening crowd throughout the 1830s and most of the 1840s until the split between Young and Old Ireland manifested itself in 1847–8. The 1848 attack on the Young Irelanders showed that a riot was likely if there was any political division among the working classes of the city. The riots of 1858–9 and 1892–5 also bear this out, when the disruptive role of the non-voting public was clearly valued by local political interests. Indeed, William Spaight – brother to James the political candidate – attested that John O'Donnell, who acted as their agent in May 1858, urged them to hire a large mob and declared that there was little hope of winning the election without one.[60] When further questioned, William Spaight protested that he was never in favour of bringing in the mob, but then appeared to forget himself, agreeing that their mob had got the better of their opponents and had 'thrashed the other well'.[61]

The riots of 1869 and 1876, again precipitated by conflicting political loyalties, were a little different in that they featured a striking numerical imbalance, with a small section of the population (the Fenians) seeking to dominate city politics in spite of the political will of the majority. In this regard these riots do not demonstrate a split in the working-class community, but rather the ability of a fringe party to push itself forward. At first glance the 1858 riots seem to bear comparison with those of 1892–5, but whereas the 1892–5 riots can be used as evidence of a citizenry strongly engaged with the political ideologies of the time, the riots of 1858 are an example of what can happen when the prevailing political ideology fails to interest the population at large. In the 1850s religious identity entered the void left by the collapse of repeal and reform, and the populace became politically apathetic, as was shown in 1851 when the Earl of Arundel was returned in the city, largely due to the fact that he was Catholic.[62]

The 1848 riot, in which Smith O'Brien was manhandled by the crowd, is extremely useful in uncovering the attitudes of that sizeable percentage of the population that the local media had largely ignored. Had the riot not occurred, an observer could have been forgiven for assuming there was no serious opposition to Smith O'Brien and the Confederation from the Catholic populace in Limerick, apart from that outspoken priest Fr Richard Baptist O'Brien. The riot served as a crucial barometer of local political allegiance, though we must not read too much into the disturbance and politics was certainly not the only factor motivating the rioters, with the provocative role of Fr O'Brien clearly significant, since he had deliberately circulated one of John Mitchel's *United Irishman* articles that was particularly condemnatory of O'Connell.[63]

Limerick was politically mobilised in the late 1890s by the release from prison of the Fenian John Daly, whose popularity seems to have been largely based on his image as a gaoled patriot. This image was reinforced by the enthusiasm generated by the 1798 centenary celebrations and by the expansion of the electorate following the 1898 Local Government Act. The trades council, working closely with John Daly from its headquarters in the Mechanic's Institute, set up a local 'Labour Party' to prepare for the 1899 municipal election, successfully achieving a large majority in the city corporation and installing Daly as mayor. This triumph soon gave way to divisions, which led to predictable rioting. There was a backlash against Daly and the Labour Party, much of it based on local rivalry. St Mary's Band nominated their own bandmaster as a candidate for the District Council elections in opposition to the Labour Party candidate, the challenge showing the importance of social and class divisions. Patsy McNamara, the St Mary's bandmaster candidate, was a general labourer living in one-room accommodation in one of the lanes in the Abbey, whereas his opponent, the Labour Party candidate Patrick Keane, was a prosperous baker living in a six-bedroom house in one of the area's main streets. In retaliation for this challenge, the Labour Party supporters launched an attack on the St Mary's band room. The attackers were repulsed by the band members, who then pursued the attackers out of the area, leading to a major riot in that part of the city.

The ingredients in this riot reveal the composition and motivation of rioting crowds in Limerick not only in 1898 but over the preceding seventy years: loyalty to one's occupation, loyalty to one's club, identification with one's area, frustration with lack of political representation and animosity between skilled and unskilled workers.

9

'A CENTRE OF TURBULENCE AND RIOTING'

The republican movement in Limerick, 1917–18

JOHN O'CALLAGHAN

The inactivity of the Irish Volunteers in Limerick during the 1916 Rising meant that the reaction of the local authorities was restrained. While the Volunteers were rendered largely impotent by their surrender of arms, most of the leading republicans in Limerick escaped police attention. Volunteer structures remained in place and reorganisation began promptly. Republicans capitalised on indecision among the police and military in Limerick about how to react to the Volunteer renaissance, and to the orchestrated public disorder which was central to that revival. Even as the Limerick Volunteers became entangled in divisive and debilitating internal splits after the Easter Rising, they demonstrated unity of purpose in bringing violence to the streets of the city and, to a lesser degree, the towns and villages of the county. Until 1920 violence between republicans and crown forces rarely involved shooting and usually took the form of rioting. Anti-police and anti-military riots were a central tactic in what, by the end of 1917, was the successful rejuvenation of the Volunteers before vigorous anti-conscription activity in Limerick in 1918 facilitated the further expansion of militant republicanism.

In the wake of the Rising the police were aware of almost immediate efforts on the part of republicans in Limerick to restore subversive momentum at frequent underground meetings and through cover organisations such as the Irish Volunteers Dependants' Fund, but they had no power to interfere with private gatherings on mere suspicion that they were held for seditious purposes. Attempts to revive most Volunteer units around the country did not begin until early 1917, whereas the Limerick City Battalion mobilised on 3 September 1916.[1] The Limerick county inspector of the Royal Irish Constabulary (RIC) suggested that 'but for martial law they would be more active than before the Rising' and he found it necessary to request the cancellation of special trains from Dublin and other counties to Limerick 'to avert the danger apprehended from a monster Gaelic Athletic Association meeting' on 24 September. There was still a large parade through the city after the GAA games, however, and a 'seditious demonstration' was held close to the main RIC barracks. The marchers flew the flag of the Irish Republic and sang rebel songs, but the police did not have sufficient numbers to disperse them.[2]

The Manchester Martyrs commemoration in Limerick on 26 November 1916 was attended by 350 people. Eighteen of the twenty-one marches held around the country were 'orderly and rather poorly attended'; Limerick was one of the three that were not.[3] The occasion marked the first public display of the City Battalion since Easter, but the Volunteers were dispersed by a police baton charge.[4] Drilling continued despite this setback and developments in Limerick replicated the national pattern. The regard in which a handful of prominent separatists (who returned to the region on their release from internment) were held gave them the authority to lead the republican campaign. Michael Brennan contrasted his departure, when the wives of British soldiers hurled insults at him, with his homecoming in early 1917, which was marked by a crowd 'numbering several thousands who cheered themselves hoarse and embarrassed me terribly by carrying me on their shoulders through the streets. It was all very bewildering, but it made it clear that the Rising had already changed the people.'[5]

At a Town Tenants meeting on 21 January 1917, between forty and fifty Sinn Féiners disrupted the proceedings by singing republican songs. About ten or twelve of this group then rushed the platform. Thomas Lundon MP received injuries that necessitated eight days in hospital. He was specifically targeted because of a speech he had made criticising the Volunteers.[6] Five men were prosecuted and imprisoned for their roles in the assault.[7] In January a Limerick solicitor, Hugh O'Brien-Moran (president of the Tom Clarke Sinn Féin club), successfully defended James Ryan, secretary of the Limerick GAA county board, on a charge of refusing police admission to a hurling match without payment. General Sir Bryan Mahon, commander-in-chief of the British forces in Ireland, subsequently ordered O'Brien-Moran and Ryan to reveal the origin of the documents that had formed the basis of the defence case. Both refused and were detained in Arbour Hill barracks under the Defence of the Realm Act. They were court-martialled and imprisoned. This case inspired much criticism of the Defence of the Realm Act in the local press and among the legal profession in Limerick and Dublin. O'Brien-Moran protested that, though the legislation 'had a very high sounding name', it was actually applied to:

Every two pence ha'penny case. At the present time if a policeman heard the word Kaiser, Kingdom, Dublin, Rebels or Volunteers uttered his feathers immediately became ruffled and he brought a case under the Defence of the Realm Act.[8]

There were frequent arrests for petty offences such as shouting 'Up the rebels' or 'To hell with the king'.[9] When Limerick men were court-martialled for wearing a uniform of a military character, carrying a sword or taking part in movements of a military nature, public admiration for them increased.

Police and military correspondence reveals a great deal of uncertainty among the authorities about how to react to the republican resurgence so soon after the apparently terminal defeat of Easter week. However, reports written by the senior British army officers in Limerick, Lt Col N. B. Grandage and Col Anthony Weldon, indicate that during a personal conversation on 11 January Michael Colivet, commandant of the Limerick Volunteers, had assured Weldon there would be no further drilling. When County Inspector Yates pressed for Madge Daly, whose brother Edward had been executed after the Rising, to be court-martialled for allowing her premises to be used by the Volunteers, Weldon – under the impression that Colivet did not approve of the resumption of Volunteer activities and would try to curtail drilling – recommended restraint. Colivet had apparently issued 'definite orders' that drilling was to be discontinued because it was 'only likely to cause unnecessary trouble'. Weldon was satisfied by Colivet's assurances because this was not the first such unofficial deal that they had struck:

I have no reason to disbelieve this gentleman's assurances as he has consistently kept his undertakings with me, as indeed have the other leaders of the Sinn Féin body here (note that he was mainly instrumental in getting in arms last May without my having unnecessarily to employ the military to seize them).[10]

Colivet's apparently conciliatory attitude, however, soon gave way to a more aggressive approach among Limerick Volunteers. On 22 February 1917, Colivet himself was found in possession of reconnaissance reports dated 5 December 1916 about the military defences of Limerick, showing the position of police and soldiers and making recommendations on how to attack the military barracks. Seán Ó Muirthile, another Volunteer, was found in possession of six detonators.[11] On the night of 22 March a party of Volunteers that went to the railway station, to meet three prisoners sent from Foynes to Limerick prison for offences against the Defence of the Realm Act, mobbed the police escort and pelted them with stones and bottles until they reached the barracks. On the night of 23 March the return to Limerick of Hugh O'Brien-Moran after his prison sentence was the occasion of further disturbances. A 'Sinn Féin mob' escorted Moran from the railway station to his home, where he made a speech. The crowd then marched through the main streets singing seditious songs and attacked two RIC patrols. A number of revolver shots were discharged but the second police patrol dispersed the crowd with batons. Two policemen were injured by stones.[12] This incident marked a significant escalation in activity, because it was the first time the Volunteers had fired at the RIC in Limerick. At the end of March Volunteer organiser Ernest Blythe, at that time incarcerated in Magherall Prison in Lisburn, was happy to hear that 'Limerick is becoming a centre of turbulence and rioting'. 'Was it true that some people in the crowd fired at the police the other night?' wondered Blythe.[13] Captain J. H. M. Staniforth certainly felt intimidated:

This city has a population of 32,000 and about a third of them are
brawny young hooligans parading the streets shouting 'Hoch der
Kaiser!', 'To hell with King George!', 'Down with the Army!', 'Up
the Germans!', and other such pleasantries, and throwing half-bricks
when they see a soldier by himself. And the women are worse.[14]

Some weeks later, he elaborated:

There's a lot of 'dark doings' over here ... This town in particular is
a nest of Sinn Féinery, and our men won't go through the riverside
streets after dark unless there are two or three of them together ...
the town is swarming with men of all ages sporting the Sinn Féin
rosettes or buttons.[15]

Nevertheless, this rampant 'Sinn Féinery' did not seem to have
inspired any great sense of urgency in Staniforth's company, for
as far as he could see 'nobody ever dreams of doing any work or
attending any parades whatever ... One subaltern hasn't been on
parade yet, and he arrived over six months ago.'[16]

The tension continued through March and April 1917. On 5
April eighteen men were arrested in Limerick and charged with
unlawful assembly and riot on the nights of 22 or 23 March.[17]
Towards the end of the month, however, an 'unlawful assembly' of
republicans in the city resulted in a confrontation with the RIC
and rioting.[18] On 23 April fourteen of them were convicted and
sentenced to two- and three-month terms of imprisonment. The
Volunteers were not as active in April as before, possibly due to the
presence of extra police in the city. Their organisation had declined
somewhat since the arrest of prominent leaders in February. Some
republican flags and copies of the Proclamation were displayed
in the city and county around the anniversary of the Rising.[19] A

republican flag flew over town hall on the morning of 25 April until it was removed by the police.[20]

While Limerick was not the scene of any of Sinn Féin's by-election victories in 1917, successes elsewhere acted as a stimulus for republican efforts in the county. The victory of Sinn Féin's Joe McGuinness in the South Longford by-election in May was celebrated in Limerick by 'seditious and turbulent demonstrations'. Sinn Féin supporters clashed with the RIC in the city, throwing stones – and in one instance an open razor – at the police. On 6 June, when three Volunteers were convicted at Galbally of unlawful assembly at Ballylanders on the night the result of the South Longford election was announced, over 100 policemen were on duty in the town, armed with rifles. While escorting the prisoners from the courthouse to the barracks, several policemen received head wounds from stones and bottles that were thrown at them. Volunteer Simon Scanlon of Galbally Company fired revolver shots from the crowd before it dispersed after two baton charges.[21] The county inspector described the Galbally incident as a 'savage attack' on the RIC. In response the police 'inflicted severe punishment' on the attackers.

A public meeting in support of the demand for the release of republican prisoners or their treatment as prisoners of war was planned for the Markets Field in Limerick City on 13 June. The meeting was 'proclaimed' and 200 extra constabulary were drafted into the city; at the same time 200 soldiers of the Leinster Regiment were moved from the New Barracks to William Street RIC station. The meeting was eventually held outside the city.[22] When the internees were released in June over a thousand 'Sinn Féiners' and two companies of Volunteers welcomed Richard Hayes and Con Collins to Limerick.[23] A feis under the auspices of the local Sinn Féin club was held at Doon on 24 June and 3,000 people attended.[24] On 24 June in Newcastlewest former internee Con Collins, on a Sinn Féin platform, said that people were sick of oratory and wanted guns and bullets, and he advised every young Irishman to get rifles and ammunition.[25]

De Valera's by-election victory in East Clare on 11 July further boosted the popularity and membership of Sinn Féin. The rapid expansion of the party in Limerick gave the police 'reason to fear that the movement will later on become both dangerous and troublesome'.[26] Quite clearly, however, the republican movement was already dangerous and troublesome for the police in Limerick. Armed Volunteer units had been sent from Limerick to about ten polling stations in East Clare.[27] These kinds of activity helped to forge closer contacts between the Volunteers in Limerick and elsewhere, which were to come to fruition in the shape of joint operations during the Tan War. The Ballylanders Feis on 22 July attracted 6,000 people. Large bodies of Volunteers marched and carried republican flags despite the presence of extra police.[28] The effect of events outside Limerick was also evident when the news of Cosgrave's success in Kilkenny in August led to celebrations in the city, as well as in Abbeyfeale and Glin, where 250 members of the Con Colbert Sinn Féin club marched with wooden rifles.[29] On 16 September, in another important escalation of Volunteer activity, three men armed with revolvers confronted two RIC men armed with rifles at Ballinacurra in a failed attempt to seize the police arms.[30] When Volunteer Edward Punch was arrested, he had keys to the back doors of three police stations and to the side entrance of the Castle barracks. Various military manuals and a rudimentary hand grenade made at a factory in Limerick were found in his house.[31] The Limerick Volunteers were preparing to intensify their efforts. Punch was convicted and sentenced to five years' hard labour but was released from prison on 17 November, having gone on hunger strike.[32]

The death of Thomas Ashe acted as another accelerator of political excitement. Demonstrations took place around the county in September. County Inspector Yates lamented the fact that, just as the 'suppressed feeling of political excitement' that prevailed around Limerick was gradually decreasing, Ashe's death had provided 'a good excuse for inflaming public opinion again'. Richard Mulcahy, chief-of-staff of the Volunteers, credited Ashe's death with being the catalyst that 'transformed a bewildered political and military situation into an effective and cohesive national movement'. The Volunteers' executive decided on a show of strength through open drilling, the main expression of this being the order to each unit to drill openly during the second week of December 1917. The Volunteers had been drilling publicly in Limerick before Ashe's death, but now they intensified their activities, with drilling, route marching and wearing of the Volunteer uniform becoming more common. Drilling took place in Croom on 26 September despite warnings from the police. There was also drilling in Galbally and the wearing of unauthorised uniforms at Hospital, where the Volunteers drilled on 28 and 30 September. Eighty men drilled in 'various bits of Volunteer uniforms' at Newcastlewest. Wooden guns were carried at Cappamore and Oola. Unauthorised uniforms were worn at Cappamore.[33] Two hundred and fifty Volunteers paraded in Limerick on 25 October and 360 on 28 October. Arms, however, were not yet being carried.[34]

This accelerated activity was matched by an increased organising drive. Police records indicated the presence of fifty-six Sinn Féin clubs in Limerick at the end of 1917 with a membership of 3,828, though the accuracy of these figures is highly questionable: Sinn Féin figures showed eighty affiliated clubs in County Limerick on 17 December 1917.[35] More importantly, the RIC were faced by an increasingly hostile and secretive population. The Volunteers' policy of selective public drilling meant that, while some companies largely escaped police scrutiny, the RIC were able to catalogue and analyse the activities of others. In January 1918 the average strength of the Limerick companies known to the police was sixty-eight, whereas in April 1916 it had been forty. By the end of 1917 the Irish Volunteers had been successfully reorganised at local and national level; recruitment was promising, morale was high and formal training and leadership structures were in place.[36] Patrickswell Company, for instance, had only eight or nine Volunteers in early 1917, but by December it had sixty men and was linked into a battalion with neighbouring companies in Adare, Kildimo, Mungret and Ballybrown.[37]

Subversive separatist newspapers published in Limerick further fanned republican sentiment and fervour. The first of these was the *Factionist* in January 1917. It proudly claimed the title of 'the smallest paper in the world' and, for the first few issues, the editor sarcastically declared that 'As we are kept up by "German Gold" we can afford to distribute our Official Journal free'. It was printed on both sides of a single sheet. The characteristic tone of the *Factionist* was a mixture of humour and acerbic invective directed against all non-republicans. It exhibited the same pious Catholicism as the *Bottom Dog* – Limerick's first socialist newspaper, published between October 1917 and November 1918 – and, on the dock labourers' strike in May 1917, the *Factionist* commented that 'We do not like to advocate syndicalism but we do think Jim Larkin is needed in Limerick'.[38] The attitude of the *Factionist* to violence was unambiguous: when the police 'severely batoned several people' at a republican demonstration in the city in May the paper recommended that:

… the police could be well taught a lesson, that they would not forget for some time, and we suggest that in future if any crowd of young men feel inclined to demonstrate they ought to come prepared to meet the peelers at their own game.[39]

Its tone became increasingly militant over time, in June stating: 'The way to Freedom is a sword-track through our enemies. Whether we hew it or whether it will be opened for us, is as may be. If we are to have National Freedom we must at least be prepared to fight.'[40]

The *Factionist*, which was circulated privately among republicans, gloried in the failure of the authorities to suppress it and defied the 'imitation detectives and fat-headed peelers of Limerick to locate us'. In their efforts to suppress the paper, the police had twice searched the printing premises of Michael Gleeson at 6 Cornmarket Row between the middle of July and the start of August. They seized copies of the paper as well as destroying the principal parts of Gleeson's machinery and all his type, though the *Factionist* (falsely) declared that Gleeson was not involved in its publication and it continued to appear after the raids. The publication was deliberately provocative, reflecting the declining respect for authority among at least some in the city: it pledged, following the raid on Gleeson's, to send a copy of each issue to Dublin Castle to save the police the trouble of doing so and to show that it had not been suppressed.[41] However, the last of its thirty-two issues was published on 6 September 1917. Both the *Chronicle* and the *Leader* reported that the *Factionist* 'had a fairly large circulation' during its brief lifetime, but its resources and possibly its circulation were obviously insufficient for survival.[42]

But underground subversive publication continued. The first issue of the *Soldier Hunter* on 23 February 1918 took a different approach, combining anti-army feeling with a strong expression of

Catholic morality by detailing its plans to guard against the moral corruption of young Limerick women by the British garrison: 'We are out to clean up the town. Social Hygiene, if you will, is our objective.' It listed 'dens of infamy where immorality stalks naked and unabashed' and advocated the use of tougher tactics to help the clergy who had been doing 'police work as well as priest's work'. The paper published a letter from a city priest about a military chaplain who had been assaulted by a Welch Fusilier when he tried 'to protect a girl of sixteen years of age against the lustful passion of this low clodhopper'. The priest called on 'the support of the young men of Limerick for the parish clergy in their efforts to uphold public morality'. A leading article described khaki-clad 'demons in human form', one of whom had apparently tried to take advantage of a young girl by offering her drugged chocolates.

In early March there were violent clashes in the city involving soldiers of the Royal Welch Fusiliers, during which at least one soldier and two policemen were seriously injured. The source of the tension was reported in the *Leader* as an issue of public morality rather than politics and concerned the conduct of soldiers towards the young women of the city. The situation in rural Limerick was apparently somewhat different; Mossie Harnett's experience was that the young women of west Limerick showed their patriotic ardour by their preference for Volunteers.[43] After the city clashes, the military were confined to barracks for three nights.[44] In reality, however, the violence may have had just as much, if not more, to do with the Volunteers' lust for weapons as it had to with protecting the virtue of the girls of Limerick. Volunteer Michael Conway of Patrickswell Company described how the Patrickswell pipers' band, accompanied by an escort of Volunteers, clashed with the Welch Fusiliers at the Crescent in early March and managed to capture some weapons. Patrickswell Company also attempted to bomb a police lorry, and successfully burnt a military lorry before the end of 1918.[45]

The leadership of the Catholic church locally was drawn into the political arena. Bishop Dennis Hallinan lent his support to Sinn Féin on condition that it did not endorse armed rebellion.[46] Hallinan understood the Sinn Féin principle to be self-reliance rather than collusion with secret societies and resort to violence.[47] Yet, what exactly the Sinn Féin principle was remained somewhat unclear. The shouting down of an attempted sale of land at Newcastlewest and a large cattle drive at Castleconnell indicate the web of issues other than politics that complicated the movement's policies.[48] Land was probably just as important as nationalism and it is clear that Sinn Féin clubs, 'whose members disregard all law and order' according to the county inspector, were involved in incidents of agrarian unrest around the county.[49]

The conscription crisis began in the spring of 1918 as British forces in France came under critical pressure from the German army and the government made moves to apply conscription to Ireland. Limerick's board of guardians used such strong language in its objection to conscription that thirty-three of its members were summoned on various charges of unlawful assembly and sedition.[50] The scale of the public reaction to conscription was obvious when up to 20,000 protestors gathered in the city on 21 April and Limerick participated in the general strike on 23 April.[51] After the arrest of a Volunteer in Newcastlewest on 15 April, when 10,000 people congregated, the police came under such heavy attack that they were forced to open fire. The telegraph wire had been cut to prevent them calling for assistance, showing that the operation was conducted with a degree of sophistication. County Inspector Yates reported that 'the whole city and county are seething with hatred against the government for passing conscription. This is egged on by the Sinn Féiners whose move-ment has swallowed all others.'[52]

The 'German plot' arrests in May put a temporary check on the progress of Sinn Féin and heralded a period of military rule. Limerick was proclaimed in June and drilling largely ceased. Apart from an increase in organised raids for arms by the Volunteers, who planned to resist conscription by force if necessary, republican activity diminished considerably and there was a strong public police and military presence.[53] The real move from potentially violent protest to the deliberate use of force came on 6 September 1918, when Volunteer Tommy Leahy of Tournafulla fired shots at a police patrol near Abbeyfeale, wounding one constable.[54] This was the first time that a Volunteer had shot a member of the crown forces in Limerick. Sinn Féin's general election manifesto demanded an Irish republic, the withdrawal of Irish representatives from Westminster and the establishment of a constituent assembly. It committed itself to achieving these aims 'by any and every means available to render impotent the power of England to hold Ireland in subjection by military force or otherwise'.[55] When set in the context of the type of speeches being made by candidates like Con Collins, it seems quite clear that an implicit, and sometimes explicit, part of Sinn Féin's pre-election policy was to condition its supporters for a campaign for independence in which the use of violence would potentially form a central method. The actions of the police, too, accelerated the move towards violence. On 2 November, the police in Broadford dispersed a crowd who had assembled to celebrate the release from prison of three Cumann na mBan members who had refused to pay a fine. Fr Tomas Wall witnessed the incident:

> The peelers at Broadford were so frightened by the magnitude of
> the turnout that they telephoned for military to Newcastlewest ...

The peelers, who had kept very quiet till then, cheered their arrival. A mess was made of the crowd, the peelers using the butt-ends of rifles and batons. The military did nothing except march up to where I was and fix bayonets ... I announced that our meeting was over and called on the crowd to go home quietly – which they did. But the peelers, wherever they came on an isolated group around the village, they batoned fiercely. The disturbance was renewed by the police on Sunday night and two quiet young men got badly beaten by them. The whole incident will do good and has done good already. The village was one of those places overrun and bossed by police and police pensioners.[56]

The general election of December 1918 showed how events had moved away from the political patterns of the past to a stage where the militant movement was in control. Sinn Féin's Michael Colivet was unopposed in Limerick City in the general election of December. The long-standing representative of the city, Irish Parliamentary Party member Michael Joyce, did not contest the seat largely because of the almost complete absence of nationalist organisation in the constituency. The Sinn Féin campaign was highly organised and enjoyed the support of the local Catholic clergy. However, Joyce also cited 'the opposition we would be faced with both inside and outside the polling booths ... the knowledge we had that many respectable citizens were afraid to sign a nomination paper for me' and the desire to preserve 'the peace and harmony of the city' as reasons for his retirement. He had been pressurised by Colivet's supporters.[57] Con Collins was unopposed in West Limerick. Internee Richard Hayes defeated the Irish Parliamentary Party candidate Thomas Lundon by 12,750 votes to 3,608 in East Limerick.[58] Lundon's re-election campaign was basically non-existent and he 'did not dare to hold an open-air public meeting'.[59] Volunteers from all over the county had canvassed for Hayes in East Limerick and were heavily involved on polling day. Sixty Volunteers from Rathkeale, for instance, stood guard at the voting booths in New Pallas, while the RIC stood by. At the close of polling the ballot boxes were conveyed by Volunteers to the county courthouse for counting.[60] Sinn Féin and the Volunteers were not only preventing the British administration from exercising its functions but acting as a substitute for that administration.

Republicans with The Republic *newspaper, one of the radical underground productions available in Limerick 1917–18. Reproduced from the Daly Papers, Glucksman Library, University of Limerick.*

10

'NOTORIOUS ANARCHISTS?'

The Irish smallholder and the Irish state during the Emergency, 1939–45

BRYCE EVANS

On St Patrick's Day 1943 Éamon de Valera delivered one of his most renowned speeches, one which came to define popular memory of the Emergency (1939–45). In the Taoiseach's dream of Ireland, her countryside would be 'bright with cosy homesteads ... with the romping of sturdy children, the contests of athletic youths, and the laughter of comely maidens'.[1] In recent times this crackly recording has been roundly derided for its rustic quality, but the conscious archaism of the Long Fella's addresses in the early 1940s was in keeping with Irish state propaganda at the time, which deliberately distinguished spiritual Ireland from the destructive materialist mêlée engulfing the outside world.

De Valera's rhetoric was sentimentalist, but it was designed to justify the deprivation that the Irish endured during the Emergency, for Ireland was not isolated from world events except in the green dreams of propaganda. In common with nearly every other European nation during the Second World War, Ireland experienced serious shortages of essential supplies. After the fall of France in June 1940, grave concerns arose that Ireland would run out of food altogether, and from early 1941 Irish people began to suffer the acute pain of a British trade squeeze aimed at bullying the neutral island onto the Allied side. By the end of that year, Ireland was importing 1,000 tons of grain a week. Consumption, though, was 1,000 tons a day.[2] This clearly unsustainable situation underlay the urgent need to increase productivity in the Irish countryside. Braving vicious maritime fighting, Ireland's plucky merchant fleet was too minuscule to reliably maintain supplies of food. To press home the importance of growing more food, government propaganda invoked a historical spectre almost 100 years old: the Great Famine.

Fianna Fáil used the impending centenary of this cataclysmic event to add legitimacy to the methods used to increase Irish food production. The government's 'Grow More Wheat!' campaign became ubiquitous: the slogan was repeated on the wireless, in newspapers and in political speeches on town-square platforms. Appealing to farmers in 1941, Seán Lemass, the Minister for Supplies, reiterated that Ireland needed increased production as a matter of urgency because 'outside sources of supply are virtually cut off' and reserves 'insufficient', yet 'people need bread'.[3] More sinisterly, from 1942 onwards official announcements insisted 'Only the Farmers are Between Us and Famine'.[4] The government message was repeated from the pulpit, too. In his Lenten pastoral of 1942, the bishop of Ardagh and Clonmacnoise attacked the 'materialistic conflict in Europe', reminding people that 'lack of co-operation with the civil authority' would result in 'a shortage of food more terrible than the failure of the potato crop in the Black Forty Seven'.[5]

There was more to this than the cynical manipulation of historical memory of famine by church and state. The Dáil heard stories of the urban poor's desperation for affordable food during the Emergency, a period when the government froze wages but the price of living skyrocketed because of wartime inflation.[6] There were reports of families of thirteen forced to share a small loaf of black bread for a week and Dublin women fainting in bread queues.[7] Furthermore, devastating famines occurred elsewhere with grim frequency in the early 1940s. About half a million people starved to death in Leningrad (1941–2) and some three million died from hunger in Bengal (1942–3). Famine also occurred nearer home, in Greece (1941–2), the Netherlands (1944–5) and the Warsaw Ghetto (1944). In February 1944, reports of the 1943 Chinese famine landed on de Valera's desk. They are likely to have sent a cold shudder through the Taoiseach's bony frame. Correspondents from China vividly depicted the erosion of a progressive, hard-working social system by hunger in provinces which had failed to grow enough rice and over-relied on imports.[8] Substituting 'wheat' for 'rice' made a chilling parallel with Ireland's supply crisis at the time.

Irish state propaganda allowed farmers to be seen as the shock troops in Ireland's private war against the apocalypse of famine. Concentration on the farmer figure continued the post-independence nationalist idealisation of the smallholder and the ruralist ethic. The smallholder-as-Ireland was embodied in the ploughman – back hunched, tilling the soil with his horses beneath a beaming sun – depicted on the Irish pound note from 1929. The state's focus on the farmer during the Emergency echoed the Irish hierarchy's concept of ruralism as the all-embracing embodiment of the very spirit of Irishness.[9] Politically, too, the national effort to overcome scarcity and the threat of starvation during the Emergency represented a unique national unity of purpose, with most parties and interest groups in agreement: more wheat had to be grown.

For much of the history of modern Ireland the countryside was the arena for battles between nationalist and crown forces. Post-independence, the compulsory purchase and distribution of land through the Land Commission continued the anti-colonial thrust. The compulsory tillage scheme represented a very different form of state intervention, aiming to get Ireland's farmers to till their land to cultivate wheat and other cereal crops rather than giving land over to dairy farming or other uses. Put simply, the government sought to use the scheme to provide people with enough bread to prevent social discord. It also sought to control prices and productivity to ensure that enough food was produced and equitably distributed. Apparently unremarkable, the scheme actually came to represent the high-water mark of state involvement in agriculture in the history of independent Ireland.

Compulsory tillage formed the centrepiece of the Irish government's emergency controls on agriculture, introduced in 1939 and periodically extended thereafter. Jim Ryan's Department of Agriculture oversaw these regulations; Seán Lemass' Ministry of Supplies dealt with prices and complaints of overcharging.[10] As with many Emergency measures, the government's hand was forced by the British precedent of rationing and a strict price-control mechanism.[11] These, together with the high insurance costs of transporting cattle during a time of marine warfare and the scarcity of feed and fertiliser, ensured that the export of livestock to Britain fetched very little profit at this time and Irish farmers' ample returns from export during the First World War became little more than a distant memory.[12]

Ryan announced the scheme in late 1939 and it was implemented from 1940 to 1948. The Department of Agriculture sent inspectors to nearly every farm in the state, to assess the holding and determine how much land the farmer should put under tillage, a quota based on the farm's size and quality. When the scheme was launched as the Emergency Powers (No. 12) Order 1939, Ryan announced that farmers with holdings below ten acres would be exempted, but the rest were required to till one-eighth of their arable land.[13] Those who failed to meet the requirements would be liable for a fine of up to £100 or six months' imprisonment.[14] Rough mountain, bog, sand dunes, forest and land subject to flooding were exempted.[15] Inspectors had the power to enter holdings, repeatedly if necessary, to provide the evidence that could result in prosecution for offending farmers.[16]

Even more significant, however, was a threat to farmers articulated by Jim Ryan shortly after the scheme was launched. Before the harvest of 1940, the minister announced that he had instructed his officers 'to enter on to and take possession of holdings' of any farmers who failed to comply with his quota.[17] This empowered the department's inspectors to act as bailiffs, enabling the state to seize private land and let it to conacre tenants considered more reliable and productive.[18] This was a bold threat indeed and it belied the cosy ruralism of government propaganda. As a derogation of property rights, the scheme evoked uncomfortable parallels with Soviet agricultural collectives of the era. Reacting to the announcement, the *Irish Independent* attacked the power to confiscate holdings with typical bluster, accusing Ryan of a 'repugnant', 'high-handed threat' which would allow the state to act as 'judge, jury, sheriff and bailiff'.[19]

The policy was not without precedent in Ireland, however. The compulsion to till built on Fianna Fáil's emphasis on tillage during the years of the Economic War (1932–8), when trade restrictions made stock unprofitable and the government vigorously encouraged wheat growing.[20] Drawing up plans for what was to become compulsory tillage in 1938, officials from the Department of Agriculture noted that the average yield for tillage crops had declined after tillage drive propaganda was relaxed from 1935.[21] During the Emergency the department therefore decided to place a premium on propaganda. They also noted that compulsory tillage had been witnessed before, if briefly and less extensively, when the imperial authorities introduced it during the Great War. Records showed that in 1915 and 1916, despite intensive propaganda, farmers were still devoting most of their time to livestock.[22] When tillage was made compulsory, under the Defence of the Realm Act in 1917, the area under tillage increased by a million acres. This convinced Agriculture officials that 'intensive tillage developments cannot be obtained without compulsion'.[23] During the Emergency, then, the state adopted a twin-pronged approach in enforcing increased tillage, combining counsel with coercion. The scheme followed that instituted in Northern Ireland in September 1939 by the Craigavon administration, itself following Westminster's lead. At the time, *The Irish Times* commented: 'farmers are notorious anarchists, and it remains to be seen how those of Northern Ireland will respond to the new discipline.'[24] When it was introduced south of the border, these proved prescient words indeed.

The issue of land repossession was particularly sensitive in Ireland. If historical memory of the Great Famine was powerful during the Emergency, so too was that of the Land War. In Ireland, historically, popular protest that was legitimated in moral economic terms centred on agrarian crime and land-based agitation, not the food riots witnessed in England.[25] Given this background, the scope of the powers now enjoyed by tillage inspectors proved contentious. Compulsory tillage, one senator claimed, was state instruction 'at the point of the bayonet'.[26] When the scheme was announced in October 1939 a number of farmers' organisations sought consultation with Ryan, but he refused.[27] This hard-headed, top-down approach typified Fianna Fáil's implementation of the scheme for the remainder of the Emergency. By 1944, tillage orders were revised to take greater account of the heterogeneity of land: the country was divided into three districts to ensure quotas reflected the quality of land.[28] This revision was, however, unlikely to have abated farmers' scorn for the scheme because it came after the considerable intensification of tillage stipulations. In 1940 Ryan upped the requirement to till one-eighth of arable land to one-sixth. In 1941 he announced that the requirement to till one-sixth had now become one-fifth; and later in the year increased this mandatory quota to one-quarter.[29] In 1942 the government had a bill passed increasing the maximum penalty for failing to comply with tillage orders from £100 to £500.[30] In 1944 the ten-acre limit was reduced to five acres and the quota increased to three-eighths.[31]

As Ireland's supply situation worsened, the government's stance in the press switched noticeably as well. Official notices changed from external legitimation of compulsory tillage, by referring to wartime disruption, to an increasingly inward and punitive focus on disobliging farmers. Addressing the Seanad on 4 October 1939, de Valera expressed his hope that compulsion in agriculture would not be necessary, yet less than a week later compulsory tillage was introduced.[32] The Department of Agriculture published statistics of farmers dispossessed of their land or fined under the order,[33] the notices usually sharing space in newspapers with calls from the bishops for greater food production.[34] In December 1943, in contrast to his conciliatory tone of four years earlier, de Valera attacked what he called the 'black sheep' among the farming community who were failing in their tillage obligations.[35] This was in keeping with a warning issued by the Taoiseach the previous year, one far blunter than the 'Grow More Wheat!' message. Now it was 'Till or Go to Jail'.[36] Fianna Fáil were making it quite clear that coercion, not cosy homesteads and comely maidens, would be the norm in the Irish countryside.

According to the writer John McGahern, son of a garda, the rule of law was relatively weak during the Emergency: 'In the Ireland of that time the law was still looked upon as alien, to be feared and avoided, and kept as far away as possible.'[37] The lowly status of the rule of law then may help to explain the actions of Stephen Dalton, a small farmer in County Leitrim, when he was visited by a tillage inspector in late 1941. Seeing the inspector approach, Dalton ran towards him 'cursing and threatening to sink his teeth into his belly'.[38] Dalton explained in court that he had reacted so violently because he thought the inspector was a member of the police. Predictably, this excuse was greeted with hoots of laughter in the courtroom. It may be that Dalton was, in the words of the judge who charged another Leitrim farmer earlier that year for not complying with a tillage order, 'a stupid bovine creature'.[39] His reasoning may, on the other hand, have rested on a common antipathy to the stifling atmosphere of officialism during the Emergency.[40] The unfortunate inspector serves as a metaphor for the evils of big government castigated by the vocationalist lobby, whose arguments formed an influential undercurrent of public opinion at the time. This popular mood was articulated in the *Irish Monthly* in 1939 thus: 'if our system of government makes it more attractive to produce more and better civil servants ... and poorer farmers, then the next generation will hardly pray for us.'[41]

Writing in 1941 to protest against petrol rationing, a Galway farmer bemoaned the 'deplorable ... position of the people especially the small farmers owing to the Government's compulsory tillage order'.[42] Others, fuelled by the widespread perception that compulsory tillage was foisted on them by a brutish and heedless Dublin bureaucracy, practised disobedience similar to the rather riotous behaviour of the Leitrim farmer. Some ploughed the required acreage and merely planted what they always had, leaving the rest fallow. Others sowed oats among the wheat or claimed ownership of fewer acres than they really had.[43] Shortly after Ryan announced the scheme, a farmer in Meath hired a private aeroplane to fly over local churches and GAA pitches on a Sunday morning, dropping thousands of leaflets opposing compulsory tillage.[44] Elsewhere, a farmer was fined for not tilling the required acreage despite claiming at his trial that he 'thought Leitrim was exempt'.[45] It is a matter of conjecture whether this response was a genuine misunderstanding or disingenuous cunning. There can be little doubt, however, over the motives of a Dingle farmer who in 1942 decided to act as if he was mentally unstable to avoid being allotted a tillage quota. While talking to a tillage inspector he began to eat horse feed and as the inspector was about to leave he smashed a lump of coal into dust with a hammer, eating the dust as he did so and encouraging the inspector to join him.[46]

Many farmers remained defiant even when in court. In February 1942 three Roscommon farmers were charged with not obeying tillage orders. It is uncertain whether these men were unable to till the required acreage because they were too old to cope and all spare local labour had been taken up on turf schemes, as they claimed, or whether they were merely idle.[47] Either way, all three challenged the fines imposed by the judge, one telling him – 'Do what you like with me. I am doing all I can and can do no more' – and another saying 'I have never had an inspector tell me what to do in my life'.[48] Such recalcitrance showed the disruption that tillage orders brought to the elderly countryman's life, a yearly round that followed the innate rhythms of the seasons and was – in some cases – unchanged in generations.

Others used more conventional litigious strategies of resistance. In several court cases, judges and justices found that the state had prosecuted prematurely. In November 1940, for instance, the judge at Longford circuit court reversed the convictions of five farmers for non-compliance with their quotas 'in 1940'. The judge reasoned that they could not be prosecuted as the year had not yet expired.[49] Similarly, in a case that went before the high court in January 1941, a Blanchardstown farmer escaped prosecution for tilling only one acre of the required 33. Once again, the defence argued that the issuing of the summons by the Department of Agriculture in October 1940 was premature.[50] Outraged that the judiciary could be so lenient, de Valera stormily claimed that judges who acquitted farmers 'did not realise the seriousness of the situation'.[51]

Such cases are in contrast to the bulk of examples, where some harsh sentences were imposed. In February 1942 the department successfully fined the owner of land which, unbeknown to him, had not been tilled by his tenant farmer.[52] By spring 1940 six holdings had been taken over by the state and sixty-eight farmers brought to court for failing to till enough land.[53] Between January and April 1941 the department announced that it had taken possession of 385 acres from seventeen farms.[54] Although a relatively small number, these figures relate to just the first few months of the scheme's operation. They also reflect the time and cost incurred in confiscating and running a farm, a point raised by politicians opposed to the measures.[55] In 1947 the *Irish Independent* reported that 300,000 farms came under compulsory tillage regulations, yet the average yearly number of convictions (1940–6) was only 236. Reproached by the government for its earlier negative appraisal of the scheme, the *Independent* had – by this stage – changed tack, reporting 'in other words, not even one farmer in a thousand failed in his duty'.[56] However, by including the data for 1946, the *Independent* distorted the figures to emphasise the extent of co-operation with tillage orders. As Dáil records showed, there were a mere ten prosecutions listed for 1946 because prosecutions were still proceeding,[57] whereas the yearly mean for 1941–5 was 305.[58] In this period the state dispossessed and cultivated some 7,365 acres of farm land.[59]

These figures indicate that the impact of compulsory tillage was widespread and, to those dispossessed, devastating. These figures do little to convey the unpopularity of state compulsion amongst farming communities, an important factor in the coalition government's abolition of the scheme in July 1948. Neither do they convey the rise in dispossessions as the Emergency progressed: a symptom of the desperate need to grow more food but also the growing bureaucracy of the Department of Agriculture's inspectorate. The unrepresentative mean of 236 convictions per year also obscures the number of cases where court action was either dismissed or threatened but not executed. The dismissal of summons in 1940 against an immobile 80-year-old farmer of 'hopelessly feeble mind' illustrates not only the unwillingness of the judiciary to summarily punish offenders but also the dour determination of the state to secure convictions against deviants, almost regardless of circumstance.[60]

Failure to comply with tillage regulations, then, represented much more than a failure to do one's duty. Frequently it signified a riotous refusal to obey outside authority, and conflict between farmers and Agriculture officials was certainly more common than censored Emergency press reports suggest. Reports of prosecutions show that those farmers who did not comply with the state's instruction were often obstinate characters but many, sadly, were old and infirm. Summoned for non-compliance with a tillage order in 1940, an aged and hard-of-hearing Meath farmer was guffawed at in court when he confessed to the judge 'Damnit, I can't hear a word at all'.[61] For the 1940s the farmer in the dock – often unfamiliar with even basic court proceedings – was an alternative symbol to the ploughman on the pound note, suggestive of the state's condescension towards its rural peripheries and those who inhabited them. Perhaps the ultimate rebuff to the ploughman idyll was the revelation that the all-Ireland ploughing champion had been forced from the land by compulsory tillage regulations and had taken up selling gravel in Dublin.[62]

Resistance to compulsory tillage within the farming community reflected the fact that cultivation was much harder without fertiliser, lime, chemicals and tractors. Irish farmers were compelled to produce more without modern productive aids. This was primarily a consequence of the British trade squeeze of 1941 but it was also, significantly, a consequence of Seán Lemass' failure to stockpile adequate reserves of essential agricultural chemicals and machinery at an early stage in the Emergency.[63] Many farmers would have concurred with James Dillon's contention that 'tillage without manure is not farming. It is mining – i.e., taking the fertility out of the soil without putting anything back.'[64] Moreover much land, particularly in the west, was unsuitable for wheat growing.[65] As The McGillycuddy of the Reeks, a County Kerry farmer, argued in a 1939 Seanad debate, compulsory tillage took little account of the variations in land nationwide and the ability of farmers to pay for seed, labour or implements. It was little more than an indifferent instruction to the farmer to 'go and till as much land as I require you to do'.[66]

During the Emergency the conflict between small farmer and government was heightened by the farming community's recurrent perception that they were viewed as small and insignificant by an arrogant and unthinking Dublin bureaucracy. This opinion was not specific to Ireland, of course, and neither was it entirely justified. The emphasis given to tillage was not only because of the demand from urban dwellers for bread but also because the extraordinarily high freight charges for maize and cattle feed greatly increased the cost of rearing cattle during the Emergency.[67] As an incentive to farmers to grow more wheat, the government increased the fixed price of wheat with every hike in the tillage quota and announced the availability of credit to help with the demands of the order. This ensured – at least – that obliging farmers received some recompense for their efforts.

Nonetheless, farmers in independent Ireland had a miserable Emergency compared to those in Northern Ireland, where Basil Brooke's Ministry of Agriculture took over control and distribution of agricultural machinery. In the short course of the Emergency old farming practices were substantially overhauled. As a County Down farmer put it, 'people said that a tractor couldn't plough like horses ... but sure the tractor was ploughing three times as much; when the horse is working he's not eating, but when a tractor's working it's eating an awful lot'.[68] Unfortunately for Ryan, widespread mechanisation of Ireland's farms was not an option since the Department of Supplies was wrong-footed by Britain reneging on trade guarantees for agricultural machinery.[69] Lemass' department also, rather irresponsibly, continued to allow the export of machinery to Britain in the first fourteen months of the Emergency, only securing a paltry barter of agricultural machinery for beer in the closing stages of the war.[70] Between 1939 and 1944 the number of tractors in the six counties rose from 550 to 7,000.[71] By contrast, the horse was still very much in evidence in the neutral state. As the official history of Northern Ireland in the war years smugly notes, 'to go south was to be transported in a matter of minutes from the twentieth to the seventeenth century'.[72] Due to the British Government's war effort, farmers in the northern statelet also had more access to fertilisers and phosphates; and, when the tillage ceiling was reached in 1943, Brooke was able to relax tillage quotas and extend the use of fertilisers.[73] A combination of poor planning and British duplicity ensured Jim Ryan could not use similar solutions to ease the tillage burden.[74]

Compulsory tillage during the Emergency disproportionately affected farmers in the lower socio-economic bands. Despite the expansion of the urban population during the Emergency, Ireland remained a nation of smallholders. According to the 1936 census, half of Ireland's working population was employed in agriculture and farms were small: about a quarter of them were under 15 acres.[75] A 1941 source claimed that 60 per cent of Irish farms were 30 acres or less.[76] In a Dáil debate of 1944 Oliver J. Flanagan asserted that the compulsory tillage scheme had not affected the 'ordinary farmer', but had succeeded in targeting the 'rancher', 'one of the greatest enemies that we have in this country'.[77] On the contrary, the evidence suggests that 'ordinary' farmers – whose farms were invariably unmechanised – were affected disproportionately by legislation that applied to farmers with as little as five acres.

Perhaps the government was unwilling to offend the patrons of the Golfing Union of Ireland, but during the six years of the Emergency the country's links were spared the plough and spade, though in 1917 Irish golf courses had not escaped compulsory tillage.[78] In Northern Ireland, by contrast, not even the lawns of Queen's University or Stormont were exempt. Newsreel footage in 1940 showed the Northern Ireland Minister of Agriculture Basil Brooke (Lord Brookeborough) overseeing the ploughing of Stormont with newly imported tractors.[79] Even Brooke's own country estate was subject to tillage regulations. Lady Brookeborough recorded in her diary '1941 – much ploughing last year … arable acreage 90 acres … have now one Ferguson, one Ford/Ferguson and only two horses'.[80]

The front cover of the Dublin Opinion *from February 1942. The magazine regularly parodied the stringency of the government's compulsory tillage order.*

Within the cabinet, it was Lemass who favoured land dispossession most strongly. In a 1944 memorandum he made a number of observations about Ireland's agricultural economy, declaring himself in favour of reorganising the entire sector.[81] Citing the high number of uneconomic holdings in the country, he argued that 'land policy must be geared towards ownership based on ability to work the land'.[82] Ominously, Lemass wanted the seizure of farmland by the state to continue after the Emergency, to complete the 'elimination of incompetent or lazy farmers'.[83] Lemass' enthusiasm for widespread dispossessions was probably only matched by that of James Larkin, the trade union leader and socialist deputy, who urged that any farmer who 'will not farm scientifically' be dispossessed by the state.[84]

This keenness to dispossess was challenged, however, by the man responsible for enforcement of tillage orders. Ryan had consistently defended such expropriations in the Dáil, but he privately quelled Lemass' enthusiasm for land dispossession. During the Emergency such displacements had proved 'a delicate and difficult matter'.[85] Ryan was perturbed by the deep-seated resentment against the coercive measures used by the department to increase the wheat yield.[86] In a further admission of the robust resistance that compulsory tillage had met with, he warned that if displacement was pursued on the same scale post-war there would be 'a danger of serious agitation and public disturbance'.[87] Ryan, who possessed not only a greater understanding of farming than either Lemass or Larkin, but also a more evident distaste than the two Dublin TDs for any scheme redolent of Soviet-style agricultural collectivisation, recognised that dispossessions were viewed by the farming community as hostile encroachment showing a fundamental misunderstanding of the nature of farming. 'Unlike coal miners', farmers did not 'slack' having attained a certain income, he contended.[88] 'There are a number of holdings in every parish falling below a reasonable productive capacity due to some fault on the part of the present farmer,' Ryan conceded. But in these cases a young family member 'would in time pull the place together and become a first class farmer'. It would, therefore, be 'unthinkable to disturb the family in such cases no matter how much below the desired standard the farm might be'.[89]

Fianna Fáil's powerful message of national unity, appealing to people to pull together to avert famine while reminding them that the geopolitical inferno causing the hardship was not of its doing, inspired many people in the Irish countryside to redouble their labour in the national interest. Commenting in 1944 on Ireland's 'essential planning problem', a contributor to the Jesuit periodical *Studies* noted: 'Except in a purely Totalitarian state no government could ... apply the regimentation necessary to ensure that the farming community on a whole would reorganise itself', but added 'except as a last resort in a national emergency'.[90] Whereas the majority of Ireland's farming community and agricultural labour force similarly regarded this 'regimentation' during the Emergency as a 'last resort' – a painful but exceptional necessity of wartime conditions – to Lemass, it seems, it was an exciting opportunity.

Lemass' mindset was at loggerheads not only with Catholic social theory but with most people's sensitivities at the time. The clash between Catholic social thought and the state's seemingly coercive methods of enforcement in the countryside never occurred, however. The 1943 *Report of the Commission on Vocational Organisation* favoured replacing 'the state's despotic control of production and labour' with 'voluntary collaboration for the good of the nation at a critical time'.[91] If the government's intention to ensure fair food distribution and increase agricultural production sat comfortably with this desire in theory, the same cannot be said of its methods. Nonetheless, the commission overlooked the elephant in the corner: compulsory tillage. Nor is there evidence of a major clash between the Catholic hierarchy and the government over compulsory tillage. In large part this can be attributed to assurances of support for the scheme that Lemass secured from John Charles McQuaid, the Catholic archbishop of Dublin, in early 1941.[92] Perhaps as an unspoken *quid pro quo*, despite their quest for greater agricultural productivity during the Emergency, Lemass and his developmentalist[93] allies in government did not antagonise Catholic sensitivities to the home and family so far as to advocate a Women's Land Army.[94]

That the land issue and agrarianism were at the heart of the independence struggle has led some commentators to speculate that agrarian radicalism died with the formation of the Irish state following the end of the Civil War in 1923.[95] This conviction was repeated by Farmers' Party senator Patrick Baxter in a 1939 Seanad debate. Farmers, he warned, had 'never got a chance to pull themselves together since 1923'. This recent peace in the countryside would only continue 'if Ministers approach this problem of getting increased production from the land ... without applying the big stick from buildings in Merrion Street'.[96] From 1939 onwards, though, many farmers perceived the big stick in the form of compulsory tillage. The growth of the Irish agrarian political party, Clann na Talmhan, during the Emergency is evidence of the re-emergence of bottom-up rural political agitation, even within state structures. The rise of Clann na Talmhan has been attributed to Emergency shortages in feed, fertiliser and fuel, and the conviction that fixed prices and rates were unfair to farmers.[97] The incompatibility of all these factors with compulsory tillage requirements was repeatedly highlighted by Clann na Talmhan before and after their strong showing in the 1943 election.[98] Resistance to the scheme was certainly, therefore, a significant and overlooked reason for the party's growth at this time.

The compulsory tillage drive of the 1940s has never been the subject of serious historical analysis. Food shortages ensured that the farmer – the archetypal hard-working, frugal man who, to quote a Victorian bishop, was 'the purest, the holiest, and the most innocent of society … high enough in the social scale to be above extreme want and below the reach of the seductive and demoralising influences of great wealth and affluence' – was again accorded primacy by the political and religious establishment.[99] The subjects of this deeply patronising rhetorical embrace, Irish small farmers, responded by raising the amount of land under corn crops from a five-year average of just under a million acres (1935–9) to one and a half million acres (1940–4).[100] As Ryan, in a typical invocation of the Famine era, contended: 'you have to go back nearly one hundred years to beat that record'.[101] While perhaps not the Stakhanovite effort desired by Lemass, this remarkable increase was achieved by the country's farmers despite the absence of modern productive aids on many farms. Meanwhile, though never reaching a collective pitch of 'notorious anarchy', the individual and collective resistance of a significant minority of farmers provides evidence that agrarian dissidence, far from being dead and buried by 1923, was alive and well during the Emergency.

11

'CONDITIONAL CONSTITUTIONALISTS'[1]

The reaction of Fianna Fáil grass-roots to the IRA border campaign, 1956–62

STEPHEN KELLY

Though not strictly speaking either riotous or based on a one-off assembly, the reaction of Fianna Fáil grass-roots to the IRA border campaign of 1956 to 1962 does enable us to explore the subculture of popular revolt. The IRA's renewed campaign in Northern Ireland exposed a major fault-line between Fianna Fáil's leadership and its grass-roots supporters on the use of physical force to secure Irish unity. For a small but vocal minority of Fianna Fáil members, the party hierarchy's crushing of the IRA border campaign signalled that the 'Republican Party' had abandoned its primary objective of a united Ireland. While most Fianna Fáil members rejected the use of violence, there were a small number of supporters, including locally elected county councillors, who were unwilling to condemn as illegitimate the use of force to secure Irish re-unification and who could be termed 'conditional constitutionalists'.

During a seven-year interlude under the leadership of Éamon de Valera and then Seán Lemass, the Fianna Fáil hierarchy desperately sought to keep control of the party's official policy towards the IRA. From County Cork to County Donegal, disgruntled Fianna Fáil grass-roots members threatened to resign from the party in protest because of the perceived 'draconian' suppression of the IRA. Ultimately, under de Valera and subsequently Lemass the Fianna Fáil party did manage to retain control of policy towards the IRA, which eventually announced an end to its border campaign in 1962.

Nevertheless, the episode demonstrated that, for some members of Fianna Fáil, ideological aspirations for a united Ireland outweighed their loyalty to their party. What they saw as the ruthless suppression of the IRA, coupled with the Fianna Fáil leadership's failure to secure Irish re-unification in the forty years since partition in 1920, brought them to breaking point. Many Fianna Fáil members viewed the IRA campaign as merely a continuation of the long quest to secure an independent, united Ireland. Indeed, for some Fianna Fáil supporters Ireland's recent history – the 1916 Easter Rising, the War of Independence and the Civil War – was justification that 'political' violence was a legitimate course of action.

The attack by the IRA on 12 November 1956 on six customs posts along a 70-mile section of the Irish border in counties Armagh and Fermanagh signalled a new border offensive, later named 'Operation Harvest'. The method was to be guerrilla warfare, with an ambitious plan to use flying columns from the Republic of Ireland to attack targets in Northern Ireland. In December of that year, the IRA began further attacks on key military positions of the Northern Ireland security forces: on 11–12 December, Counties

Armagh and Fermanagh were again the targets, and a BBC transmitter site and the courthouse in Magherafelt, County Derry were also attacked. On 14 December, the IRA exploded four bombs outside Lisnaskea Royal Ulster Constabulary (RUC) police station in County Fermanagh.[2] The renewed IRA campaign shook the foundations of Fianna Fáil and demonstrated how far a minority in the organisation openly sympathised with the use of physical force to help achieve Irish unity. Since the early 1930s, de Valera had maintained an almost missionary zeal against the use of physical force to this end. At Fianna Fáil Ard Fheiseanna (annual party conferences) and in Dáil Éireann he habitually spoke of the 'futility'[3] and 'impracticality' of violence.[4] For a vocal anti-partitionist wing of Fianna Fáil, however, de Valera's campaign against the use of force to win re-unification was traditionally greeted with outward contempt; grass-roots delegates at Ard Fheiseanna regularly demanded that the Irish government 'invade the six counties'.[5]

From the mid-1950s Fianna Fáil headquarters in Dublin's Mount Street increasingly received letters from despondent local supporters criticising the Fianna Fáil leadership's willingness to back the second inter-party government's suppression of the IRA. In early 1955, an agitated party member from County Wexford demanded that, in view of Fianna Fáil's 'republican outlook', the party should support the IRA and use 'every opportunity as forcibly as possible' as a means of resolving partition.[6] In March 1955, a concerned party follower from County Waterford informed Seán Lemass, deputy leader of Fianna Fáil and TD for Dublin South, that at a recent debate on partition at a local meeting of a Law and History symposium at Carrick-on-Suir, County Tipperary, a large number of young people between the ages of eighteen and twenty-five had made insulting remarks about de Valera and Fianna Fáil over the party's approach to partition, instead vocally lending their support to the IRA campaign.[7]

In response to the renewed IRA attacks, Lemass believed the party was at a 'crossroads', warning that if supporters did not 'speak in the same voice' they might as well 'wind up Fianna Fáil'.[8] The party leaders routinely spoke against the use of violence to end partition and the 'illegality' of the IRA campaign.[9] Lionel Booth, Fianna Fáil councillor for Dún Laoghaire-Rathdown and future TD, a Protestant and respected businessman,[10] believed the time had arrived for the organisation to educate those 'hot heads',[11] supporters who were sympathetic to the 'irresponsible' actions of the IRA.[12]

It was the military shambles of 1 January 1957, following an IRA ambush of Brookeborough RUC police station, County Fermanagh, which exposed a growing divergence of opinion within Fianna Fáil on the use of violence to end partition. In the ambush two IRA men, Seán South and Fergal O'Hanlon, were killed.[13] The raid became a legend overnight, South and O'Hanlon were martyrs within the week and their deaths became the source of numerous ballads sung through the years.[14]

Their deaths caused serious problems in the Fianna Fáil parliamentary party and demonstrated just how strong the mystique of self-styled 'republicanism' was in the Republic of Ireland in the 1950s. As Dermot Keogh has noted, South and O'Hanlon enjoyed the status of popular martyrs and were viewed by many, including many traditional Fianna Fáilers, as part of the 'purer, unsullied "republican" tradition which was contrasted with politicians caught up in the materialist world of Yeats' "greasy till"'.[15] A founding member of Fianna Fáil and TD for Roscommon, Gerry Boland later eloquently described this mindset which inspired the Irish nationalist community with a 'philosophy of death rather than life'.[16]

The funerals of South and O'Hanlon were a public relations coup for the IRA. Their coffins, draped with the Tricolour once they crossed the border, were removed from Enniskillen to St Macartan's cathedral, Monaghan.[17] At the funeral emotional speeches were made, with the wholehearted participation of a number of clergymen in support of 'Volunteer Fergal O'Hanlon'.[18] Thousands of people lined the streets of Drogheda, Dundalk and Dublin to pay their last respects as the remains of South made their way to his native city and his funeral in Limerick on 5 January was a huge affair. The funeral pictures in the *Irish Press* spoke for themselves, reflecting a clear ambivalence in Irish society about the use of violence.[19]

The public reaction to the two young men's deaths forced Taoiseach John Costello to make a radio broadcast that doggedly refuted accusations that the IRA border campaign had the support of the Irish government;[20] the public statement was supported by de Valera.[21] The widespread public outburst of sympathy for the two dead 'Volunteers' was apparent at numerous meetings of county councils throughout the country. In Dublin city council and Clare county council there were differences of opinion when some councillors appealed for an 'unqualified vote of sympathy' for the relatives of the dead men.[22] In Clare, Councillor Vincent McHugh remarked that it was not a 'regrettable thing to find young men ready to fight the common enemy'.[23]

In January 1957 the Seán MacDermott cumann [party branch], Dublin North-East, wrote to party headquarters – and the letter reached Lemass – advising that they had passed a resolution by majority vote in 'adoration of the courage and selflessness of Seán South and Fergal O'Hanlon in fighting for Ireland and giving their lives in the cause'.[24] The resolution expressed a desire for 'a leadership that will not hesitate to adopt the most radical measures to secure the re-unification of our Country'.[25] Referring to the increased support for recent IRA activities, the resolution stated that 'it was not surprising that the youth of Ireland, sick of platitudes and hungering for a new more visile [sic] leadership should turn to the IRA'.[26]

Evidently, some in Fianna Fáil had followed party policy only as long as it proved effective. For many, the partition of Ireland looked like 'unfinished business' and, while condemning the use of force as ill-advised, they were reluctant to regard it as immoral.[27] Indeed, the very fact that local representatives agreed that a vote of sympathy should be passed by their county council was a worrying development. Lionel Booth, in a letter to the *Irish Press*, objected to any vote of sympathy for anyone who did not recognise the authority of the Oireachtas and was a member of an illegal organisation. Booth put it in a refreshingly simple way:

> If these two men had survived, they would, if found by the Gardaí, have now been under arrest on a criminal charge … anyone, therefore, who attempts to glorify the actions of this illegal organisation is joining in the present defiance of our Constitutional Government.[28]

Booth's comments caused offence among many in his own constituency of Dún Laoghaire-Rathdown, as two cumainn threatened to resign from the party.[29] The Meaghen Neary cumann and Joseph Hudson cumann, Sallynoggin, wrote to Fianna Fáil headquarters to protest that Booth had 'shown that he is not a loyal member of Fianna Fáil'.[30] Lemass, however, fully supported Booth, having similarly remarked that the passing of a vote of sympathy by public representatives would 'only do more harm'.[31] He advised that such expressions of sympathy should be voiced so 'as to make clear beyond doubt or ambiguity that Fianna Fáil did not endorse the IRA's actions'.[32] Seán Moylan, the frontbench Fianna Fáil TD for Cork North, sullenly remarked that if party members accepted 'speeches made at those gravesides, as future policy' there was no future for the party.[33]

In early January 1957, Donogh O'Malley, Fianna Fáil Limerick East TD and future cabinet minister, wrote to de Valera suggesting that, since many party representatives had been 'making goats of themselves' and showing the party in a 'bad light', a meeting of the parliamentary party should be held so as to make sure that any votes that were passed in local county councils were in accordance with official party policy.[34] The Fianna Fáil TD for Clare and future president of Ireland, Patrick Hillery, recalled that many Fianna Fáil deputies, including himself, were coming under pressure in their constituencies because of the renewed IRA campaign, and urged that the Fianna Fáil government clarify its position against the use of violence in the national drive to end partition.[35]

The increasing disquiet among Fianna Fáil members, as noted by John Bowman, showed that many of those originally recruited to the party were only 'conditional constitutionalists'.[36] Though the majority of party members understood the futility of violence, a small number of supporters still had an 'each way bet' on the use of force.[37] The recent events highlighted the difference between policy and ideology, a difference that was central to the Fianna Fáil position on Irish unity. Matthew Feehan, a member of the Fianna Fáil national executive, wisely explained that the 'young generation is unable to distinguish between the physical force tradition and the national tradition ... Fianna Fáil as the true "Republican Party" must endeavour to win over the young IRA'.[38]

In an effort to restate official Fianna Fáil policy on the use of force and to prevent a possible backbench revolt, de Valera scheduled a meeting of the parliamentary party for 15 January

1957. It lasted an unprecedented eight hours.[39] John Horgan notes that during the meeting, at a critical juncture, one TD suggested that peaceful methods had failed. At this, Lemass, 'in a quite untypical display of emotion, erupted'. The problem with peaceful methods, he told the meeting, was they had not been tried. He explained that 'every time there was the prospect of some advance in North–South relations, the IRA surfaced to blow it out of the water'.[40]

Lemass was himself an ex-revolutionary and his passionate words on the futility of armed struggle would have most certainly resonated among his fellow deputies. His intervention, in both form and timing, helped de Valera significantly in his task of stiffening the resolve of the parliamentary party at a difficult time.[41] Lemass believed the party should not 'pussyfoot about' and should instead focus its attention on practical ways to end partition.[42] As a public representative his job was to 'lead public opinion and not to follow it slavishly'.[43]

During the meeting, the majority of party deputies present contributed to the debate on the recent raids in Northern Ireland. It was decided that 'there could be no armed force here except under the control and direction of the government' and that the 'employment of force at any time in the foreseeable future would be undesirable and likely to be futile'.[44] Patrick Hillery remembered that, while it was a 'decision not easily arrived at', party members had 'definitely' agreed that 'whatever happens in the North we're not going in there'.[45] His recollection was, however, at variance with the official minutes of the meeting, which recorded that 'concerning the feasibility of the use of force by any future government as a means of solving partition … no definite decision was taken'.[46] It is apparent, therefore, that at the conclusion of the meeting de Valera had failed to secure agreement from those present that the use of physical force to secure Irish unity was not a legitimate objective – if in the future the suitable circumstance arose. This was interesting, not least because the meeting had lasted over eight hours.

Such lengthy meetings were a classical example of de Valera's leadership technique, in which he always wanted to achieve unanimity and sought this by the simple process of keeping the debate going until those who were in the minority, out of sheer exhaustion, conceded the case made by the majority.[47] On this occasion, however, the technique did not work, because too many deputies refused to agree that the use of force by a future government was not a legitimate policy.

In an attempt to present a united front in the Fianna Fáil parliamentary party at the close of the meeting, a frontal assault was made by leading members of the front bench to remind both the general public and party supporters that the use of force was not Fianna Fáil policy. Gerry Boland remarked that 'it was the height of folly to think that we in the Twenty-Six Counties had force enough, if we wished to use it, to compel the Six Counties to join our State'.[48] Seán Moylan announced that he could 'see no possible value for the nation in the policy of the use of force in the Six Counties'.[49] Indeed, de Valera's son, Vivian de Valera, speaking in January 1957 during the general election campaign, which Fianna Fáil won, stressed that the young men of the IRA needed 'friendly sympathy and advice' to desist from violence.[50]

Fianna Fáil's return to government in February 1957 was a defining moment for the party's policy on both the IRA and the use of physical force to secure Irish unity. Guided by de Valera, the party hierarchy sought once again to dispel the general misconception that Irish unity was a realistic short-term aim. The Minister for External Affairs, Frank Aiken, and the Minister for Health, Seán

MacEntee, acknowledged it would be naive to say that partition would be ended in their lifetime.[51] The new Fianna Fáil deputy for Dublin County and Minister for Defence, Kevin Boland, later conceded that on the party's return in 1957 it was obvious that a solution to partition was 'not being undertaken with any degree of urgency'.[52]

Publicly, de Valera conceded that there was 'no clear way' to end partition and said that 'the man or men that would solve partition would deserve an outstanding place in Irish history'.[53] Such public declarations, although logical, were viewed by a vocal minority of the party grass-roots as acts of treachery. A representative of the Fianna Fáil cumann in Mountmellick, County Laois, accused de Valera and his cabinet colleagues of 'not giv[ing] an answer to the question of partition'.[54] Under the current Fianna Fáil government, a dejected supporter from Nenagh, County Tipperary, complained, 'any ray of hope in the quest to find a solution to the problem had lapsed'.[55]

The first signs of a rift between the new Fianna Fáil government and the rank-and-file surfaced when de Valera decided to enact the Offences Against the State Act in July 1957 in response to renewed IRA violence in Northern Ireland. His action led to the imprisonment of most of the republican leadership, the Sinn Féin Ard Comhairle, the IRA army council and the GHQ staff of the IRA.[56] De Valera viewed the IRA campaign as undermining the government's official approach to partition and seriously threatening the stability of the Irish state, and this justified the heavy-handed approach taken by the Fianna Fáil government.

On the same day that the legislation was enacted, 25 July 1957, de Valera issued a public statement on the recent wave of IRA violence and maintained that the arrest of Sinn Féin activists was because they were believed to be members of the IRA.[57] He explained that a Fianna Fáil government could not tolerate a secret army which denied the legitimacy of the state and undermined the authority of the cabinet and the Dáil. The Taoiseach was widely praised for his 'no nonsense' stand against the IRA.[58] The British Secretary of State for Commonwealth Relations, Lord Home, described de Valera's actions as 'extremely courageous'.[59] For the vast majority of the Irish public, it was the constitutional, gradualist pragmatism of Fianna Fáil, rather than the vanguardist violence of the IRA, that proved more appealing.[60] The party offered an avenue of expression for those Irish nationalists who were no longer willing to endorse physical force; the significant factor in the party's success and endurance was that it offered a credible alternative to hard-line republicanism – 'if militant republicans were anti-partitionist, comradely, ethnically rooted, cultural and historical nationalists, with a sense of moral superiority and an implicit exclusivism, then so too were Fianna Fáilers'.[61]

However, de Valera's actions were greeted with resistance from a small section of Fianna Fáil. At a meeting of Cork county council in late July 1957, the vocal anti-partitionist Fianna Fáil TD for Cork South, Seán McCarthy, spoke in defence of a Sinn Féin councillor, Tomás Mac Curtáin, who had been arrested as part of the government crackdown on IRA activity.[62] In late December 1957 at a meeting of Dublin county council, some Fianna Fáil councillors were said to have supported a motion demanding that all persons imprisoned under the 'Provisions of the Offences Against the State Act' should be accorded the status of political prisoners.[63] In the same month, in the border county of Monaghan, at a meeting of Clones urban council, Councillor S. O'Connor unsuccessfully proposed a resolution calling for the immediate release of IRA internees from the Curragh.[64]

Given such public displays of sympathy for the IRA campaign

by elected representatives, de Valera realised that recent events could have a destabilising effect on Fianna Fáil – as had been the case in January 1957 following the deaths of the IRA activists Seán South and Fergal O'Hanlon. Therefore, in April 1958, de Valera scheduled a meeting of the Fianna Fáil parliamentary party to re-affirm government policy. In response to the Cork deputy McCarthy's defiance in July 1957, de Valera warned all those present at the parliamentary meeting that any deputy who wished to disagree with government policy on the IRA 'could resign from Fianna Fáil'.[65] During de Valera's remaining years as Taoiseach, at meetings of the parliamentary party and national executive, the Fianna Fáil leadership – working closely with a small group of cabinet ministers including Frank Aiken, Oscar Traynor (TD for Dublin North-East) and Jack Lynch (TD for Cork Borough) – pleaded with party TDs to adhere to government policy on the IRA, because to do otherwise would result in the 'loss of everything that has hitherto been gained'.[66] Local party canvassers also received instructions from party headquarters to notify grass-roots supporters that official Fianna Fáil policy was resolutely against the use of private armies and that if 'the use of force were desirable, only the government would be entitled to employ it'.[67]

Speaking in 1959, on the eve of his retirement from active politics, de Valera again appealed to party supporters to realise that the alternative to non-violence was 'anarchy and national frustration'.[68] Indeed, de Valera's final years as Taoiseach can be characterised as an almost relentless campaign in his lectures to the Dáil and the annual Fianna Fáil Ard Fheiseanna against the 'useless sacrifices' of the IRA.[69] His efforts, however, failed: a small number of Fianna Fáil elected representatives still publicly sympathised with the IRA campaign, Counties Tipperary and Cavan being most inclined this way. At meetings of their county councils in late 1958 and early 1959, Fianna Fáil councillors voted in favour of resolutions calling for the release of IRA internees.[70]

During a meeting of the South Tipperary county council in early January 1958, six Fianna Fáil councillors voted in support of, and four other party councillors abstained from, a motion calling on de Valera to grant a political amnesty for IRA internees.[71] The successful motion was proposed by the prominent Fianna Fáil activist John Ahessy and seconded by his party colleague T. Duggan.[72] Abuse was hurled across the council floor against those opposing the motion, in particular against William Ryan, Fianna Fáil councillor and future party member of the Seanad. In bitter scenes not witnessed in intensity since the Treaty debates in 1921, Ahessy, who had previously spent time in gaol and on hunger strike, labelled his fellow party representative, Ryan, an 'Armchair Republican'.[73]

De Valera received criticism for his handling of partition and his firm stance against the IRA. In early February 1958 an outraged grass-roots Fianna Fáil member from County Tipperary wrote to the *Kerryman* accusing de Valera of helping to 'openly maintain partition'.[74] In July 1958, an irate Kerry native living in Derbyshire, England, wrote to de Valera personally to express his 'amazement, regret and disgust at the Fianna Fáil government's shameful treatment of patriotic' IRA men. Comparing the government tactics to those of the Gestapo, he warned de Valera that 'back in Kerry' many prominent Fianna Fáil supporters were 'outraged and disgusted at their Party's persecution of Republicans'.[75]

On hearing of the unrest locally de Valera immediately instructed that copies of his Dáil statement, originally issued in July 1957, be sent to every registered Comhairle Ceantair and Comhairle Dáilcheantair throughout the Republic of Ireland. Attached to the statement was a cover letter that gave details of an amendment that could be used by Fianna Fáil councillors if a resolution in defence of internees was moved at any future local county council meeting.[76] However, the situation was perceived to have become so unstable in south Tipperary that in early 1959 de Valera arranged secret meetings with the three local party TDs, Daniel Breen, Michael J. Davern and Francis Loughman.[77]

Seán Lemass' succession as Fianna Fáil president and Taoiseach in the summer of 1959 was widely welcomed by party supporters. During his first term in government (1959–61) the IRA was relatively inactive, allowing Lemass the comfort of not clashing with the grass-roots over the party's official policy on the IRA. This drastically changed when Lemass began his second term as Taoiseach (1962–5). Within weeks of assuming power, he announced that the major objective of Fianna Fáil's term in office was the crushing of the IRA. Led by Lemass' son-in-law, the Minister for Justice, Charles Haughey, Dublin waged a campaign against the IRA leadership.[78] Haughey re-activated the special criminal courts and, working closely with Lemass and Aiken, mounted a publicity campaign which sought to portray the IRA as an illegal organisation which did not 'serve the cause of national unity'.[79]

The Fianna Fáil government's ruthless crackdown on the IRA was not welcomed by a vocal minority in the party. In the summer of 1962 a Fianna Fáil supporter living in London wrote to Lemass expressing his anger that the government had done nothing about partition, but instead imprisoned those IRA men who had fought for Irish unity. 'Instead of sending soldiers to the Congo', he pronounced, 'couldn't they send them into Northern Ireland?'[80] In early February 1962, a disgruntled Fianna Fáil sympathiser, Rev. P. F. Malone, from Roshery, Westport, County Mayo, wrote to Lemass denouncing the government's decision to imprison 'freedom fighters'. Rev. Malone asserted that those IRA men arrested had acted on the 'same principles' that caused many within Fianna Fáil to fight the British during the Irish War of Independence. He was angry that 'even tinkers' (members of the Travelling community) had the right to trial by jury, but not members of the 'once historic Sinn Féin',[81] and he could not forgive politicians for constantly expressing their desire to end partition but never offering any plan to achieve this:

> I honestly say – that if certain members of the Dáil came to confession to me and admitted that they were lax regarding it [ending partition] – and that suffering is caused by it, I could not in conscience absolve them ... some make a terrible error. They think there's no practical sin – that anything 'put over' is o.k. They believe that what they don't do is no harm in politics – whereas sins of omission can be and are frequently the greater sins of all.[82]

Rev. Malone's closing comments epitomised the ambiguous attitude of many supporters of Fianna Fáil to the use of violence to secure Irish unity. For some anti-partitionists, constitutionalism had merely been a strategy, worth trying just as long as 'it proved promising'.[83] The renewed IRA campaign resonated in the collective consciousness of Fianna Fáil supporters. Many of them began articulating anew the party's underlying obsession with the perceived injustice of partition; some of them allowed emotion to distort their grip on the reality of the situation. As Seán MacCarthy, Fianna Fáil TD for Cork South, told Lemass: 'if you listen to the ordinary citizens in the bars and buses ... they have become increasingly supportive to the IRA activity.'[84]

This was the first occasion since becoming Taoiseach that Lemass had been strongly criticised by party supporters over his approach to the renewed IRA and the government's Northern Ireland policy. Like his predecessor, Lemass was determined to retain absolute control of the government's handling of the latest IRA campaign. In a strongly worded reply to an American attorney in Buffalo, New York, in November 1961, Lemass made clear his policy against the resurgent IRA. He condemned suggestions from Mr Heaney that IRA members were 'brave men', explaining: 'A government which failed to take action to protect their people's democratic rights would not be worthy of the name.'[85]

Speaking at the Fianna Fáil Ard Fheis in January 1962, Lemass returned to his theme that the use of violence by 'irresponsible elements' was a futile exercise and 'such actions cannot serve the cause of national unity'. What was required, he insisted, was 'for all Irishmen of all classes and creeds to work together through democratic institutions to achieve re-unification'.[86] Privately, he saw the recent IRA campaign as putting the goal to end partition 'back generations'.[87] By February 1962 the Fianna Fáil government's actions proved successful and the IRA leadership, realising that its military position was futile, issued orders for the movement to 'dump arms'. Its campaign had resulted in the deaths of six members of the RUC and eleven members of the IRA, the introduction of internment in Northern Ireland and in the south, and the mobilisation of 13,000 B-Specials.[88]

Lemass had been fortunate not to experience the levels of discontent over the party's official stance towards the IRA that de Valera faced in his final years in government; indeed, an examination of the records of the parliamentary party minutes while Lemass was Fianna Fáil leader reveal that Northern Ireland policy was never discussed.[89] He had nevertheless seen for himself how some in Fianna Fáil felt they must live up to the aspirations of a bygone generation. For this minority in the party, ideological reverence for the past, and specifically for the popular narrative of Ireland's struggle for independence, outweighed the pragmatic consideration (generally accepted by informed opinion then) that the use of physical force in pursuit of Irish unity was a futile exercise.

In conclusion de Valera's last years as Taoiseach had witnessed unprecedented levels of discontent among Fianna Fáil grass-roots members over his handling of partition policy. The unrest among party supporters challenges the perceived opinion, as put forward by de Valera's official biographers, that he secured the 'devoted loyalty of his followers'.[90] Indeed, the observation by Tom Gallagher that under de Valera Fianna Fáil was seen as united, loyal and unshakable is misleading.[91] In fact, de Valera was routinely attacked by grass-roots supporters for not adopting 'an active policy' on partition.[92]

During Lemass' period in office as Fianna Fáil leader and Taoiseach, the party leadership did manage to retain control over the anti-partitionist wing. The IRA's decision to end its campaign in 1962 no doubt came as a relief to Lemass. Nevertheless, like his predecessor, Lemass had been confronted with the reality that, whatever the party did to counteract rank-and-file support for the IRA, the party was always going to have an anti-partitionist wing that viewed physical force as a legitimate policy.

For that vocal anti-partitionist minority, the IRA campaign was logically the next step following years of perceived failure by Fianna Fáil to make any concessions – or indeed any progress – on partition. How small was that minority? The resolutions passed by Fianna Fáil county councillors and cumainn and the numerous letters of protest written by party members could not be dismissed as the work of an extremist fringe. The IRA border campaign exposed the fact that many within Fianna Fáil sympathised with the use of physical force to achieve Irish re-unification. To the 'conditional constitutionalists' of Fianna Fáil, the armed struggle remained a logical and legitimate option until a united Ireland was achieved; perhaps more significantly, it carried such emotional force that it clouded their judgement.

12

BELFAST, AUGUST 1969

The limited and localised pattern(s) of violence

LIAM KELLY

Belfast, Sunday 16 August 2009: smoking bandsmen, families, neighbours, community leaders and political representatives gather at the base of Divis Tower, West Belfast. Less than a mile away, the transatlantic Tall Ships slip their moorings and set sail down Belfast Lough after a four-day festival in which three quarters of a million people visited the re-imaged capital of Northern Ireland[1] – the city of the B-shaped heart.[2] A few hundred feet up, two aerobatic planes (with coloured smoke tracking their gravity-defying movements) entertain the thousands gathered below on the banks of the River Lagan. For those forming up in procession this display proved a distant distraction, for they were assembling to remember an event which, in the tourist-friendly Belfast of 2009, seemed even further away than those planes: the fortieth anniversary of August 1969. In that month a different type of smoke and spectacle gripped the city as hundreds of buildings (mostly people's homes) blazed, seven people lost their lives, hundreds of households were displaced and British soldiers first set foot on the streets of Belfast.[3]

As this description of the march by Sinn Féin's publicity department attests, the procession carefully recounted a historical and communal narrative:

> It progressed up the Falls Road, passing Saint Comgall's Primary School which was attacked by unionist mobs ... It made its way through Conway Street and Cupar Street where homes were burned out, before moving up Clonard Street past Clonard Monastery which was targeted by petrol bombs ... The march ended in Clonard Gardens and Bombay Street which was completely destroyed in the burnings.[4]

At the parade's destination a number of speeches were made to the thousand or so people assembled and a mural was unveiled. In the small, intimate space of now-reconstructed Bombay Street, overshadowed by a 40-foot-high 'peace wall' (a direct legacy of 1969),[5] Daniel Jack of the Commemoration Committee reiterated the 'significance' of the journey they had just made: it 'incorporated all the area that was on the receiving end of the pogrom'.[6] The story of 1969 was being re-traced, re-told and re-inscribed upon the narrow streets of the Lower Falls and Clonard for the benefit of the 2009 generation.

During that same summer of 2009 two further events (both photographic exhibitions) were put on in Belfast to mark and reflect upon the awful violence that defined 1969 in the city. The first was a series of 'fifty stunning images' taken by Gerry Collins, a keen local amateur photographer, in and around Bombay Street in the immediate aftermath of its destruction and the arrival of British troops in the district.[7] These pictures had not been viewed in public before and only came to light when Collins approached Frankie Quinn (director of Belfast's Red Barn Gallery) in early 2009 to tell him about the photographs. Quinn recalled how he thought nothing more of it until Collins turned up some time later with, in his words, an 'incredible box of history'.[8]

The success of the subsequent exhibition ('Bombay Street – Taken from the Ashes') and the publicity it attracted led the family of Hugh McKeown to present the gallery with a number of pictures that he too had taken forty years previously. This second collection recorded the effects of rioting in Ardoyne in 1969 and was displayed alongside Collins' originals under the title: 'Ardoyne – The Aftermath'. In the book that accompanied the exhibition, the foreword picked out one particular snapshot for further comment:

> In one ironic image, two young children play at the driver's seat of a bus with its route – Falls Road via Ardoyne [*sic*] – clearly visible. As Ardoyne burned, so did Bombay Street on the Falls. Indeed, at one point the following day, Hugh [McKeown] travelled to West Belfast to witness and photograph the devastated Falls, and the powerful pictures he took there reflect the shared experience of the two communities.[9]

A damaged bus used by two children for play © Hugh McKeown

One of the most noticeable characteristics of all the above reflections is how geographically limited and spatially concentrated in scope they were. The march from Divis Towers to Bombay Street conspicuously ignored events outside that district. The speeches made a few fleeting (almost apologetic) mentions of events in Ardoyne, but the individuals commemorated on the new mural were all from the Greater Clonard area and the image used was that of a burnt-out Bombay Street.[10] The titles and contents of the two photographic exhibitions showed the horrific concentration of destruction wrought upon these two tightly packed Catholic working-class neighbourhoods, but the lens did not move beyond those areas to contextualise these pictures. The 'one ironic image' of the two boys in the burnt-out bus may have symbolically reflected the 'shared experience of the two communities' (the Falls and Ardoyne) but it did not capture what the majority of Belfast's residents and most of its neighbourhoods experienced during that tumultuous summer. The fact that these retrospectives told only part of the narrative(s) of August 1969 in the city of Belfast can be understood within the general processes of selectivity that surround all commemorative acts. However, this chapter argues that the nature and shape of these commemorative events tells us much more: in fact they highlight a defining characteristic of that year's disturbances – their limited and localised nature.

In 1969 the city of Belfast was divided into six police districts, A to F. The majority of disturbances in August 1969 occurred in police districts B and C (the northern and western parts of the city).[11] Police district A remained the 'most peaceful part of the City' despite having at times only a dozen or so policemen available for patrol.[12] District A covered the central parts of Belfast, including two potential sectarian flashpoints: the working-class neighbourhoods of Sandy Row (predominantly Protestant), and the

Market(s) (predominantly Catholic). There was no 'sharp dividing line' between the two; instead a 'mixed area', made up of people from both religious groups, separated them.[13] Both Sandy Row and the Market(s) remained 'quiet' during August and relationships between residents were noted as being 'very good'. In fact on 16 August 1969 two peace committees were created, one operating out of Sandy Row and the other from the Market(s), and in time they 'collaborated well and worked together to maintain peace'.[14]

Police district D covered the greater part of north Belfast, from Peter's Hill/York Street to the west of the city centre and the docks to the east, going as far north as the city's boundary.[15] Its main residential roads included the Antrim Road, York Street and the Shore Road. There were a number of 'sensitive' points within the division, all of which saw a general 'heightening of tension' but no violence at the peak of the unrest in mid-August.[16] This was somewhat surprising as significant rioting had occurred in and around the Unity Flats on 12 July and again in early August. In fact the disturbances there, and in the Crumlin Road/Ardoyne area, in early August led to British troops being 'quietly posted … in police stations surrounding the trouble areas'.[17] The only sign of potential violence in district D in the mid-August period was after 16 August when rival crowds gathered and barricades were erected at the New Lodge/Tiger's Bay interface. However, there were no signs of 'serious' disturbance and the rival crowds merely exchanged 'catcalls, shouts and songs'.[18] Head Constable Thomas McCluney, in his testimony to the Scarman Tribunal (the inquiry established to explore the events of that year in Northern Ireland), highlighted the co-operation between the various Protestant and Catholic streets directed through Newington Presbyterian church and St Patrick's church, respectively, as being key to taking the 'whole explosive tension out of the area'.[19]

Police district E covered much of the (predominantly Protestant) eastern part of the city. Its western boundary was marked by the River Lagan, which it followed northwards from the Albert Bridge and Beersbridge Roads.[20] The only major Catholic area in the district was the Short Strand, a small tightly packed working-class neighbourhood surrounded mainly by Protestant streets. This area did see some unrest when tension became 'dangerously high' on the nights of 14 and 16 August, but on both occasions Protestant mobs were stopped from entering the neighbourhood by the police and 'no clashes between civilians' occurred.[21] It was only after the second attempt to attack the district on 16 August that the first barricades were erected by Catholic vigilantes. The local Catholic street committee and the (mainly Protestant) 'East Belfast Peace Committee' worked well with one another and with the RUC. Again, like police district A, what makes the events in that area even more remarkable is that the police presence was 'at the barest minimum' as reinforcements had been sent to other parts of the city and to Derry.[22]

Finally, police district F, although the scene of a number of attacks upon properties, in particular Catholic-owned licensed premises, 'remained outside the area of civil disturbances'. This district included most of the southern part of the city, with a population between 100,000 and 120,000. There were two potential flashpoints within the district: the Protestant Woodstock Road boundary with the Catholic Short Strand; and the Protestant Donegall Road, near the motorway, which faced onto the Catholic Falls Road. In August a number of barricades were put up in certain parts of the district but interestingly those on the Donegall Road 'were manned by both Catholics and Protestants working in harmony'. Subsequently there was no occurrence of violence in this 'sensitive' area and 'clergy of all denominations came together and achieved a measure of success in keeping the peace during August and September'.[23]

This brief overview of events outside the major riot areas during July and August 1969 shows how remarkably limited (in geographic terms) the disturbances actually were. The violence which did occur in police districts B and C was further concentrated in three areas: the 'Orange–Green' line separating the Shankill and Falls neighbourhoods (from Divis Street to the Springfield Road); the Hooker Street/Crumlin Road area; and the Unity Flats/Peter's Hill/Upper Library Street interface. On the surface this pattern seems understandable in that the riots occurred in places where Catholic and Protestant working-class streets abutted each other. The 'extremely constricted physical spaces' which this type of terrace housing created have been seen as significant in providing 'conditions ripe for sectarian conflict'.[24] When densely populated Catholic and Protestant neighbourhoods were established within these tightly knit urban spaces a principle of 'territorial dominance' began to underwrite communal rioting,[25] and there was an emphasis on the use of violence as a mechanism for marking out the future development of single-denomination areas.[26] Seemingly these 'seismic zones'[27] were where disturbances would inevitably manifest themselves during periods of civil unrest, so that the violence was literally 'embedded' in Belfast's built environment.[28]

On further initial analysis, the location of rioting in August 1969 seems to be explicable in terms of the role played by local collective histories of violence, which have been noted as another key factor determining the spatial shape of communal disturbances in the north of Ireland. For example, Mark Doyle has described how in 1919 local journalist James Winder Good noted the significance of 'a peculiar sort of folk memory among the working-class Protestants and Catholics of Belfast'. Good went on to argue that this knowledge was passed down from generation to generation:

> Gates scarred with bullet holes from long-ago riots, a corner where a sniper had once operated, a cul-de-sac in which an unfortunate company of dragoons had been successfully repulsed by stone-throwing crowds – these became landmarks of communal identity for the coming generations, reminders of collective victories or humiliations, urban monuments evoking feelings of triumph or recalling grievances to be avenged.[29]

The commemorative march from Divis Towers to Bombay Street, described above, is a good example of how such 'working-class memories' are formed and communicated. It is not insignificant that the parade route passed by St Comgall's school where, even today, bullet marks caused by police gunfire in August 1969 are still visible on the front of the building – a symbolic repertoire (or 'urban monument') of past transgressions against that community.

However, if one were to take a map of Belfast as it looked in January 1969 with the Catholic neighbourhoods coloured in green and Protestant districts in orange, and then marked those areas with long histories of collective violence, it would only partly correspond to the map produced by the Scarman Tribunal of the 'Main Riot Areas'.[30] The spatial distribution of the disturbances, therefore, reveals that the nature of communal violence in Belfast is a much more complicated phenomenon than initially suggested by either the city's sectarian topography or its 'peculiar sort of folk memory'. This is reflected in the fact that potential flashpoints like the Short Strand and the New Lodge/Tiger's Bay interface witnessed little unrest in that period. It is also shown in the way districts like Sandy Row, which had long histories of fraught community relations, saw little violence in the summer of 1969.[31]

To fully understand the nature of the disturbances that summer we should first focus on their local aspects, much as the fortieth anniversary commemorations did; and then we need to conceptualise these events as a series of localised narratives which played out simultaneously (and sometimes independently of one another), rather than being fixed within a general temporal framework starting with the 5 October 1968 Civil Rights march in Derry and marked by Burntollet, the 'Crossroads' election, the Apprentice Boys' march and the 'Battle of the Bogside', before culminating in the Belfast 'pogroms' that we are examining here. In so doing we begin to see a plethora of triggers and small details which tell us a great deal more about why, when and where violence erupted in the city. This allows us to understand how, in the words of the Scarman Report, the 'disturbances in Belfast were confined to a relatively small area'.[32]

Police actions and decisions made in and around certain 'sensitive' points during this period also played a key role in shaping events. There are numerous examples where police judgement and approaches in a certain neighbourhood had a positive effect on events, and also (tragically) many other instances where they did not.

In their submission to the Scarman Tribunal the Catholic residents of Ardoyne stated that 'the major responsibility for the happenings ... must lie with the police'.[33] Tellingly the germ of the deteriorating relationship between police and local Catholic residents lay in the mishandling of a seemingly innocuous bar-room incident.[34] On 16 May 1969 a crowd gathered outside the Edenderry Inn – a public house with 'a thoroughly bad reputation' – to watch a customer who had fallen down some stairs being taken away by ambulance.[35] They became agitated shortly after when an RUC patrol dressed in riot gear arrived and arrested a man.[36] Stones and other missiles were thrown at the police, who called in reinforcements.[37]

There were disturbances outside the Edenderry the next night and the following weekend, and the public house (at the junction of Hooker Street and Crumlin Road) continued to be the main 'site of violence' in Ardoyne throughout the rest of that year. In analysing this incident, Vivian Simpson, Stormont MP for the area, noted how this 'ill-feeling against the police tended to be localised'.[38] However, as Simpson's solicitor rightly pointed out, the 'resentment such as existed in Hooker Street before the major troubles broke out always ran the risk of developing into something much more serious'.[39] And so it proved, with this sensitive spot becoming a 'running sore' from May up until the arrival of British troops in the area in mid-August.[40]

By then, criticism of police actions was not limited to Ardoyne's Catholic residents. The *Sunday Times* investigative team was highly dismissive of the RUC's actions on 14/15 August, concluding that: '[t]he ultimate tragedy of Belfast is that, given better standards of policing that night, bloodshed need never have happened on the scale that it did'.[41] The journalists were correct to reprimand the police over their use of Browning machine-guns in 'the huddled streets' of the Falls and Divis areas.[42] The fact that some of the bullets fired from these heavy-calibre weapons landed up to a mile away, hitting a police station whose incumbents (ironically) believed they were under attack, attests to the reckless nature of this reaction.[43] However, if RUC actions in the Lower Falls and Ardoyne helped feed into the violence being played out in those localities, the same cannot be said of other 'sensitive' parts of the city.

For example, the residents of Unity Flats – a 'Catholic fortress in Protestant territory'[44] – in their submission to the Scarman Tribunal paid tribute to the police for stopping an attempted attack on their area on 3 August and for doing so 'in a determined and forceful manner'.[45] Harold Wolseley, Belfast City police commissioner, described his force's reaction to the assault thus: 'Let's face it, my Lord [Scarman], we took on the Shankill for two nights and beat them to their knees, putting it rather crudely, and made 100 or something arrests. There was no bias in that.'[46] In fact the ferocious nature of the confrontations between the RUC and Protestant rioters in the Shankill in that period led to the police withdrawing from the district; it was only the introduction of the Special Constabulary and Loyalist institutions (both Orange Order and Royal Black members) patrolling the streets that brought calm to the area.[47]

Events in and around the predominantly Catholic Short Strand, which was isolated and vulnerable in much the same way as Unity Flats, were also telling. On three successive nights from 14 to 17 August, Protestant mobs tried to enter Catholic streets and on each occasion the police were able to stop these incursions. Indeed the RUC officer in charge of that area praised the role played by Catholic vigilantes in helping to prevent 'a clash between the different factions'.[48] The good relationship between local Catholic residents and the police can be gauged by the fact that when barricades were constructed on 16 August, blocking off all access routes into the Short Strand, the area did not become a 'no-go' for the RUC (unlike 'Free Derry' and 'Free Belfast'). In return the police seemed to show a high degree of sensitivity in how they approached their duties in that locality:

We did not go into the area unnecessarily for the purpose of 'flag

showing'. We went in there when we had to go in and dealt with ordinary matters and we went up and down Seaforde Street [in Short
Strand] every day at different times.[49]

Good working relationships between police and other Catholic
working-class neighbourhoods where barricades were set up can
be seen elsewhere in the city. For example, on the two occasions
when barricades were constructed in the Market(s) the police
were able to successfully negotiate with the residents and reassure
them that if they took them down no attacks would follow.[50] Such
dialogue would not have been possible if relations between the
RUC and local residents had deteriorated in the way they had in
Ardoyne and the Falls.

The above examples are not meant to provide a comprehensive
analysis of the RUC and policing in the city of Belfast during 1969;
instead they are meant to be one prism of many through which we
can view the unrest of that year. They highlight how the nature
of those events, in particular the nature of the violence, may be
better understood within a local conceptual framework rather than
within a general narrative structure. So, for instance, in the case of
Ardoyne we see a situation where a small event in a specific locality
could become a defining trigger. The evidence suggests that the
arrival of the police in the aftermath of the Edenderry Inn incident
changed the nature of the crowd which had gathered there. What
is less clear is whether it was just the police presence or the fact
that they were clothed in riot gear that caused the atmosphere to
become agitated. What is certain is that by the following night (17
May) the RUC's visibility in the area was being viewed by (some)
patrons of the public house as a provocative act, with a crowd
from the Edenderry Inn attacking two 'uniformed constables' who
during the course of their 'normal patrol' were standing opposite

the establishment.[51] A full-scale riot broke out and, tellingly, residents from the Hooker Street/Herbert Street area were drawn to this 'site of violence', driving up the number of citizens involved in the riot from 80 to 200.[52]

With these two incidents we can see the beginnings of the dynamics of future disturbances in that area, particularly the fact that the junction of Hooker Street and the Crumlin Road became the locale for much of the violence that followed. The way the RUC policed the neighbourhood also began to change as these events informed the force's perceptions (at institutional and individual levels) of the district. Just as significantly, these events similarly influenced local (Catholic) residents' attitudes to the police. The relationship between the police and Catholic residents in that area, though not across the whole of Belfast, was now fundamentally altered. We should not completely separate these events from the city's recent experience of rioting (in the Falls from 20 to 22 April) or the tumultuous political and social changes in the rest of Northern Ireland, but the fact is that the contours of these events (in this example, in Ardoyne) were defined at a street and neighbourhood level, not at a city-wide or national one.

I have put forward two arguments about August 1969 in the city of Belfast. Firstly, I argue that the violence in that period was significant not only in and of itself but also because it was spatially quite limited. The highly concentrated nature of the rioting (geographically) was what the Scarman Report described as the 'one remarkable fact' of the Belfast disturbances that year, and this characteristic continued to define much of the violence during the subsequent 'Troubles'.[53] As John Darby noted, Northern Ireland as a case study was interesting for 'the limitations of its violence rather than for the violence itself'.[54] Similarly, Elliott Leyton emphasised that the 'true enigma' facing researchers working on the Troubles was 'not why so many have died: rather, it is why so *few* have been killed'.[55]

Secondly I am arguing that, though Belfast's intricate sectarian geography and its collective folk memory together help explain the shape and distribution of the violence that marred the city in that period, they do so only to an extent. In fact, to gain a fuller understanding of these disturbances we need to begin to view them from another perspective – the local. As Niall Ó Dochartaigh has rightly argued, in 'conditions of civil disorder and conflict the world contracts and the local situation becomes the central political concern of many more people'.[56] It has been easy when exploring the long history of communal rioting, intimidation and violence in Belfast to analyse events somewhat too deterministically, identifying and rarefying a number of causal factors.[57] By looking at these events through the prism of multiple local narratives (each instructive in its own way) we can start to gain a fuller understanding of the nature of communal violence – and communal non-violence – in Northern Ireland's largest city.

13

WHEN IS AN ASSEMBLY RIOTOUS, AND WHO DECIDES?

The success and failure of police attempts to criminalise protest

EALÁIR NÍ DHORCHAIGH & LAURENCE COX

This chapter explores the sensitive topic of police violence at political protests in Ireland in more recent times and in particular the question of when and how it is legitimised. Long experience of discussing the matter with students, colleagues, journalists and members of the public makes it clear that many people see police acts using force as per se legitimate and therefore not 'violent', a term thus reserved for illegitimate acts. Yet police behaviour can be contested publicly and on occasion found to be illegitimate (by expert opinion, by media commentators, by internal inquiries or indeed by courts of law). The question of how the use of force is legitimised – and what conditions make this achievement of legitimacy more or less likely – is then an interesting one, as is the broader question of why a police decision is made to use force in the first place, and at what level.

Thus a central theme of our chapter is the need to separate

acts involving force (injury to civilians on Dublin's Dame Street, for example) from the question of whether or not they are subsequently legitimised (in the case of Dame Street in 2002 they were not; in the case of Rossport in Mayo in the years up to 2010 they consistently have been). In the contexts in question, police acts of force – far from being seen as automatically legitimate – have been widely condemned in the media and, on occasion, by internal inquiries; they have also been denied (rarely) or ignored (far more commonly), and (on occasion) explicitly justified.

Our general argument here is that (a) police officers commit violent acts, but are (sometimes) licensed to do so; (b) the question of when they are licensed to do so is an interesting one and worthy of research; (c) it has to do with a range of social actors, notably the media, courts and politicians; (d) all of this is separate again from the question of whether in some other sense they are justified or not, on which opinions will no doubt continue to differ.

A separate question centres on why particular acts of police violence are committed. A particular act may originate with a strategic decision by senior police management (or indeed a general directive by politicians); it may also be a decision by the immediate commander or it may indeed represent a loss of 'command and control' over individual officers. Given that some policing decisions will never be recorded, and others will be fully discoverable only in the event of independent legal inquiries or the subsequent release of state papers, a whole series of problems arise.

In this context, researchers have to draw on the available evidence and make reasonable arguments about (i) when genuine choices are being made – as with the 'no-arrests' policy, which was publicly stated in *Garda Review*, or the withdrawal of batons from front-line police at protests, visible between May and September 2002; (ii) at what level such choices are made – for example, the involvement of the navy in responding to the Erris protests and the borrowing of water cannon from the PSNI for the May Day protests were clearly not decisions within the remit of junior officers; and (iii) what explanations for such decisions can plausibly be suggested.

In other words, as citizens or (sociological) researchers, we have to do the best we can to understand why, when citizens protest, they are occasionally attacked (legitimately or not), though we remain aware that in some cases we may never know the answer. Comparable limitations, of course, apply to events in the past, where the data is also limited (albeit differently) and researchers also need to rely on chains of evidence, assumptions and reasoning to make convincing arguments about the reasons for particular acts.

Here we discuss some choices in the recent policing of protest in the Republic, and possible explanations for these choices; we also ask about the processes through which the outcomes of such choices – in terms of the use of particular levels of violence against citizens – have been found legitimate or otherwise, and the conditions which influence these outcomes. We start, however, in the eighteenth century.

In 1787, Irish law introduced the 'reading of the Riot Act'. In this ritual, once the Act was read, a popular gathering – irrespective of the participants' actions – became illegal, and subject to physical attack by the authorities. Similar 'warnings to disperse' are still employed by the Irish police at demonstrations in Ireland today, and the charge of 'refusal to obey the instructions of a garda' is routinely brought against protestors, whereas the 1994 Criminal Justice Act makes 'riot' an offence in itself, separate from any specific actions. In other words, if the police publicly define protests or other collective actions as riotous, they are entitled to make extensive use of force in repressing them, and both participation and mere physical presence become criminal. Another way of describing such laws is to say that an assembly is riotous when the authorities say that it is. Such statements are what Jürgen Habermas calls 'performative utterances', statements which make something real by saying that it is so, like 'I do' at a wedding.[1] The implication is that the state can legitimate its use of violence against social movements, restrict the freedom of assembly and criminalise participants just by saying so.

However, police decisions to define a specific protest as illegitimate and illegal – and hence a legitimate target of violence – is not automatically the end of the matter. Protestors try, sometimes successfully, to undermine such decisions; and other social groups like the media and courts do not always give the consent needed to legitimise coercion. As the broad history of the popular assertion of political rights like the right of assembly suggests, the authorities' routine attempts to restrict such rights often fail.

The key feature of all these events – as with the series of simultaneous protests around the use of Shannon Airport by the US military, which deserve separate discussion – is their combination of peaceful protest with disruptive tactics (non-violent direct action) and a consequent refusal to negotiate protest events in advance with the police. This disruptive power is one of the major tools that those who are formally powerless have at their disposal.[2] Struggle over the legitimacy of such action is therefore a key site of political conflict. It is also important that we are discussing events which broadly fit within the 'alter-globalisation' (anti-capitalist, global justice, etc.) movement; policing strategies are very different in relation to different movements.[3] Our analysis leads us to ask three further questions:

- Why should police seek to criminalise the alter-globalisation movement in the first place?
- What conditions enable or prevent legitimation of the use of force by the police?
- What do police and protestors learn from these events?

Considering its origins, the Republic of Ireland is a remarkably peaceful state, as shown by international comparisons of murder rates or the availability and use of weapons, official and unofficial. This is tied to the successful pacification of the state during the post-Treaty 'counter-revolution' and more recently to the Northern Ireland 'Troubles', which have had a massive impact on political violence in the republic. The key security institutions of the state have – or at least had until the Good Friday agreement of 1998 – been justified by the Northern Ireland conflict (and, by extension, the supposed subversive threat to state power in the republic), to which they have directed most of their attention, with the support of most political forces and media in the south.

One major implication of this preoccupation was a sharp division in policing style for protest in the republic in the last third of the twentieth century. 'Routine' political demonstrations of whatever colour were (until 2000) essentially self-policing, with very low police presence and organisers determined that their protest should be fundamentally non-disruptive, in contrast to the routinely tolerated disruptive protests by insider interest groups like farmers and taxi drivers. Conversely, other kinds of political protest – notably republican events, but also working-class and Traveller protest, and rural protests against the development plans of multinational corporations – were met with a massive and coercive police presence as a matter of course.

Political riots have been rare in the republic's recent history.

After the 'Bloody Sunday' killings of protestors by soldiers in Derry in 1972, a crowd set fire to the British embassy in Dublin. It was again a target during the 1981 hunger strikes, but this time the crowd of 15,000 met a brutal response. This zero-tolerance security operation is seen as a watershed in Irish policing history.[4] Conversely, non-political collective violence on a small scale has long been a fairly routine feature of Irish life. For example, at the time of the 2004 EU summit protests in Dublin (twenty-nine arrests, but only half reached trial), the 'Rally of the Lakes' resulted in forty-three arrests in Killarney,[5] where one incident was reported thus:

> Officers were targeted by thugs when they arrived at the scene of a fight at the busy junction linking Main Street and Plunkett Street at 1.30 a.m.
>
> As they moved in to apprehend two culprits, other bystanders got involved and Gardaí were targeted with missiles when reinforcements arrived to break up the row. 'It was basically the crowd that couldn't get into the nightclubs that had congregated on the street – these were people who had come out of the pub and couldn't get in anywhere,' Sergeant Tom Tobin told *The Kingdom*.
>
> Around 300 people were present at the scene as Gardaí broke up the fight. Seven people were arrested under the Public Order Act as a result of the fracas, making up a quarter of the 28 public order arrests made on Saturday night and Sunday morning. Nobody was injured as a result of the street fight and those arrested will be brought before the courts.[6]

The contrast between the policing of the Killarney event and that of the EU protest, for which over half the republic's police force was deployed, is stark.

Similar conflicts at Traveller weddings and funerals have been a feature of life in the Republic, and routinely provoke a 'moral panic' in the media as well as intensive policing. Yet another kind of response marks the frequent encounters between police and groups of youths on council estates in west Dublin and elsewhere, which are typically occasions for the deployment of state force but without any media fanfare. Such 'social violence' took an explicitly political form in 2006, with the so-called 'Dublin riots' in which an apparently spontaneous gathering of marginalised working-class youth prevented the loyalist Love Ulster organisation from marching past the GPO. This event highlighted both the organisational capacity of those involved and the separation of their networks from those of traditional republicanism: both republicans and the police were caught by surprise.[7] This event, however, stands out as exceptional, and is best understood as a transposition to the city centre of normally hidden conflicts on peripheral estates.

Despite this peaceful history, the alleged likelihood of anti-capitalist violence has frequently resulted in high-scale policing of protest, justified by implausible information fed to the media.[8] Equally interestingly, the co-operation of courts and media – routinely available to criminalise working-class youth and Travellers – has often been withheld. What is it about the alter-globalisation movement that seems to make the Irish police want to criminalise it and yet makes their attempts to do so fall flat? By 2002, senior Irish police officers were familiar with their European colleagues' picture of alter-globalisation protestors as 'the new subversive threat', a perspective highlighted in 2001 by the near-fatal shooting of three protestors in Gothenburg and the killing of one in Genoa. Dublin's 'Reclaim the Streets' (RTS) protests were equally international in inspiration and were by now traditional in

Dublin, highlighting the privatisation of public space by car traffic and disrupting it with street parties.

The 2002 street party began with about 400 people listening to music played from a rig blocking one of the city's busiest roads. Banners against car culture and commodification of the city called for free public space. Numbers rose to 700 and the party continued for three hours until the police became hostile and began making arrests. Partygoers decided it would be safer to walk *en masse* to Stephen's Green and disperse there but, as they began to move, an unmarked police car drove into the march, breaking it up. Several police vans arrived and participants alleged that gardaí started indiscriminately attacking people – partygoers, bystanders and passing shoppers. As police numbers rose to about 150, the crowd, now only 200, was still moving towards the park, but was blocked by police vans and bikes. One protestor recalled:

> This was the worst of the baton charges I saw. Previously they had been happy taking a few swings at a couple of people to frighten people back. This time they were knocking people to the ground and continuing to baton and kick people once they had gone down. I saw a young man being thrown against the side of a bus and batoned there by at least five gardaí ... One advertising executive reported that he had been hit three times before seeing two motorbike cops banging a young man's head off a wall. A woman was knocked off her bike and beaten on the ground before being arrested, and many people were sent to hospital at this point.[9]

These events fitted into an increasing police hostility to alter-globalisation activism. On European Car Free Day in September 2001, a well-established and generally tolerated event in other EU states, five Dublin activists were arrested for obstructing traffic. Three weeks later a protest against privatisation was met by a baton charge, with fourteen protestors being arrested and held overnight – a then unprecedented measure in relation to minor public order disturbances. A journalist recording the event was arrested and had his equipment confiscated. By the time the police attacked the Dame Street party, arresting twenty-four and hospitalising over a dozen people, a pattern of aggressive policing of anti-capitalist movement activity had already emerged. The *Irish Times* journalist William Hederman commented:

> Since last summer, there has been a remarkable shift in the garda's approach to dealing with protests by the 'anti-capitalist' or 'internationalist' movement. Activists report that gardaí have been moving in suddenly and aggressively, making arrests and bringing criminal charges under the controversial Public Order Act (POA).[10]

Protestors also noted that the riot units that attacked the crowd were not wearing numbers, a serious breach of discipline if it had not been sanctioned by senior officers.

What marked this event out from previous incidents was the availability of high-quality video footage of the events and the willingness of national television to broadcast images of police violence, resulting in what is now widely seen as one of the major police legitimacy crises in recent Irish history.[11] Uniquely, tabloid headlines the next day criticised the police rather than the protestors, and it became clear that the traditional licence accorded to students in particular to engage in unusual and colourful behaviour was widely accepted even among traditional, 'middle-class' supporters of the gardaí. A crowd of almost 1,000 marched the following week to demonstrate against the treatment of RTS protestors, the marchers representing a broad mix of socialists, anarchists, republicans and the travelling community.

There were serious repercussions for the police: over €1 million was paid out in compensation to victims, while the Garda Complaints Board denounced the behaviour of the police involved in attacking the RTS protest. An internal inquiry was held (in which officers unanimously claimed not to be able to identify any of their colleagues as having taken part) and batons were taken away from the police at the next RTS demonstration, six months later. For their part, police participants in the September events held that they had been 'hung out to dry' by management. Plans to hold the European meeting of the World Economic Forum in Dublin the following year were scrapped after the Irish Social Forum and Grassroots Gathering mounted an anti-summit campaign. If, as activists believed, this represented an official acknowledgement of police inability to deal successfully with new kinds of protest, this was clearly a problem for the police (not to mention an embarrassment for senior politicians) and required a new strategy on their part, as well as a substantial investment in training.[12] As an aside, we can observe that Dame Street was by 2010 partially closed to private transport and used only by buses and taxis.

Two years after the events of May Day 2002, Ireland was scheduled to hold an EU summit meeting in Dublin's Phoenix Park. The old left used this opportunity to hold a conventional march against neo-liberalism in a location approved by the police, whereas the libertarian left established the 'Dublin Grassroots Network' and called for a march to the summit itself. Following the model of Argentinean *cacerolazos*, the aim was to 'bring the noise' – whistles, pots and pans – to discover whether dissenting citizens could in fact be heard by EU leaders. The key issues were opposition to what were seen as racist 'Fortress Europe' policies, the privatisation of basic services, neo-liberalism's perceived contribution to social injustice and the increased militarisation of the European Union.

Although May Day 2004 was officially framed as a 'day of welcomes', anticipatory media coverage of the summit protests – drawing on the usual unattributed 'security sources' – warned the Irish public that hordes of EU citizens were planning to travel across the Irish Sea to protest. Elsewhere in the EU, similar attempts by citizens to exercise the right to demonstrate have routinely been met with the suspension of the Schengen agreement, the detaining of protestors at frontiers and the systematic demonisation of 'foreign' protestors. The Garda Representative Association claimed that everyone who had been in Genoa (some 250,000 according to standard estimates) would come to Ireland; another claimed that there were '20,000 anarchists' travelling from the UK. Rather more accurately, the final *Garda Review* analysis suggested a figure of twenty visitors intent on causing trouble.[13] The bizarre inflation of numbers seems to have been part of a disinformation campaign, which ran for months before the event, attacking alter-globalisation demonstrations and aiming to legitimise militarised policing. Stories were leaked of secret armies, arms dumps, a threatened gas attack on the Taoiseach and plans to burn down Blanchardstown shopping centre; journalists wrote of infiltrating 'secret meetings' which turned out to be publicly advertised and open to all.[14] Aisling Reidy of the Irish Council for Civil Liberties said they were 'very concerned that gardaí, through stories fed to the media, [were] trying to soften up public opinion for a show down, by talking of potential violence and well-planned attacks by subversives'.[15]

The summit's location, close to a residential area, was marked off by a four-mile exclusion zone, with between 4,000 and 6,000 police officers – half the national force – deployed on summit-related duties, 1,000 in riot squads. Overtly alarmist measures included the deployment of over 2,500 troops, the use of the navy and air corps, placing the army's chemical, biological, radiological and nuclear unit on stand-by, detailing other troops to help gardaí secure key installations around the capital, including the airport, tightening immigration checks at ports and airports, cancelling all garda leave and borrowing water cannons from the Northern Ireland police, from whose tactics gardaí have historically preferred to dissociate themselves. More disturbingly, senior gardaí told hospitals to have their emergency contingency plans ready in case of serious civil unrest, space was cleared at the city morgue and body bags[16] were said to have been ordered, a wing of a Dublin prison was emptied in readiness, and gardaí visited city-centre businesses warning of serious violence and encouraging them to shut up shop for the weekend, producing a frightened, silent and militarised city.[17]

The right to protest was directly suspended with the announcement, two days before the protest, that the riot squad would be deployed at the march's starting point with orders to break up any attempt to assemble – a serious threat to those who might not hear of this in time. In the face of this, and the usual anonymous announcements in the media that the protest had been cancelled, Dublin Grassroots Network declared a new starting point. The eventual march brought 5,000 marchers within a mile of the summit venue, well inside the supposed exclusion zone, and safely back to the city centre, a distance of some eight or nine miles. In the confrontation at Phoenix Park's Ashtown gate between some protestors and police, the apparently overwhelming force available to police was restrained in the face of a massive media presence, legal observers, memories of 2002 and the presence of large numbers of interested local working-class men on a warm Saturday evening. An attempt by a group of protestors to push through police lines was met with the use of water cannon, producing a stalemate, and protestors retreated in good order in the face of baton charges.

Police strategies were also less than successful in the public arena. Banning the march almost certainly boosted the number of protestors who were defending the freedom to protest. Serious media used the more ludicrous claims fed to journalists to mock the alarmism of the tabloid press. Journalist Harry Browne commented that the event was 'actually a garda riot control operation without a riot … and the virtual erasure of people who were involved in peaceful protest in a public place and were subjected to assault by baton and cold bath, then arrest by gardaí'. The denial of bail to the handful of protestors arrested (usually on trivial charges, and held over the bank holiday weekend) was the subject of newspaper editorials and it was rapidly reversed.[18]

Far from the organisers being charged with conspiracy to organise a riot, as would have been logical if the police had believed their own claims, only trivial charges were brought (most for 'breach of the peace' and 'refusal to obey the instructions of a garda'). The courts refused to entertain police requests to take into account the political context of the supposed offences. The most serious charge (of possessing stencils) was thrown out because the police had failed to bring any evidence to show their purpose.[19] We may note that four years later the Irish electorate rejected the EU's Lisbon Treaty and was 'sent back' the next year to vote again until the officially approved result was achieved.

The year after the EU protest, five men from an isolated rural community in north-west Ireland were jailed for refusing to comply with an injunction against interference with Shell's plans, using the first compulsory purchase orders awarded to a private company in the history of the state, to construct a gas pipeline on their land. Local residents, supporters and much expert opinion considered the experimental pipeline and refinery to pose a significant danger. After years of organising, local people resorted in 2005 to civil disobedience in a desperate attempt to halt the development. They picketed the gates of the refinery construction site on the day of the jailing, preventing any work from taking place. Following the imprisonments, a major national and international mobilisation ensued in support of the locals, and Shell quickly changed tack, enabling their release and ending a serious PR disaster. The Shell to Sea campaign now came to be seen as an international example of local struggle against global capital.

In October 2006, the situation changed. Smears against the campaign were spread to the press, claiming that it had been hijacked by dissident republicans,[20] and the policing operation changed. That month, the picket line which had been held for nearly a year and a half was violently broken by hundreds of police who were brought into the area and remained there for the next couple of years. In an interview Superintendent Gannon explained the changed strategy:

> The entrance to the site was blocked for a year and a half. Local people had a veto on who went in and out of the site: it was out of this situation that the current operation was born … There were no arrests. That was part of our strategy: we did not want to facilitate anyone down there with a route to martyrdom. That has been the policy ever since.[21]

The net result of this 'no arrests' policy was the use of police violence rather than risking the uncertain support of the courts and media. It clearly followed from the major mobilising effect of the imprisonment of the Rossport Five, which drew criticism from many quarters in Irish society. Other elements of the new policy evidently included the targeted use of off-camera violence and the intimidation of individuals through intense surveillance and harassment – this, however, was counter-productive, in that the local residents who were the main victims became more, rather than less, committed to their protests. The situation was intensified by the appearance of groups of masked individuals who hospitalised one local fisherman and sank his boat; it is hard to imagine this could go unnoticed by the massive police presence. Ironically, following the end of the 'no-arrests' policy, this same fisherman found himself targeted for imprisonment.[22]

The period of no arrests, but off-camera violence, ended in 2009. Though a full clarification of this strategy must await the release of state papers, the ending of the 'no-arrests' policy and the use of the military can hardly have been within the discretion of local commanders, and presumably represented a decision that the time had come to force the pipeline through at any cost. To this end, a substantial part of the Irish navy was brought in to protect the ship laying the pipeline. Fishing boats and kayaks had previously been used to prevent this; now there were targeted arrests of protestors with access to these skills and equipment. Leading protestors were given severe sentences, and a local judge even required a psychiatric examination of one protestor. When the mass arrests of less high-profile campaigners were brought before higher courts, however, twenty-five out of twenty-seven people had their cases withdrawn or dismissed, with criticism both of the local judge's refusal of bail and of the unlawful detention of another activist; evidently the breach between police and courts was not so easily mended.[23]

In this new strategy, media attacks on protestors continued –

no doubt reflecting the fact that much of the broadcast and print media is owned either by the state or by individuals with interests in offshore energy exploration. As before, most journalists assigned to the case were still crime reporters, reliant on the police for information. Nevertheless, it is worth noting that by 2010, some eleven years after the saga began, despite the best efforts of the police and corporations, planning permission had still not been granted for the onshore section of the pipeline. Let us now return to the three questions we asked earlier.

1. Why criminalise the alter-globalisation movement?

Police respond differently to different protest groups; and the treatment of campaigners involved in the anti-globalisation movement changed substantially around 2001–2. How should we understand this? Neo-liberal states reject on principle the kinds of investments and concessions needed to win popular consensus. This policy entails an attack on gains won by previous movements from below, including, importantly, political rights such as the right to protest or to exercise control over government policy.[24] This thus marks a shift from consent to coercion.

From this perspective, it is no coincidence that at this point in history a global anti-capitalist movement should develop, with a critical approach to state power and a willingness to adopt disruptive tactics as popular movements become increasingly distanced from decision-making; nor is it a surprise that these movements against neo-liberalism encountered an approach to policing protest that had not been seen since the early 1970s. The recent standard policing of transnational, alter-globalisation protest involves:

- The use of 'less-lethal' arms; databanks of 'travelling troublemakers' have been constructed; special anti-insurgent units have been created; and in some cases the military has also been deployed for public order tasks.[25]
- Even though this shift came from the executive arm of the state, it had to overturn previous norms in the media and courts. To this end, alter-globalisation protestors were branded as terrorists, by association with foreign 'anarchists' or dissident republicans. Just as, in the USA, the end of the Cold War created the need for a new campaign – the 'war on drugs' – to legitimate the neo-liberal increase in state coercion, so in Ireland the alter-globalisation movement was chosen, we suggest, to fill the gap created by the Northern ceasefire.[26]

2. What conditions enable or prevent legitimation of the use of force by the police?

The failure of the Irish establishment to legitimise the use of force on May Day 2002 can be explained in part by the use of activist media, and in particular the ability of activists to produce TV-quality footage of police assaulting people who fitted popular images of 'young, middle-class students'. While the Irish police had a clear idea that RTS needed to be beaten down, as anti-capitalist subversion and as a threat to the free flow of private traffic in Dublin, journalists did not agree that it was acceptable to use such force against these particular groups.

Gramsci writes that power consists of 'consent armoured by coercion': in other words, the routine deployment of coercion against particular groups depends on the consensual relationship between the state and other groups. 'Bad' protestors, in the sense of protestors subject to heavy policing and the sudden use of force, are a social category rather than a category representing a particular type of behaviour. It is worth reiterating that very few demonstrations in Dublin show any propensity to violence or rioting; not a single window was broken on May Day 2004.

While the new Irish policing tactics followed international models, they could not be successfully applied without a shift in the way anti-capitalist protestors were perceived by Irish society. Hence the anticipatory coverage of the EU protests, aimed at discrediting anti-capitalists and generating a moral panic to justify massive policing; hence too the media smear campaign in Erris, aimed at delegitimising the community through accusations that they were pawns in a subversive plot against the state.

The success of these strategies has been uneven. One suggestion is that the tabloid media had to be 'turned around' or influenced by some agency to change them from their 2002 hostility towards police violence to their 2004 crediting of implausible stories about the protests.[27] The serious media have been somewhat more resilient, and have on occasion used this process for an attack on tabloid journalism. In the case of Rossport, however, the apparent interest of economic and political elites in the transfer of offshore wealth to multinationals has seriously constrained both print and broadcast media, whether owned by the state or by wealthy individuals.

The courts present a similar picture: district courts, in which the police are routinely the de facto prosecutors and the only witnesses, have on the whole been more receptive to the police version of events, whereas higher courts have been willing to crack down on serious challenges to state interests but have shown little willingness to criminalise 'ordinary protestors' on the evidence of gardaí alone.

Public opinion, finally, remains contested and contradictory: at one point accepting the use of the navy against a small rural community, at another point outraged by the imprisonment of members of that same community; willing to provisionally believe scare stories about EU protests but also to enjoy serious journalists' demolition of those same stories; less willing to engage in protest themselves but more willing to come out to defend the right to protest. In this respect, the right to political protest in Dublin probably remains better supported than the right of marginalised communities to resist development by large business interests.

3. What do police and protestors learn from these encounters?

Firstly, the Europeanisation of the policing of protests was part of a general 'professionalisation' of the gardaí, reflected in tactics like borrowing water cannons from the PSNI, using training by the London Metropolitan police, collaboration with Interpol in the use of spotters and the identification of known activists, the use of the military and the militarisation of police functions. At the broadest level, of course, it was reflected in the identification of anti-capitalists as 'the new subversives'.

This strategy, however, has met with limited success. There were severe constraints on using force of a kind unusual in UK or continental protest policing. On the other hand, a media offensive relying on police interdependence with crime journalists and local socio-historical factors helped to delegitimise protestors' claims. In particular, in the case of Erris, the argument that protestors were influenced or infiltrated by republicans and were against development (and hence jobs) made this offensive easier.

By contrast, there is little evidence of any improved police strategy in the courts: interdependence between police and judges in low-level proceedings continues to produce some convictions, but police are still failing to convince senior, or more sceptical, judges in higher court appearances. Nor have police efforts at public relations proved uniformly effective at influencing 'serious' media. Rather, political controls – such as the refusal by Radio Telefís Éireann to broadcast the AfrI (Action from Ireland) advertisement campaign about Erris, or the private ownership of much of the Irish media – have meant that silence has been the more common 'serious' response.

Finally, the apparent outsourcing of state violence to private companies in Erris represents a worrying trend, perhaps a response to this blockage. Some aspects, such as night-time attacks on local campaigners by masked groups, have apparently been too sensational for 'serious' journalism. Independent media journalists have raised questions over IRMS (Integrated Risk Management Services), a security company which operates in conjunction with the gardaí in policing protest and whose staff appear to have very dubious records abroad, but again mainstream journalists have avoided this story.

Movement activists, for their part, have shifted towards disruptive but non-violent protest as an effective strategy in a neo-liberal context where access to decision-making is increasingly constrained. This move is supported by the development of independent media sources in place of state and corporate media, and the development of solidarity and alliances with other groups on a national and transnational level, replacing two decades of 'partnership' politics in which most alliances were at best confined to a single sector.

The use of video technology and legal observers, with careful documenting of police behaviour, has become important in attempts to limit coercive policing, as has an increased willingness to engage with media and courts. An awareness that in such battles protestors are sometimes successful also raises the costs (in both money and legitimacy) of attempts at repression. Attempts at widening the arena have also been significant, such as the use of human rights observers, academic and non-academic researchers, and the development of trade union and international links.

As in the past, the right to protest – and, when institutions block effective democratic control of decisions, the attempt to disrupt their normal functioning – remains an inherently contested area. What stands out most obviously from this Irish experience is that the result is not a foregone conclusion, but depends on the attitude of other social groups – themselves internally divided – and the learning processes of both police and protestors.

NOTES

Chapter 1

1. Many thanks to David Edwards and John Walter for discussion of protest and references and to Bill Frazer for comments. Thanks also to Donal Ó Drisceoil and Gillian O'Leary for assistance in sourcing the image.

2. NAUK, S.P. 63/58/25.

3. J. Walter, 'A "rising of the people"? The Oxfordshire Rising of 1596', *Past and Present* 107 (1985), pp. 95, 137.

4. J. Brewer and J. Styles, 'Popular attitudes to the law in the eighteenth century', in M. Fitzgerald *et al.* (eds), *Crime and Society: readings in history and theory* (London, 1981), p. 29; see also I. M. W. Harvey, 'Was there popular politics in fifteenth-century England?' in R. H. Burtnell and A. J. Pollard (eds), *The MacFarlane Legacy: studies in late medieval politics and society* (New York, 1995), pp. 155–74; J. C. Scott, *Domination and the Arts of Resistance* (New Haven CT, 1990); E. H. Shagan, *Popular Politics and the English Reformation* (Cambridge, 2003); M. J. Braddick and J. Walter, 'Introduction: grids of power: order, hierarchy and subordination in early modern society', in *idem*, *Negotiating Power in Early Modern Society* (Cambridge, 2001), pp. 1–42; J. Walter, *Crowds and Popular Politics in Early Modern England* (Manchester, 2006); C. Hill, *Change and Continuity in Seventeenth-Century England* (New Haven CT, 1991), pp. 181–204; D. Underdown, *Revel, Riot and Rebellion* (Oxford, 1987), especially chapter 5; E. P. Thompson, *Customs in Common* (London, 1993); W. Beik, *Urban Protest in Seventeenth-century France: the culture of retribution* (Cambridge, 1997).

5. S. Hindle, *The State and Social Change in Early Modern England, 1500–1640* (Basingstoke, 2002), p. 67.

6. R. Gillespie, 'Negotiating order in early seventeenth-century Ireland', in Braddick and Walter, *Negotiating Power*, pp. 188–

205; Gillespie, 'The political nation and political history in early modern Ireland', paper presented at 'Constructing the Past' symposium, Hertford College, Oxford, 14 March 2008.

7. D. Edwards, 'Beyond reform: martial law and the reconquest of Tudor Ireland', *History Ireland* 5 (1997), pp. 16–21; D. Edwards, 'Ideology and experience: Spenser's *View* and martial law in Ireland', in H. Morgan (ed.), *Political Ideology in Ireland, 1541–1641* (Dublin, 1999), pp. 127–57; D. Edwards, 'Two fools and a martial law commissioner: cultural conflict at the Limerick assize of 1606', in D. Edwards (ed.), *Regions and Rulers in Ireland, 1100–1650* (Dublin, 2004), pp. 237–65.

8. Many of the records are reproduced in J. G. Crawford, *A Star Chamber Court in Ireland: The Court of Castle Chamber, 1571–1641* (Dublin, 2005); on the 'strategic allegation of riot and assault' in the English Court of Star Chamber, see Hindle, *State and Social Change*, p. 79.

9. C. Lennon, *The Lords of Dublin in the Age of Reformation* (Dublin, 1989); C. Lennon, *The Urban Patriciates of Early Modern Ireland: a case study of Limerick* (Dublin, 1999); A. Sheehan, 'Irish towns in a period of change, 1558–1625', in C. Brady and R. Gillespie (eds), *Natives and Newcomers: the making of Irish colonial society, 1534–1641* (Dublin, 1986), pp. 93–119; R. A. Butlin, 'Irish towns in the sixteenth and seventeenth centuries', in Butlin (ed.), *The Development of the Irish Town* (London, 1971), pp. 61–100; R. Gillespie, 'Small towns in early modern Ireland', in P. Clark, *Small Towns in Early Modern Europe* (Cambridge, 1995), pp. 148–65; J. Bradley, 'From frontier town to renaissance city: Kilkenny 1500–1700', in P. Borsay and L. Proudfoot, *Provincial Towns in Early Modern England and Ireland* (Oxford, 2002), pp. 29–52; W. Smyth, 'Ireland a colony: settlement implications of the revolution in military-administrative, urban and ecclesiastical structures, c.1550–1730', in T. Barry (ed.), *A History of Settlement in Ireland* (London, 2000), pp. 158–86. On the meaning of civic freedom to urban populations, see J. Barry, 'Civility and civic culture in early modern England: the meanings of urban freedom', in P. Burke *et al.* (eds), *Civil Histories: essays presented*

to Sir Keith Thomas (Oxford, 2000), pp. 181–96; P. Withington, 'Two renaissances: urban political culture in post-Reformation England reconsidered', *Historical Journal* 44 (2001), pp. 239–67; see also P. Withington, *The Politics of Commonwealth: citizens and freemen in early modern England* (Cambridge, 2005). A. Thomas, *The Walled Towns of Ireland* (2 vols, 1992) gives a good sense of the geography and size of Irish towns.

10.   On relationships between nobles/gentry, towns and the crown in England, see C. F. Patterson, *Patronage in Early Modern England: corporate boroughs, the landed elite, and the crown, 1580–1640* (Stanford CA, 1999).

11.   Lennon, *Lords of Dublin*; C. Lennon, 'Civic life and religion in early seventeenth-century Dublin', *Archivium Hibernicum* 38 (1983), pp. 14–25; B. Bradshaw, 'The Reformation in the cities: Cork, Limerick and Galway, 1534–1603', in J. Bradley (ed.), *Settlement and Society in Medieval Ireland* (Kilkenny, 1988), pp. 445–76.

12.   Another attempt to take Youghal, in 1582, was eventually repulsed, though considerable damage was done. R. Bagwell, *Ireland Under the Tudors* (3 vols, London, 1885–90), 3, pp. 33–5, 107; R. Day, 'Cooke's memoirs of Youghal, 1749', *Journal of the Cork Historical and Archaeological Society* 9 (1903), pp. 43–4.

13.   C. Brady, 'The captains' games: army and society in Elizabethan Ireland', in T. Bartlett and J. Jeffrey (eds), *A Military History of Ireland* (Cambridge, 1996), pp. 136–59.

14.   S. G. Ellis, *Ireland in the Age of the Tudors, 1447–1603* (London, 1995), pp. 186–8; C. Brady, *The Chief Governors: the rise and fall of reform government in Ireland* (Cambridge, 2002), especially chapters 2 and 6.

15.   These riots are dealt with in detail in C. Tait, 'Broken heads and trampled hats: rioting in Limerick in 1599', in L. Irwin and G. Ó Tuathaigh (eds), *Limerick: history and society* (Dublin, 2009), pp. 91–112.

16.   *Cal S.P. Ire., 1586–1588*, pp. 361–2.

17.   *Cal. Carew MSS*, 2, no. 414.

18.   Tait, 'Broken heads and trampled hats'.

19. The deputy initially threatened to 'discharge the cannon upon them as they stood upon the Castle bridge', but changed his mind: NAUK, S.P. 63/152/45, S.P. 63/152/49. The names of Norreys' men in April 1589 are listed at NAUK, S.P. 63/143/34; *Cal. Carew MSS*, 3, nos. 76, 78, 79, 80, 85.

20. A foot cloth was 'a large richly ornamented cloth laid over the back of a horse and hanging down to the ground on each side. It was considered a mark of dignity and state' (*OED*).

21. C. L. Falkiner (ed.), *Calendar of the Manuscripts of the Marquess of Ormonde,* new series (London, 1902), vol. 1, pp. 17–18; D. Edwards, 'The poisoned chalice: the Ormond inheritance, sectarian division and the emergence of James Butler, 1614–1642', in T. Barnard and J. Fenlon, *The Dukes of Ormonde, 1610–1675* (Dublin, 2000), pp. 55–82; D. Edwards, *The Ormond Lordship in County Kilkenny, 1515–1642: the rise and fall of Butler feudal power* (Dublin 2003), especially pp. 287–8.

22. Descant can mean a discourse, or to criticise or carp at someone (*OED*).

23. *Cal. S.P. Ire.*, 1588–1592, pp. 178–9; on Bingham, see R. Rapple, 'Taking up office in Elizabethan Connacht: the case of Sir Richard Bingham', *English Historical Review* 123 (2008), pp. 277–99.

24. NAUK, S.P. 63/257/45.

25. *Cal. S.P. Ire.*, 1611–1613, pp. 344, 350, 360–64; *Desiderata Curiosa Hibernica, or a select collection of state papers* (Dublin, 1772) prints many of the papers relating to the elections, and also those recounting disturbances surrounding the election of a speaker and over precedence at the start of the Parliament; for the 'British' context of riots at elections, see L. Bowen, *The Politics of the Principality: Wales, c.1603–1642* (Cardiff, 2006); in Wales prominent gentlemen would muster armed retinues to secure the result they desired.

26. *Cal. Carew MSS*, 4, no. 197.

27. J. Lynch, *Portrait of a Pious Bishop: the life and death of the Most Rev. Francis Kirwin, Bishop of Killala,* ed. and trans. C. P. Meehan (Dublin, 1848), p. 27; J. Hardiman, *The History of*

the Town and County of the Town of Galway (Dublin, 1820), pp. 93–4.

28. C. Tait, 'Riots, rescues and "grene bowes": Catholic popular protest in Ireland, 1570–1640', in R. Armstrong and T. Ó hAnnracháin (eds), *Catholics and Presbyterians: alternative establishments*, forthcoming; C. Tait, 'Adored for saints: Catholic martyrs and the Counter-Reformation in Ireland, c. 1560–1655', *Journal of Early Modern History* 5 (2001), pp. 128–59.

29. C. Tait, *Death, Burial and Commemoration in Ireland, c.1550–1650* (Basingstoke, 2002), pp. 54–6.

30. B. Whelan, 'The impact of warfare on women in seventeenth-century Ireland', in C. Meek and C. Lawless (eds), *Studies on Medieval and Early Modern Women: victims or viragos?* (Dublin, 2005), p. 129; *Cal. S.P. Ire.*, 1633–47, pp. xxxvi, 274. It is difficult to tell how common food riots were in early modern Ireland. Suggestions that they were rare are taken to task in R. Wells, 'The Irish famine of 1799–1800: market culture, moral economies and social protest', in A. Randall and A. Charlesworth (eds), *Markets, Market Culture and Popular Protest in Eighteenth-Century Britain* (Liverpool, 1996), p. 179.

31. Day, 'Cooke's memoirs of Youghal', pp. 45, 47; the townsmen had gained the right to organise themselves into companies in 1610; in 1616 prices for candles and tallow were fixed, so the attack on 'foreign' butchers may have been part of a wider campaign to prevent undercutting of prices within the industry.

32. Crawford, *A Star Chamber Court in Ireland*, pp. 527–8. On the Sextons, see C. Tait, 'A trusty and wellbeloved servant: the career and disinterment of Edmund Sexton', *Archivium Hibernicum* 56 (2002), pp. 51–64; C. Lennon, 'Religious and social change in early modern Limerick: the testimony of the Sexton family papers', in Irwin *et al.*, *Limerick: history and society*, pp. 113–28.

33. Thompson, *Customs in Common*.

34. *Cal. Carew MSS*, 4, no. 197.

35. For the way such a conflict played out in Limerick in the 1590s, see Tait, 'Broken heads and trampled hats'.

36. J. Walter, 'Faces in the crowd: gender and age in the early mod-

ern crowd', in H. Berry and E. Foyster (eds), *The Family in Early Modern England* (Cambridge, 2007).

37.   R. A. Houlbrooke, 'Women's social life and common action in England from the fifteenth century to the eve of the Civil War', *Continuity and Change* 1 (1986), pp. 171–89; A. Wood, '"Poore men woll speke one daye": plebian languages of defer-ence and defiance in England, *c*. 1520–1640', in T. Harris (ed.), The Politics of the Excluded, *c*. 1500–1850 (Basingstoke, 2001), pp. 76–7.

38.   M. Harrison, *Crowds and History: mass phenomena in English towns, 1790–1835* (Cambridge, 2002), p. 140.

39.   D. L. Horowitz, *The Deadly Ethnic Riot* (Berkeley, 2001).

40.   See Tait, 'Broken heads and trampled hats' for a fuller discussion of this.

41.   Day, 'Cooke's memoirs of Youghal', p. 49.

42.   R. Ruff, *Violence in Early Modern Europe, 1500–1800* (Cam-bridge, 2001), p. 170; S. Ó Suilleabháin, *Irish Wake Amusements* (Cork/Dublin, 1976), pp. 125–6.

43.   B. McGrath (ed.), *The Minute Books of the Corporation of Clon-mel, 1608–1649* (Dublin, 2006), pp. 271–2.

44.   Ruff, *Violence in Early Modern Europe*, p. 191.

45.   M. Ingram, 'Ridings, rough music and the "reform of popular culture" in early modern England', *Past and Present* 103 (1984), pp. 79–113.

46.   E. P. Thompson, 'Rough music reconsidered', *Folklore* 103 (1992), pp. 3–26, and quotation on p. 16.

47.   In England and parts of Ireland, Ascension Thursday and Rogation (the three days beforehand) were a time for 'beating' boundaries (processing around parish limits to bless and mark them) and giving to the poor. K. Danaher, *The Year in Ireland* (Cork/Dublin 2001), p. 128; R. Hutton, *The Stations of the Sun* (Oxford, 1998), pp. 277–88.

48.   Hutton, *Stations of the Sun*, pp. 134–45.

49.   Danaher, *Year in Ireland*.

50.   Hutton, *Stations of the Sun*.

51.   *Desiderata Curiosa Hibernica*, p. 157.

52. On gesture, see J. Walter, 'Gesturing at authority: deciphering the gestural code of early modern England', in M. Braddick (ed.), *The Politics of Gesture: historical perspectives* (Past and Present, Supplement, 4, 2009).

53. Skrimishe = scrimish or scrimmage in the obsolete meaning of 'an outcry, alarm' (*OED*).

54. J. T. Gilbert, 'Archives of the town of Galway', *HMC Tenth Report, Appendix, Part V* (London, 1885), p. 391.

55. C. B. Herrup, 'New shoes and mutton pies: investigative responses to theft in seventeenth-century East Sussex', *Historical Journal* 27 (1984), pp. 811–30; B. Rich, *The Irish Hubbub or the English hue and crie* (London, 1618); F. Moryson, *Shakespeare's Europe: unpublished chapters of Fynes Moryson's Itinerary*, ed. C. Hughes (London, 1903), p. 484; E. Spenser, *A View of the Present State of Ireland*, http://www.ucc.ie/celt/published/E500000–001/index.html, accessed 26 March 2010; B. K. Smith, *The Acoustic World of Early Modern England* (1999), pp. 303–12.

56. Crawford, *A Star Chamber Court in Ireland*, p. 479; another case of raising the cry is found on p. 478.

57. Spenser, *View*.

58. See C. Tait, *Death, Burial and Commemoration in Ireland, 1550–1650* (Basingstoke, 2002), pp. 35–38, 175–6; Marie-Louise Coolahan deals with 'literary keens' written by Irish women as a means of both lament and petition to patrons: M. L. Coolahan, *Women, Writing and Language in Early Modern Ireland* (Oxford, 2010), pp. 14–62.

59. B. Rich, *A Catholicke Conference betweene syr Tady MacMareall a popish priest of Waterforde, and Patricke Plaine a young student in Trinity Colledge by Dublin in Ireland* (London, 1612), pp. 5–6; P. F. Moran (ed.), *Spicilegium Ossoriense* (Dublin, 1874), p. 123.

60. W. Brereton, *Travels in Holland and the United Provinces, England, Scotland and Ireland* (London, 1844), p. 155.

Chapter 2

1. I wish to thank Dr Eamon Darcy and Dr Robert Armstrong for

commenting on early drafts of this chapter. Dates are Old Style (Julian Calendar) with the calendar year taken to begin on 1 January. Spelling has been modernised.

2.   W. Farmer, 'Chronicles of Ireland, 1594–1613', ed. C. Litton Falkiner, *English Historical Review,* 20 (1907), p. 546.

3.   *Calendar of the ancient records of Dublin, in the possession of the municipal corporation of that city* (Dublin, 1892), III, pp. 523–36.

4.   NAUK, S.P. 63/217/95, printed in *Calendar of State Papers in Ireland, 1603–06* (London, 1872), p. 355.

5.   C. Lennon, *The Lords of Dublin in the Age of Reformation* (Dublin, 1989), p. 176.

6.   *Ibid.,* p. 171.

7.   J. McCavitt, 'Lord deputy Chichester and the English government's "mandates policy" in Ireland, 1605–1607', *Recusant History,* 20 (1991), p. 328.

8.   As quoted in Lennon, *Lords of Dublin,* p. 178.

9.   NAUK, S.P. 63/218/45, printed in *Cal. S.P. Ire.,* 1603–06, p. 453; NAUK, S.P. 63/229/108, printed in *Cal. S.P. Ire.,* 1608–10, p. 475.

10.   *Cal. S.P. Ire.,* 1611–14, pp. 96–7.

11.   Lennon, *Lords of Dublin,* pp. 197–8; NAUK, S.P. 63/217/49, printed in *Cal. S.P. Ire.,* 1603–06, p. 302.

12.   V. Treadwell, 'The establishment of the farm of the Irish customs, 1603–13', *English Historical Review,* 93: 368 (1978), pp. 591–2. Poundage was a customs tax whereby a duty of 1 shilling was imposed on every pound of goods imported or exported.

13.   *Ibid.,* pp. 598–9.

14.   V. Treadwell, 'Sir John Perrot and the Irish parliament of 1585–6', *Proceedings of the Royal Irish Academy,* section C, 85 (1985), pp. 259–63.

15.   As quoted in Lennon, *Lords of Dublin,* p. 199.

16.   'Letter-book of Sir Arthur Chichester, 1612–14', ed. R. D. Edwards in *Analecta Hibernica,* 8 (1938), pp. 95–6.

17.   *Cal. Carew MSS* (London, 1873), vol. VI, 1603–1624, pp. 164–70.

18. B. McGrath, 'The membership of the Irish House of Commons, 1613–1615' (MLitt dissertation, TCD, 1986), p. 26.

19. NAUK, S.P. 63/232/12, printed in *Cal. S.P. Ire.*, 1611–14, p. 249.

20. *Desiderata Curiosa Hibernica; or, a select collection of state papers*, ed. [John Lodge], (Dublin, 1772), vol. I, pp. 158–60.

21. D. Hirst, *Representative of the people? Voters and voting in England under the early Stuarts* (Cambridge, 1975), p. 14.

22. M. Kishlansky, *Parliamentary Selection: social and political choice in early modern England* (Cambridge, 1986), p. 56.

23. *Ibid.*, p. 61.

24. *Ibid.*, p. 229.

25. V. Treadwell, 'The Irish parliament of 1569–71', *Proceedings of the Royal Irish Academy*, section C, 65 (1966), p. 86, and *idem*, 'Sir John Perrot and the Irish parliament of 1585–6', pp. 260–3.

26. NAUK, S.P. 63/232/12, printed in *Cal. S.P. Ire.*, 1611–14, p. 362.

27. Bodleian Library, Oxford, Carte MS 62, fo. 132.

28. Farmer, 'Chronicles of Ireland', p. 546.

29. *Cal. S.P. Ire.*, 1611–14, p. 441.

30. *Calendar of the ancient records of Dublin*, iii, p. 28.

31. J. McCavitt, *Sir Arthur Chichester: Lord Deputy of Ireland, 1605–16* (Belfast, 1998), p. 67, Lennon, *Lords of Dublin*, p. 199, 'Letter-book of Sir Arthur Chichester, 1612–14', p. 19.

32. Carte MS 62, fo. 132.

33. Lennon, *Lords of Dublin*, pp. 201–2.

34. B. McGrath, 'The membership of the Irish House of Commons, 1613–1615', p. 21.

35. Carte MS 62, fo. 132.

36. NAUK, S.P. 63/232/12, printed in *Cal. S.P. Ire.*, 1611–14, p. 362.

37. Farmer, 'Chronicles of Ireland', p. 546.

38. J. Barry, 'Civility and civic culture in early modern England: the meanings of urban freedom', in P. Burke, B. Harrison and P. Slack (eds), *Civil Histories: essays presented to Sir Keith Thomas* (Oxford, 2000), pp. 186–9, 194.

39. Farmer, 'Chronicles of Ireland', p. 546.

40. Carte MS 62, fo. 132.

41. Farmer, 'Chronicles of Ireland', p. 546.

42. *Calendar of the ancient records of Dublin*, p. 534.

43. Carte MS 62, fo. 133.

44. *Ibid.*

45. Farmer, 'Chronicles of Ireland', p. 546.

46. C. Blair and I. Delamer, 'The Dublin civic swords', *Proceedings of the Royal Irish Academy*, section C, 88 (1988), p. 130.

47. British Library, Cotton MS Titus B.X, 222, printed in *Cal. S.P. Ire.*, 1611–14, p. 354.

48. Lambeth Palace Library, London, Carew MS 616, fo. 122, printed in *Cal. S.P. Ire.*, 1611–14, p. 342.

49. Farmer, 'Chronicles of Ireland', p. 546.

50. Carte MS 62, fo. 132.

51. N. Garnham, 'Riot acts, popular protest, and Protestant mentalities in eighteenth-century Ireland', *Historical Journal* 49 (2006), p. 418.

52. R. Bolton, *A Iustice of Peace for Ireland* (Dublin, 1638), pp. 205–6.

53. Carte MS 62, fo. 132.

54. Carte MS 62, fo. 132; Farmer, 'Chronicles of Ireland', p. 546; NAUK, S.P. 63/232/12, printed in *Cal. S.P. Ire.*, 1611–14, p. 362.

55. NAUK, S.P. 63/232/12, printed in *Cal. S.P. Ire.*, 1611–14, p. 362.

56. *Cal. S.P. Ire.*, 1611–14, p. 441.

57. Farmer, 'Chronicles of Ireland', p. 546; Carte MS 62, fo. 132.

58. Lennon, *Lords of Dublin*, p. 59.

Chapter 3

1. Patrick Comerford, bishop of Waterford, to Luke Wadding, guardian of St Isidore's in Rome, 24 February 1630, in G. D. Burtchaell and T. U. Sadleir (eds), *Report on the Franciscan MSS preserved at The Convent, Merchants' Quay, Dublin*, Dublin: Historical Manuscripts Commission, 1906, p. 20. I would like to express my gratitude to the Humanities Institute of Ireland for the facilities they have put at my disposal. I would also like to give a special word of thanks to the editor for his continued patience.

2.   For example, Sir Walter Aston to Lord Conway, 5 June 1624, *Cabala, Mysteries of State in Letters of the great Ministers of K. James and K. Charles*, printed for M. M. G. Bedell and T. Collins, London, 1653, p. 49; information concerning the relations between the Irish and Spanish [1626], *Cal. S.P. Ire.*, 1647–60, pp. 67–9; Falkland and the Irish Privy Council to Charles, 11 August 1628, *Cal. S.P. Ire.*, 1625–32, p. 219.

3.   See G. Redworth, 'Perfidious Hispania? Ireland and the Spanish match, 1603–23', in H. Morgan (ed.), *The Battle of Kinsale* (Bray, 2004), pp. 255–64; M. Empey, 'Ireland, Spain and "the protection and defence of the Christian religion", c. 1622–35', in D. M. Downey and J. C. MacLennan (eds), *Spanish-Irish Relations through the Ages* (Dublin, 2008), pp. 103–22.

4.   In 1630 there were only seventeen bishops, following the deaths of Hugh MacCaghwell of Armagh (1626) and Edmund Dungan of Down and Conor (1629); see D. F. Cregan, 'The social and cultural background of a Counter-Reformation episcopate, 1618–60', in A. Cosgrove and D. MacCartney (eds), *Studies in Irish History presented to R. Dudley Edwards* (Naas, 1979), pp. 85–117.

5.   Archbishop Matthews' report to the Congregation of Propaganda, 4 February 1623; P. F. Moran, *History of the Catholic Archbishops of Dublin, since the Reformation* (Dublin: James Duffy Printers, 1864), pp. 289–92.

6.   Some of the leading citizens of Drogheda to Propaganda Fide, 27 May 1623; B. Millett OFM (ed.), 'Catalogue of Irish material in fourteen volumes of the *Scritture originali riferite nelle congregazioni generali*, in Propaganda Archives', in *Collectanae Hibernica*, x (1967), pp. 50–1.

7.   Letter from the superior of the Carmelite order, March 1628; Moran, *History of the Catholic Archbishops of Dublin*, pp. 313–14. One Catholic bishop wrote: 'our countrie is so furnished with clergiemen that ere it be long we are like to have one against every house' – Patrick Comerford, bishop of Waterford and Lismore, to Luke Wadding, 30 October 1631, *Wadding Papers, 1614–38*, ed. B. Jennings (Dublin, 1953), p. 609.

8. John Roche, bishop of Ferns, to the Congregation of Propaganda, 1 December 1629; Moran, *History of the Catholic Archbishops of Dublin*, pp. 396–9.

9. Bishop Bedell to Archbishop Ussher, 18 September 1630; R. Parr, *The life of the Most Reverend Father in God, James Ussher, late Lord Arch-Bishop of Armagh, Primate and Metropolitan of all Ireland*, printed for Nathaniel Ranew (London, 1686), p. 453.

10. [Sir John Bingley's] account of the state of the Church in Ireland, [21 March] 1629, *Cal. S.P. Ire.*, 1625–32, p. 442; such was the impact of the Counter-Reformation in Dublin that Archbishop Bulkeley could even name Catholic parish priests and calculate how many recusants there were in his report on the state of the Protestant church in 1630; M. V. Ronan, 'Archbishop Bulkeley's visitation of Dublin, 1630', *Archivium Hibernicum*, viii (1941), pp. 56–98.

11. Proclamation for the banishment of Jesuits, &c., 21 January 1624, *Cal. S.P. Ire.*, 1615–25, p. 459; R. Steele (ed.), *A Bibliography of Royal Proclamations of the Tudor and Stuart Sovereigns, 1485–1714*, 2 vols (Oxford, 1910), ii, p. 26.

12. Irish Privy Council to the king and English Privy Council, 31 January 1629; Moran, *History of the Catholic Archbishops of Dublin*, p. 315.

13. Proclamation of the Lord Deputy and Council, 1 April 1629, *Cal. S.P. Ire.*, 1625–32, p. 445; Steele (ed.), *A Bibliography of Royal Proclamations … 1485–1714*, ii, p. 31; P. J. Corish (ed.), 'Two seventeenth-century proclamations against the Catholic clergy', *Archivium Hibernicum*, xxxix (1984), pp. 53–7.

14. Lord Deputy [to the Privy Council] touching the regulations against papists, 5 April 1629, *Cal. S.P. Ire.*, 1625–32, p. 446; similar claims were made a month later: Falkland [to Lord Dorchester], 2 May 1629, *ibid.*, p. 450.

15. Falkland to Ussher, 14 April 1629; Parr, *The Life of the Most Reverend Father in God, James Ussher*, p. 407.

16. *Ibid.*

17. Draft of [Lord Dorchester] to the Lord Deputy touching his Majesty's purpose to recall him, 3 April 1629, *Cal. S.P. Ire.*,

1625–32, pp. 445–6. Falkland petitioned the king for a reprieve, but his removal was confirmed in August 1629; the king to Falkland, *ibid.*, p. 475.

18. Draft of instructions for Adam Viscount Loftus of Ely, and Richard Earl of Cork, the King's Lords Justices for Ireland [n.d.], *Cal. S.P. Ire.*, 1625–32, pp. 471–2.

19. F. X. Martin, *Friar Nugent: a study of Francis Lavalin Nugent (1569–1635), agent of the counter-Reformation* (London, 1962), p. 270. Propaganda Fide was the department of the Roman Curia responsible for missionary work and related activities, including the safeguarding of the Catholic faith in areas where it was threatened.

20. Cork to Dorchester, 22 December 1629, *Cal. S.P. Ire.*, 1625–32, p. 499; see also the comments of Sir Thomas Dutton who claimed that 'the whole of Ireland is now more addicted to popery than it was in the time of Queen Elizabeth'; Dutton to the king, 20 December 1629, *ibid.*, p. 498.

21. Sir Charles Wilmot, general of the Irish army, to Dorchester, 17 December 1629, *ibid.*, p. 498.

22. N. Archbold, 'Evangelic Fruict of the Seraphicall Franciscan Order', BL (British Library), Harleian MS 3888, p. 212.

23. Cork to Dorchester, 9 January 1629[/30], HMC, Report no. 12, Appendix, Part II: *Report on Manuscripts of Earl Cowper, K.G.*, preserved at Melbourne Hall, Derbyshire, 3 vols (London: Eyre & Spottiswoode, 1888), i, pp. 398–9: 'there were many active spirits descended of good houses who held dangerous principles'.

24. Sir James Ware's diary of events and occurrences, 1623–47, Dublin City Library, Gilbert MS 169, fo. 197; in his diary, Cork specifically stated that the archbishop and mayor 'by direction of us, the Lords Justices, ransackt the howse of ffryer in Cook-street'; Richard Boyle, Earl of Cork, *The Lismore Papers (first series) viz. autobiographical notes, remembrances and diaries of Sir Richard Boyle, first and 'great' Earl of Cork, never before printed*, ed. A. B. Grossart, 5 vols (London, 1886), iii, p. 13.

25. Events at the Franciscan Chapel in Dublin, 4 January

1629[/30], *Wadding Papers, 1614–38*, ed. Jennings, p. 330; Anonymous letter, 4 January 1629[/30], Historical Manuscripts Commission, *Franciscan MSS*, p. 17.

26. Archbold, 'Evangelic Fruict'; BL, Harleian MS 3888, p. 213.

27. Events at the Franciscan Chapel in Dublin, 4 January 1629[/30], *Wadding Papers, 1614–38*, ed. Jennings, p. 330; Anonymous letter, 4 January 1629[/30], HMC, *Franciscan MSS*, p. 17.

28. Archbold, 'Evangelic Fruict'; BL, Harleian MS 3888, p. 213.

29. Dutton to Dorchester, 30 December 1629, *Cal. S.P. Ire.*, 1625–32, pp. 500–1.

30. Wilmot to Dorchester, 6 January 1630, *ibid.*, p. 504.

31. Anonymous letter, 4 January 1629[/30], HMC, *Franciscan MSS*, p. 17. Alderman Mapas was put under house arrest on account of his illness.

32. Cork to Dorchester, 9 January 1630, HMC, *Cowper MSS*, i, p. 399.

33. Wilmot to [Dorchester], 17 December 1629, *Cal. S.P. Ire.*, 1625–32, p. 498; Cork to Dorchester, 22 December 1629, *ibid.*, p. 499; Wilmot to Dorchester, 23 December 1629, *ibid.*, p. 500.

34. B. Fitzpatrick, *Seventeenth-century Ireland: the war of religions* (Dublin, 1988), pp. 39–41.

35. Anonymous letter, 4 January 1629[/30], HMC, *Franciscan MSS*, pp. 17–18.

36. It is worth comparing Cork's recommendations for suppressing friaries and convents in his letter to Dorchester with Charles' orders to clamp down on the houses in the city confines. See Cork to Dorchester, 9 January 1630, HMC, *Cowper MSS*, i, p. 399; Minute of the king to Lord Justices and Council of Ireland, 25 January 1630, *Cal. S.P. Ire.*, 1625–32, p. 508.

37. T. Ranger, 'The career of Richard Boyle, first Earl of Cork, in Ireland, 1588–1643', DPhil thesis, University of Oxford, 1959, chapter 8.

38. Catholics were particularly fearful of Cork as deputy: 'the inauguration of Lord Boyle as viceroy, who being hitherto associated with another only as justiciary, will now no longer

have the check of rival authority, but may freely execute his plans against the Church and Catholic faith', Francis Matthews OFM to Wadding, 20 December 1630, *Wadding Papers, 1614–38*, ed. Jennings, p. 455.

39. Cork to Dorchester, 9 January 1630, HMC, *Cowper MSS*, i, p. 399; Sir James Ware's diary of events and occurrences, 1623–47, Dublin City Library, Gilbert MS 169, fol. 197; Archbold, 'Evangelic Fruict', BL, Harleian MS 3888, p. 211.

40. Sir James Ware's diary of events and occurrences, 1623–47, Dublin City Library, Gilbert MS 169, fol. 198.

41. English privy council to the lords justices and council of Ireland, 31 January 1630; J. Rushworth, *Historical Collections of Private Passages of State, Weighty Matters in Law, Remarkable Proceedings in Five Parliaments: Beginning the Sixteenth Year of King James, anno 1618, and ending … [with the death of King Charles the First, 1648]*, 6 vols, printed by J.A. for Robert Boulter (London, 1680), ii, p. 33.

42. Sir James Ware's diary of events and occurrences, 1623–47, Dublin City Library, Gilbert MS 169, fol. 199; [The Earl of Cork to Lord Dorchester], 2 March 1630, *Cal. S.P. Ire.*, 1625–32, p. 521; Archbold, 'Evangelic Fruict', BL, Harleian MS 3888, p. 211.

43. Sir James Ware's diary of events and occurrences, 1623–47, Dublin City Library, Gilbert MS 169, fo. 203; Provost Ussher of Trinity College, Dublin, to the Bishop of London [William Laud], 27 July 1630, *Cal. S.P. Ire.*, 1625–32, p. 560; see also R. Loeber and M. Stouthamer-Loeber, 'Kildare Hall, the countess of Kildare's patronage of the Jesuits, and the liturgical setting of Catholic worship in early seventeenth-century Dublin', in E. Fitzpatrick and R. Gillespie (eds), *The Parish in Medieval and Early Modern Ireland*, FCP (Dublin, 2006), pp. 242–65.

44. W. Brereton, *Travels in Holland, the United Provinces, England, Scotland and Ireland, 1634–5*, ed. Edward Hawkins (Chetham Society, vol. i, 1844), pp. 141–2.

45. St Leger [to the lords justices], 15 January 1630, *Cal. S.P. Ire.*, 1625–32, p. 510.

46. Roche to Wadding, 7 February 1629[/30], *Wadding Papers, 1614–38*, ed. Jennings, p. 337; see also Roche to Francesco Ingoli, 9 February 1630, in B. Millett OFM (ed.), 'Catalogue of Irish material in vols 132–139 of the *Scritture originali riferite nelle congregazioni generali* in Propaganda Archives', *Collectanae Hibernica*, xii (1969), pp. 14–15.

47. William Farrily to Hugh de Burgo OFM, 15 February 1629[/30]; Millet (ed.), 'Catalogue of Irish material in vols 132–139 of the *Scritture originali*', p. 341; equally grim reports from Cork were still being made nearly two months later by Eugene Field: 'the persecution begun in Dublin on St Stephen's Day grows in extent and degree'; Owen [Eugene] Field to [anonymous recipient], 10 April 1630, HMC, *Franciscan MSS*, p. 22.

48. Valentine Browne to Wadding, 28 April 1630, *Wadding Papers, 1614–38*, ed. Jennings, p. 360.

49. Rev. Joseph Mead to Sir Martin Stuteville, 20 March 1629[/30], in T. Birch (ed.), *The Court and Times of Charles the First*, 2 vols, London: Henry Colburn, 1848, ii, p. 69; a week later Mead claimed: 'five hundred priests and friars were said to be fled out of Ireland for Spain, and more following them'. *Ibid.*, ii, p. 69.

50. Thomas Strange OFM, to Wadding, 3 August 1630, HMC, *Franciscan MSS*, p. 29; Francis Matthews to Wadding, 4 September 1630, *Wadding Papers, 1614–38*, ed. Jennings, p. 408.

51. Strange to Wadding, 10 May 1630, HMC, *Franciscan MSS*, p. 23; see also similar concerns expressed by Thomas Messingham, rector of the Irish college in Paris, Messingham to Wadding, 15 July 1630, *ibid.*, p. 28

52. See, for example, Dutton to King Charles, 4 April 1630, *Cal. S.P. Ire.*, 1625–32, p. 528.

53. J. R. Turner (alias Bishop Roche) to Wadding, 26 May 1630, HMC, *Franciscan MSS*, p. 25.

54. *Ibid.*

55. Francis Matthews claimed in September 1630 'the confiscation of religious houses proceeds apace throughout Ireland', but Matthews lived in the Irish College at Louvain (Leuven) and

his reports were usually outdated by the time he sent them on to Luke Wadding in Rome. Matthews to Wadding, 4 September 1630, *Wadding Papers, 1614–38*, ed. Jennings, p. 408; Matthews to Wadding, 28 September 1630, HMC, *Franciscan MSS*, p. 30; except for threats, I have found no evidence that friaries or chapels were still being confiscated.

56. Father Barnabas [Barnewall], superior of the Irish Capuchins, to [Francis Nugent, OFM Cap?], 3 April 1631, Millett (ed.), 'Catalogue of Irish material in fourteen volumes of the *Scritture originali*', p. 37.

57. M. Empey, 'Paving the way to prerogative: the politics of Sir Thomas Wentworth, c. 1614–1635', PhD thesis, University College Dublin, 2009, chapter 7; J. McCafferty, *The Reconstruction of the Church of Ireland* (Cambridge, 2007), pp. 170–4.

58. B. Mansfield ODC, 'Fr Paul Browne, ODC, 1598–1671', *Dublin Historical Record*, xxxvii (1984), pp. 54–8.

59. Browne provided an account of the riot in his *Brevis Relatio* which he completed in 1670; see M. Glynn ODC and F. X. Martin OSA (eds), 'The "Brevis Relatio" of the Irish Discalced Carmelites, 1625–1670 by Father Paul Browne, ODC', in *Archivium Hibernicum*, xxv (1962), pp. 149–50.

60. Sir James Ware's diary of events and occurrences, 1623–47, Dublin City Library, Gilbert MS 169, fos. 200, 203, 206.

61. Wentworth to Archbishop Laud of Canterbury, 28 August 1633, Wentworth Woodhouse Muniments (WWM), Sheffield City Library, Strafford MS, vol. 8, fo. 13; though Wentworth's appointment was announced in January 1632, it took him another eighteen months to arrive in Ireland. I wish to acknowledge the trustees of the Fitzwilliam Settled Estates and the head of Leisure Services for permission to quote from the Strafford papers in their custody.

62. Wentworth even thought the offence was punishable by hanging, Wentworth to Coke, 2 March 1634[/5], WWM, Sheffield City Library, Strafford MS, vol. 5, fo. 190; Sir James Ware's diary of events and occurrences, 1623–47, Dublin City Library, Gilbert MS 169, fo. 214; Glynn and Martin (eds), 'The "Brevis

Relatio" of the Irish Discalced Carmelites, 1625–1670 by Father Paul Browne, ODC', p. 138.

63.   Sir Thomas Wentworth to Secretary John Coke, 2 March 1634[/5], WWM, Sheffield City Library, Strafford MS, vol. 5, fo. 190.

64.   J. T. Gilbert, *A History of the City of Dublin* (Dublin, 1861), p. 304.

65.   *Ibid.*, p. 254.

Chapter 4

1.   Book of Numbers, 18, verses 23–4.

2.   J. S. Fry, *A Concise History of Tithes, with an inquiry how far a forced maintenance for the ministers of religion is warranted by the example and precepts of Jesus Christ and His apostles* (London, 1820), p. 13.

3.   D. Ó Corráin, L. Breatnach and A. Breen, 'The laws of the Irish', *Perditia: Journal of the Medieval Academy of Ireland*, vol. 3, 1984, p. 409.

4.   C. Twinch, *Tithe War, 1918–1939: the countryside in revolt* (Norfolk, 2001), p. 263.

5.   M. Bric, 'The tithe system in the eighteenth century', *Proceedings of the Royal Irish Academy*, vol. 86, 1986, p. 272.

6.   Select Committee on Tithes in Ireland [hereafter: *Tithe Inquiry*], HC 1831–2 (663), vol. XXII, 181, 1835 (179), p. 110.

7.   *Ibid.*, p. 117.

8.   A. J. Coughlan, 'The Whiteboy origins', *Mallow Field Club Journal*, 17, 1999, pp. 65–6.

9.   M. Beames, *Peasants and Power: the Whiteboy movement and their control in pre-Famine Ireland* (New York, 1983), p. 52.

10.   S. Katsuta, 'The Rockite movement in County Cork in the early 1820s', *Irish Historical Studies*, XXXIII, no. 131, 2003, p. 286.

11.   P. O'Donoghue, 'Causes of the opposition to tithes, 1830–1838', *Studia Hibernica*, no. 5, 1965, p. 9.

12.   *State of Ireland. Minutes of Evidence taken before the Select Committee appointed to inquire into the disturbances in Ireland*, HC

1825 (20), vol. VII, 1 [hereafter: *Disturbances in Ireland*], p. 58.

13. G. Curtin, 'Religion and social conflict during the Protestant crusade in West Limerick, 1822–1849', *Old Limerick Journal*, 2003, pp. 48–9.

14. Katsuta, 'The Rockite movement in County Cork', pp. 283–5.

15. *Freeman's Journal*, 7 July 1823.

16. *Disturbances in Ireland*, pp. 375–77, 396.

17. Katsuta, 'The Rockite movement in County Cork', p. 278.

18. An Act to provide for the establishing of Compositions for Tithes in Ireland for a limited time, 19 July 1823, 4 Geo. IV, c. 99, p. 843.

19. A. McIntyre, *The Liberator: Daniel O'Connell and the Irish Party, 1830–1847* (London, 1965), p. 170.

20. An Act to amend an Act of the last Session of Parliament, for the providing for the establishing of Compositions for Tithes in Ireland, 17 June 1824, 5 Geo. IV, c. 63, pp. 290–7.

21. An Act to amend the Acts for the establishing of Compositions for Tithes in Ireland, 2 July 1827, 7 & 8 Geo. I, c. 60, p. 325.

22. *Tithe Inquiry* (508), vol. XXXI, 245, p. 484.

23. *Tithe Inquiry* (177), vol. XXI, 1, p. 9.

24. *Tithe Inquiry* (663), vol. XXII, p. 79.

25. *Tithe Inquiry* (177) vol. XXI, 1, p. 154.

26. M. O'Hanrahan, 'The tithe war in County Kilkenny 1830–34', in W. Nolan (ed.), *Kilkenny: history and society* (Dublin, 1990), p. 485.

27. M. O'Brien, 'The Lalors of Tenakill, 1767–1893', unpublished MA dissertation, NUI Maynooth, 1987, pp. 5–6.

28. NAI, CSO, OP 1830, Affidavit of A. Williams of Barnavidawn sworn before Rev. L. McDonnell, 11 November 1830.

29. *Kilkenny Journal*, 17 November 1830.

30. O'Hanrahan, 'The tithe war in County Kilkenny', p. 487.

31. *Tithe Inquiry* (663), vol. XXII, 181, pp. 73, 96.

32. P. O'Donoghue, 'Opposition to tithe payment in 1830–31', *Studia Hibernica*, no. 6, 1966, p. 69.

33. O'Hanrahan, 'The tithe war in County Kilkenny', pp. 489–90.

34. *Tithe Inquiry* (177), vol. XXI, 1, p. 184.

35. *Tithe Inquiry* (271), vol. XXII, 1, pp. 82–4.

36. O'Hanrahan, 'The tithe war in County Kilkenny', p. 490.

37. *Tithe Inquiry* (663), vol. XXI, 181, p. 38.

38. *Ibid.*, p. 9.

39. *Freeman's Journal*, 1 August 1831.

40. *Tithe Inquiry* (271), vol. XXII, 1, pp. 8–9.

41. O'Donoghue, 'Opposition', p. 70.

42. *Freeman's Journal*, 4 January 1831.

43. W. J. Fitzpatrick, *The life, times and correspondence of the Rt Rev. Dr Doyle, Bishop of Kildare and Leighlin* (Dublin, 1880) vol. 2, p. 239.

44. *Tithe Inquiry* (177), vol. XXI, 1, p. 190.

45. *Tithe Inquiry* (508), vol. XXI, 245, p. 378.

46. O'Brien, 'The Lalors of Tenakill', pp. 28–30.

47. J. Gough, *Some Brief and Serious Reasons why the people called the Quakers do not pay tithes and other ecclesiastical demands* (Dublin, 1818), pp. 3–6.

48. *Ibid.*, p. 12.

49. *Tithe Inquiry* (271), vol. XXII, 1.1, p. 27.

50. *Tithe Inquiry* (508), vol. XX, 245, p. 441; *Freeman's Journal*, 18 July 1823.

51. *Tithe Inquiry* (271), vol. XXII, 1, p. 14.

52. An Act for the better Administration of Justice at the holding of Petty Sessions by Justices of the Peace in Ireland, 7th & 8th George IV (1827), c.67, s.24.

53. *Tithe Inquiry* (271), vol. XXII, 1, p. 127.

54. *Connacht Journal*, 23 June 1831.

55. Séamus S. de Vál, 'The battle of the pound', *The Past: The Journal of the Uí Cinsealaigh Historical Society*, no. 9, 1972, p. 43.

56. T. Coldwell, *A Full Report of the Evidence produced at a coroner's inquest held at Newtownbarry in the county of Wexford on the 20th, and continued till the 30th of June 1831* (Dublin, 1831), pp. iii–vi.

57. *Connacht Journal*, 13 July 1831.

58. *Tithe Inquiry* (177), vol. XXI, 1, p. 187.

59. *Ibid.*, p. 21.

60. *Kilkenny Moderator*, 5 September 1832.

61.   *Ibid.*, 10, 17 October 1832.

62.   *Freeman's Journal*, 4 December 1832.

63.   *Ibid.*, 16, 26 March 1833.

64.   *Ibid.*, 4 December 1834.

65.   *Kilkenny Moderator*, 12 September 1832.

66.   *Freeman's Journal*, 16, 26 March 1833.

67.   *Ibid.*, 24 November 1832.

68.   *Ibid.*, 10 January 1833.

69.   *Cork Mercantile Chronicle*, 5 May 1834; *Freeman's Journal*, 1 May 1834.

70.   *Cork Mercantile Chronicle*, 5 May 1834.

71.   *Freeman's Journal*, 2 May 1834.

72.   Carrickshock was celebrated in ballads and local folklore. In 1926, a Celtic cross was erected to mark the famous victory. It was dedicated to the memory of the three local men, Treacy, Phelan and Power; it did not mention the twelve policemen. In August 2006, the Battle of Carrickshock was re-enacted to commemorate the 175th anniversary, complete with souvenir book and DVD. See also Gary Owens, 'The Carrickshock incident, 1831: social memory and an Irish *cause célèbre*', *Cultural and Social History*, 2004, 1, pp. 36–64.

73.   J. Mongon, *Report of the Trial of John Delany for the shooting of Mr Bailey tried before the Right Honourable The Lord Chief Justice and the Hon. Baron Sir Wm. C. Smith at the Special Commission at Maryborough, on Thursday 24 May to which is prefixed, the Chief Justice's charge to the Grand Jury* (Maryborough, 1832), pp. 10–13.

74.   E. W. Drea, *Carrickshock: a history of the tithe times* (Waterford, 1924), pp. 22–4.

75.   Mongon, *Report of the Trial*, pp. 10–13.

76.   Drea, *Carrickshock*, p. 25.

77.   *Freeman's Journal*, 23, 27 December 1831.

78.   The Terry Alts were a militant secret society that grew out of agrarian unrest in County Clare.

79.   G. Broeker, *Rural Disorder and Police Reform, 1812–1836* (London, 1970), p. 195; *Return of Persons Killed or Wounded in Affrays with the Constabulary Force in Ireland*, HC 1830–1 (67), vol.

VIII, p. 403.

80.   C. E. Tonna, *Irish Recollections* (London: Seeley, Jackson & Halliday, 1841; Dublin, 2004), p. 172.

81.   *Ibid.*

82.   E. Larkin (ed.), *Alexis de Tocqueville's Journey in Ireland, July–August 1835* (Dublin, 1990), p. 76.

83.   *Ibid.*

84.   Proceedings of an Investigation held at Armagh of the Transactions which took place in the neighbourhood of Keady, between the Police and Country People, December 1834, on collecting an arrear of tithe due to Reverend James Blacker, wherein one man was killed and several wounded; with a copy of the inquest, and all other documents connected with that transaction [hereafter: *Keady Inquiry*], HC 1835 (179), XLVII, 99, pp. 101, 121.

85.   *Freeman's Journal*, 12 May 1835.

86.   *Ibid.*, 4 December 1834.

87.   *Keady Inquiry*, p. 111.

88.   *Freeman's Journal*, 23 December 1834.

89.   O'Brien, *Tithe War*, p. 10.

90.   *Freeman's Journal*, 23 December 1834.

91.   *Ibid.*

92.   E. Garner, *Massacre at Rathcormac* (Midleton, 1984), pp. 26–7.

93.   *Freeman's Journal*, 23 December 1834.

94.   *Ibid.*, 12 May 1835.

95.   M. O'Connell (ed.), *The Correspondence of Daniel O'Connell, 1833–36*, vol. V (Shannon/Dublin, 1972–80), pp. 317–18.

96.   *Freeman's Journal*, 1 January 1835.

97.   Garner, *Massacre at Rathcormac*, pp. 49–57.

98.   *Ibid.*

99.   *Keady Inquiry*, pp. 133–4. Goulburn was chief secretary for Ireland 1821–7, and home secretary December 1834 to April 1835, when Peel's minority Tory government fell because the Irish secretary Hardinge's Tithe Bill did not include the principle of appropriation – that is, using some of the Irish tithe revenue to pay for general education in Ireland.

100. *Ibid.*

101. G. Locker Lampson, *A Consideration of the State of Ireland in the Nineteenth Century* (London, 1907), p. 170.

102. *Return of Number of Bills filed in the Court of the Exchequer in Ireland for the recovery of tithe composition*, HC 1835–36 (420), vol. XL, 101, pp. 7–8.

103. R. B. O'Brien, *Thomas Drummond: Under-Secretary in Ireland, his life and letters* (London), pp. 203–4.

104. *Ibid.*, p. 228.

105. *Freeman's Journal*, 11, 14 January 1836.

106. *Ibid.*, 19 July 1837.

Chapter 5

1. M. Cronin, 'Of one mind? O'Connellite crowds in the 1830s and 1840s', in P. Jupp and E. Magennis (eds), *Crowds in Ireland, c. 1720–1920* (London, 2000), pp. 139–72.

2. J. Bardon, *A History of Ulster* (Belfast, 1992), p. 254.

3. *Ibid.*, p. 254.

4. *Ibid.*

5. *Correspondence on meeting of inhabitants of County Tyrone, in Dungannon*, p. 1, HC 1835 (120), XLV, p. 511.

6. *Ibid.*, p. 1.

7. *[First] Report of the select committee appointed to inquire into the nature, character, extent, and tendency of Orange Lodges, associations or societies in Ireland; with the minutes of evidence and appendix [hereafter First report on Orange lodges]*, p. 371, HC 1835 (377), xvi.

8. *The Londonderry Journal and Tyrone Advertiser* [hereafter *LJ*], 4 July 1837.

9. *The Star of Brunswick*, 7 March 1829.

10. *Royal Commission on the Condition of the Poorer Classes in Ireland*, Appendix F, pp. 419, 427, 643, 657 [Command Papers 35–42], HC 1835, vol. xxx, 35, 221, vol. xxxi, 1, vol. xxxiii, 1, vol. xxxiv, 1.

11. A. Day and P. McWilliams, *Ordnance Survey Memoirs of Ireland*, vol. xx (Belfast, 1993), p. 42.

12. *Electors registered Ireland. Return of electors registered as qualified*

to vote at the last general election in Ireland, p. 8, HC 1836 (227), XLIII, p. 469.

13. Bardon, *History of Ulster*, p. 254.

14. *Correspondence on Meeting of Inhabitants of County Tyrone, in Dungannon* [hereafter *Corresp. on Meeting in Dungannon*], p. 2, HC 1835 (120), XLV, 511.

15. *The Enniskillen Chronicle and Erne Packet* [hereafter *ECEP*], 25 December 1834. Given its area of 6,700 sq. yd, if each person had a space 2ft by 1½ft to stand in, the square would hold 20,000 people. That seems a credible maximum, since there were horses and wagons there too.

16. Day and McWilliams, *Ordnance Survey Memoirs*, p. 40.

17. G. Owens, 'Nationalism without words: symbolism and ritual behaviour in the repeal "monster meetings" of 1843–45', in J. S. Donnelly Jr and K. A. Miller (eds), *Irish Popular Culture, 1650–1850* (Dublin, 1999), pp. 242–69.

18. *First report on Orange lodges*, p. 345, HC 1835 (377), XVI.

19. *Ibid.*, p. 323.

20. *Ibid.*, p. 324.

21. Owens, 'Nationalism without words', pp. 242–69.

22. *The Star of Brunswick*, 7 March 1829.

23. *First report on Orange lodges*, HC 1835 (377), XVI, p. 324.

24. *LJ*, 23 December 1834; *Strabane Morning Post* [hereafter *SMP*], 23 December 1834.

25. *LJ*, 23 December 1834.

26. *Ibid.*

27. *SMP*, 23 December 1834.

28. Cronin, 'Of one mind?', pp. 139–72.

29. *ECEP*, 25 December 1834.

30. *First report on Orange lodges*, HC 1835 (377), XVI, p. 371.

31. *ECEP*, 25 December 1834.

32. *Corresp. on Meeting in Dungannon*, HC 1835 (120), XLV, 511, p. 2.

33. *First report on Orange lodges*, HC 1835 (377), xvi, p. 371.

34. *Corresp. on Meeting in Dungannon*, HC 1835 (120), XLV, 511, pp. 2–3.

35. *First report on Orange lodges*, HC 1835 (377), xvi, pp. 371–2.

36. *Belfast Newsletter*, 26 December 1834.

37. Cronin, 'Of one mind?', pp. 139–72.

38. PRONI, Inspection books, patrol books and returns from Dungannon police station, 1833–62, D804/3.

39. *Corresp. on Meeting in Dungannon*, HC 1835 (120), XLV, 511, p. 2.

40. *First report on Orange lodges*, HC 1835 (377), XVI, p. 325.

41. Day and McWilliams, *Ordnance Survey Memoirs*, p. 40.

42. *LJ*, 6 July 1841.

Chapter 6

1. S. Clark, 'The political mobilisation of Irish farmers', *Canadian Review of Sociology and Anthropology*, 12 (1975), pp. 483–99.

2. There has also been an absence of studies of the broader political mobilisation of Irish workers, though see F. Lane, 'Rural labourers, social change and politics in late nineteenth-century Ireland', in D. Ó Drisceoil and F. Lane (eds), *Politics and the Irish Working Class, 1830–1945* (Basingstoke, 2005).

3. D. McAdam and D. A. Snow (eds), *Social Movements: readings on their emergence, mobilisation, and dynamic* (Los Angeles, 1997), p. xxiv.

4. B. Nedelmann, 'Individuals and parties: changes in processes of political mobilisation', *European Sociological Review*, 3 (1987), pp. 181–202.

5. See V. Crossman, *The Poor Law in Ireland, 1838–1948* (Dundalk, 2006).

6. Outdoor relief was introduced in response to the Great Famine; when that ended in the early 1850s, outdoor relief was reduced to very small numbers, but then rose gradually from 1,500 in 1859 to 33,500 by 1877.

7. M. R. Beames, 'Rural conflict in pre-Famine Ireland: peasant assassinations in Tipperary, 1837–1847', *Past and Present*, 81 (1978), pp. 75–91.

8. In the 1860s only about 200,000 Irish men had a parliamentary

vote and the second Reform Act had no direct equivalent in Ireland: K. T. Hoppen, *Elections, Politics and Society in Ireland, 1832–1885* (Oxford, 1984). In the 1870s about half a million Irish ratepayers (including some women) had a vote in Poor Law elections.

9. Given the somewhat chaotic state of the Irish franchise up to the late 1860s, it is likely that some poor persons did have a vote in parliamentary elections. Reports of the Galway demonstrations in 1865 suggest that some of those demonstrating did have a parliamentary vote.

10. W. L. Feingold, *The Revolt of the Tenantry* (Boston, 1984); M. Cousins, 'Poor Law politics and elections in post-Famine Ireland', *History Studies*, 6 (2005), pp. 34–47. There is little indication that agricultural labourers tried to win seats on the boards; when they did, they were largely unsuccessful. See F. Lane, 'P. F. Johnson, nationalism and Irish rural labourers, 1869–82', *Irish Historical Studies*, vol. xxxiii, no. 130 (November 2002), pp. 191–208. Few labourers would have had a vote in Poor Law elections and even fewer would have satisfied the property qualification to serve as a guardian.

11. Hoppen, *Elections, Politics and Society in Ireland*.

12. As another instance of such action, delegations of poor labourers frequently met with the boards of guardians to request, for example, the provision of work or outdoor relief.

13. See S. Tarrow, *Power in Movement: social movements, collective action and politics* (Cambridge, 1994).

14. See, for example, G. Rudé, *The Crowd in History, 1730–1858* (New York, 1964); C. A. Bouton, *The Flour War: gender, class, and community in late Ancien Régime French society* (Pa, 1993); D. Béliveau, 'Les grains de la colure: geographie de "l'émotion populaire" en France au sujet de la cherté des céréales (1816–1847)', *Criminologie*, XXVII, 1 (1994), pp. 99–115; L. Taylor, 'Food riots revisited', *Journal of Social History*, vol. 30, no. 2 (Winter 1996), pp. 483–96; N. Bourguinat, 'L'État et les violences frumentaires en France sous la Restauration et le Monarchie de Julliet', *Ruralia* [online] 1997–01.

15. R. Wells, 'The Irish famine of 1799–1801: market culture, moral economies and social protest', in A. Randall and A. Charlesworth (eds), *Markets, Market Culture and Popular Protest in Eighteenth-Century Britain and Ireland* (Liverpool, 1996).

16. E. Magennis, 'In search of the "moral economy": food scarcity in 1756–7 and the crowd', in P. Jupp and E. Magennis (eds), *Crowds in Ireland* (Basingstoke, 2000).

17. C. Kinealy, *The Great Irish Famine: impact, ideology and rebellion* (Basingstoke, 2002), chapter 5.

18. This event is described in more detail in J. Cunningham, *'A Town Tormented by the Sea': Galway, 1790–1914* (Dublin, 2004), pp. 197–8.

19. For details of these events, see Appendix 1. A food riot was expected in Mitchelstown, County Cork in 1863 but I have been unable to establish whether one occurred. I have excluded two actions: a crowd in Loughrea burning a workhouse cart intended to convey a smallpox patient to the workhouse, apparently a public health not poor relief issue (CSORP/1875/18580); a riot in Mount Bellew in 1870, seemingly the result of ratepayer opposition to paying a dispensary doctor's pension (Mount Bellew minute book, Galway county archives).

20. In Galway the leaders were described as 'local petty agitators amongst the mechanics'.

21. *Limerick Reporter*, 12 January 1861.

22. See, for example, J. A. Goldstone and B. Useem, 'Prison riots as microrevolutions: an extension of state-centered theories of revolution', *American Journal of Sociology,* 104 (1999), pp. 985–1029; E. Carrabine, 'Prison riots, social order and the problem of legitimacy', *British Journal of Criminology,* vol. 45, no. 6 (2005), pp. 896–913.

23. E. Goffman, *Asylums* (Harmondsworth, 1968).

24. See, for example, A. Scull, *The Most Solitary of Afflictions: madness and society in Britain, 1700–1900* (New Haven CT, 1993) on asylums; J. R. Walkowitz, *Prostitution and Victorian Society* (Cambridge, 1980) on lock hospitals.

25. D. R. Green, 'Pauper protests: power and resistance in early

nineteenth-century London workhouses', *Social History*, vol. 31, no. 2 (2006), pp. 137–59. Green looks at pauper protests in early nineteenth-century London workhouses, including individual actions, so his study is not fully comparable with that undertaken here.

26. H. Burke, *The People and the Poor Law in Nineteenth-century Ireland* (Littlehampton, 1987), pp. 210–18; A. Clark, 'Wild workhouse girls and the Liberal imperial state in mid-nineteenth century Ireland', *Journal of Social History*, vol. 39, no. 2 (2005), pp. 389–409.

27. This episode deserves more detailed study than it has received to date.

28. It seems in South Dublin these were largely separate from (though perhaps encouraged by) the longer-term resistance of young women inmates, which began as early as 1857 and continued into the 1860s, though by 1862 those young women were largely contained in a separate refractory ward and do not appear to have been involved in the serious rioting and significant violence between inmates and officials of that year.

29. Although the 1863 report of the Poor Law commission refers to violence in the Clonmel workhouse, I have not to date managed to locate further details of this in the local newspapers which, unfortunately, contain quite summary accounts of the meetings of the boards of guardians. Further research in the minute books of the union would be required.

30. NLI, Balrothery minute book, 10 March 1873.

31. Ryan's evidence to a later investigation by a Poor Law inspector; report in *Waterford Mail*, 11 October 1861.

32. *Ibid*. Also *Waterford Mail*, 29 March 1861, 13 September 1861; and *Waterford News*, 20 December 1861, when the matron complained to the board that despite efforts to stop it the inmates could not be prevented from doing muslin work without the active co-operation of all female officers.

33. *Waterford Mail*, 10 January 1862.

34. The more serious violence appears to have been committed by the officials rather than the inmates.

35.   *Cork Examiner,* 5 March 1863.

36.   *Ibid.,* 24 March 1863.

37.   It appears, for example, that there were workhouse riots in Belfast before the Famine (see the *Belfast Timeline* at www.belfasthistoryproject.com/belfast-timeline.html) and in the pre-Poor Law Dublin house of industry.

38.   It is notable that the master's account of the resistance at Waterford is to be found in the report of a Poor Law inspector several months later; there is little indication of such problems in the detailed reports of the meetings of the boards of guardians in the local papers of the time.

39.   J. Holmes, 'The role of open-air preaching in the Belfast riots of 1857', *PRIA* section 2, 2002, p. 102 (3); C. Hirst, *Religion, Politics and Violence in Nineteenth-Century Belfast* (Dublin, 2002).

40.   Fr Alessandro Gavazzi (1809–89), a former Barnabite monk, became religious leader of the national crusade in Italy. Driven from Rome, he took refuge in England; in 1853 he visited America, leading to riots in Canada (D. Horner, 'A barbarism of the worst kind: negotiating gender and public space in the aftermath of Montreal's Gavazzi riots', Canadian Historical Association conference, London, Ont., 31 May 2005); his visit to Ireland in 1859 led to riots in Galway and Tralee. I wish to thank Daniel Horner who kindly sent me a copy of his paper.

41.   See Hoppen, *Elections, Politics and Society in Ireland.*

42.   *Cork Examiner,* 11, 17 and 24 March 1863.

43.   See NLI, Larcom MSS 7756–8.

44.   It would be interesting to compare this resistance to that which occurred during the tithe war just over a decade earlier; see P. O'Donoghue, 'Causes of the opposition to tithes, 1830–38', *Studia Hibernica* 5 (1965), pp. 7–28; *idem*, 'Opposition to tithe payments in 1830–31', *Studia Hibernica* 6 (1966), pp. 69–98; *idem*, 'Opposition to tithe payments in 1832–3,' *Studia Hibernica* 12 (1972), pp. 77–108.

45.   S. Clark, *Social Origins of the Irish Land War* (Princeton NJ, 1979).

46.   W. L. Feingold, *The Revolt of the Tenantry* (Boston, 1984).

47. NAI, CSORP/1880/7865. In Strokestown in February 1880, for example, an estimated 500 able-bodied men with a black flag of distress marched into the workhouse yard while the board was sitting. It was estimated that only one in six were labourers; the rest included 'well-to-do' farmers, shopkeepers and their assistants.

48. *United Ireland*, 16 January 1886.

49. S. Clark, *Social Origins of the Irish Land War*.

50. *Ibid.*, pp. 309–11.

51. Burke, *The People and the Poor Law*, pp. 210–18; Clark, 'Wild workhouse girls and the Liberal imperial state'.

52. J. Robins, *The Lost Children: a study of charity children in Ireland, 1700-1900* (Dublin: Institute of Public Administration, 1980).

Chapter 7

1. Much of the information about the episode was found in one file, NAI, CSORP 1874/8773, evidence gathered for a Board of Trade inquiry held in Galway in August 1873, including material relating to a coroner's inquest and a manslaughter trial. References to items in this file are prefixed 1F.

2. 1F, 'Notes of evidence taken before a Court of Inquiry ... in pursuance of the instructions of the Board of Trade', deposition of George Bond.

3. See, for example, 1F, Captain Bedingfield to Admiralty Secretary, 30 April 1873, and 'Notes of evidence', deposition of Joseph Semple.

4. C. R. Browne, MD, 'The ethnography of Garumna and Lettermullen, in the County of Galway', *Proceedings of the Royal Irish Academy*, vol. 5 (1898–1900), pp. 243–5.

5. C. Payne, 'Smugglers, poachers and wreckers in nineteenth-century English painting', *Cahiers Victoriens et Edouardiens*, vol. iii, no. 61, April 2005; G. P. Landow, *Images of Crises: literary iconology, 1750 to the present* (London, 1982), pp. 35–130; M. Lincoln, 'Shipwreck narratives of the eighteenth and early nine-

teenth century', *British Journal for Eighteenth-Century Studies*, XX, 1997, pp. 155–72.

6. B. Bathurst, *The Wreckers: a story of killing seas, false lights and plundered ships* (London, 2005), p. 20.

7. T. J. Schoenbaum, *Admiralty and Marine Law*, 4th edn (St Paul, 2004), pp. 831–44.

8. E. P. Thompson, *Whigs and Hunters: the origins of the Black Act* (London, 1975), pp. 258–69; H. Laird, *Subversive Law in Ireland, 1879–1920: from 'unwritten law' to the Dáil courts* (Dublin, 2005), pp. 23–5, 59.

9. Laird, *Subversive Law*, pp. 24–5; R. Guha, *Dominance without Hegemony: history and power in colonial India* (Cambridge MA, 1997), pp. 63–72, passim; R. Grave and M. Kale, 'The empire and Mr Thompson: making of Indian princes and English working class', *Economic and Political Weekly*, vol. XXXII, no. 36 (6–12 September 1997), pp. 2273–88; D. Lloyd, *Ireland after History* (Cork, 1999), pp. 54, 77–88; J. Cunningham, 'Popular protest and a "moral economy" in provincial Ireland in the early nineteenth century', in F. Devine, F. Lane and N. Puirséil, *Essays in Irish Labour History* (Dublin, 2008), pp. 26–48.

10. J. G. Rule, 'Wrecking and coastal plunder', in Hay *et al.*, *Albion's Fatal Tree: crime and society in eighteenth-century England* (London, 1975), pp. 167–88.

11. 'The wreck register of 1859', *Illustrated London News*, 20 October 1860; K. Brady, *Shipwreck Inventory: Louth, Meath, Dublin, and Wicklow* (Dublin, 2008), pp. 45–6.

12. For example, T. Ó Criomhtháin, *An tOileánach* (Dublin, 1929), p. 12; A. Powell, *Oileáin Árainn: stair na n-oileáin anuas go dtí 1922* (Dublin, 1984); B. Dornan, *Mayo's Lost Islands: the Inishkeas* (Dublin, 2000), pp. 144–7; É. Langford, *Cape Clear Island: its people and landscape* (Cork, 1999); C. Kruger, *Cape Clear: island magic* (Cork, 1994), pp. 28–34.

13. For evidence of the abandonment of the *Julia*, see 1F, Report to the Board of Trade of an inquiry chaired by James O'Dowd.

14. 1F, 'Notes of evidence', deposition of Joseph Semple; D. Fitzpatrick, 'The disappearance of the Irish agricultural labourer',

Journal of the Economic and Social History Society of Ireland, vol. vii, 1980, pp. 90–2.

15.   1F, 'Notes of evidence', deposition of Frederick St Clair Ruthven.

16.   *Ibid.*, depositions of Henry Warren and St Clair Ruthven.

17.   Congested District Board, Baseline Reports: South Connemara, p. 483.

18.   Browne, 'Ethnography of Garumna and Lettermullen', p. 223.

19.   *Coimisiún na Gaeltachta*, 1925, p. 2.

20.   British parliamentary papers, *Census of Ireland for the year 1891: vol. IV, province of Connacht*, 1892, vol. XCIII, county of Galway, table vii.

21.   M. Ó Conghaile, *Conamara agus Árainn: gnéithe den stair shóisialta* (Béal an Daingin 1988), pp. 102–4, 171. Causeways were later built to join Garumna to Lettermullen (1886) and Lettermore to the mainland (1891). Only in 1897 was a bridge built between Lettermore and Garumna (Browne, 'Ethnography of Garumna and Lettermullen', p. 267).

22.   J. M. Synge, *In Connemara*, 1979 edn, Cork, p. 32; Browne, 'Ethnography of Garumna and Lettermullen', p. 248.

23.   P. O'Dowd, *In from the West: the McDonogh dynasty* (Galway, 2002), pp. 2–11; interview with Beartla King, local historian, 20 September 2005.

24.   E. Keogh, 'In Garumna island', *New Ireland Review*, June 1898, p. 194.

25.   Rundale is a system where the land is divided into discontinuous plots, cultivated and occupied by a number of tenants.

26.   Browne, 'Ethnography of Garumna and Lettermullen', pp. 249, 254.

27.   *Ibid.*, pp. 259–60; Congested Districts Board, Baseline report for South Connemara, Appendix J, 'Boats'.

28.   British Parliamentary Papers, *Thirty-seventh report of the Commissioners of National Education in Ireland, with appendices*, 1871, vol. xxiii, p. 607; Duvally deposition.

29.   *The Nation*, 9 October 1886.

30.   Máire Uí Ráine, 'Ceantar na nOileán', in G. Ó Tuathaigh, L. Ó Laoire and S. Ua Súilleabháin (eds), *Pobal na Gaeltachta: a scéal*

agus a dhán (Indreabháin, 2000), pp. 383–94; Browne, 'Ethnography of Garumna and Lettermullen', p. 240.

31. Browne, 'Ethnography of Garumna and Lettermullen'.

32. 1F, 'Notes of evidence', depositions of Denis Duvally and Michael Connolly.

33. *Ibid.*, depositions of John Clarke Drew and Richard George Jago.

34. 1F, Connolly and Duvally depositions; Fitzpatrick, 'Rural labourers', pp. 90–2.

35. 1F, Connolly deposition; the 1871 census recorded ninety-eight inhabited houses on Lettermullen.

36. 1F, Duvally deposition.

37. 1F, Connolly and Jago depositions.

38. 1F, Duvally and Jago depositions.

39. *Ibid.*; *Galway Vindicator*, 23 August 1873.

40. 1F, Peacock, Drew and Jago depositions.

41. 1F, 'The Queen versus Drew and Jago', evidence of Steven Mulkerrin; depositions of Jago, Drew, George Bond, James McDonough and John Kelly.

42. 1F, Mitchell Henry to Lord Hartington, chief secretary for Ireland, 18 February 1873; Lord Hartington to Burke, 14 May 1873; *Galway Vindicator*, 23 August 1873; K. Villiers-Tuthill, *Beyond the Twelve Bens: a history of Clifden and district, 1860–1923* (Galway 1986), pp. 51–6.

43. 1F, Patrick John O'Loughlin to Chief Secretary's Office, 15 May 1873.

44. 1F, Statement of 2nd Head Constable Mullen: enclosure in correspondence with chief secretary's office, 24 May 1873.

45. 1F, Patrick John O'Loughlin to chief secretary's office, 15 May 1873. The jurors were: Thomas Mahon (foreman), Pat Davies, James Folan, Pat Folan, Pat Fitzpatrick, James Green, John Green, Pat Hynes, Midie Lee, Bartley Mulkerrins, Colman Mulkerrins and John Nee. Beartla King identified several as relatives of the deceased.

46. 1F, St Clair Ruthven to constabulary office, Dublin Castle, 17 February 1873.

47. Beartla King interview; S. MacGiollarnáth, *Annála beaga ó Iorrus Aithneach*, Dublin, 1941, pp. 256: 'He was a sporting and a drinking man; as a dancer, he was unsurpassed.'

48. 1F, St Clair Ruthven to constabulary office, Dublin Castle, 7 March 1873.

49. 1F, Patrick John O'Loughlin to under-secretary, Dublin Castle, 28 March 1873; J. Scully, R.M. to attorney-general, 24 April 1873.

50. 1F, St Clair Ruthven to constabulary office, Dublin Castle, 8 May 1873.

51. 1F, Information sworn by Michael Cloherty and Joseph Semple, 15 May 1873; Semple, Peacock and Bond depositions.

52. 1F, Deposition of John Smith.

53. 1F, Semple deposition.

54. *Ibid.*

55. *Ibid.*

56. 1F, Drew deposition.

57. 1F, Capt. Norman Bedingfield to the Admiralty, 13 May 1873.

58. 1F, J. Scully to Chief Secretary's Office, 17 May 1873.

59. 1F, St Clair Ruthven to Chief Secretary's Office, 18 June 1873; *Galway Vindicator*, 2 August 1873.

60. *Galway Express*, 12 July 1873.

61. *Tuam Herald*, 2 August 1873.

62. *Galway Vindicator*, 2 August 1873.

63. 1F, cited in Duvally deposition.

64. 1F, Galway Assizes, 28 July 1873, transcription of evidence.

65. *Ibid.*; *Galway Vindicator*, 30 July 1873.

66. *Galway Vindicator*, 23 August 1873.

67. *Ibid.*, 20 August 1873.

68. *Ibid.*, 23 August 1873.

69. 1F, O'Dowd report to Board of Trade.

70. 1F, St Clair Ruthven deposition.

71. 1F, Drew deposition.

72. Beartla King interview; *The Nation*, 9 October 1886.

73. *The Nation*, 22 January 1876.

74. 1F, 'Notes of evidence', deposition of Joseph A. Peacock.

75.   1F, 'Notes of evidence', deposition of the Rev. Roderick Quinn.

76.   For the 'battle of Carraroe', see M. Davitt, *The Fall of Feudalism in Ireland, or the story of the Land League revolution* (London, 1904), pp. 213–19; for Nolan–Trench, see G. Moran, *A Radical Priest in Mayo: Fr Patrick Lavelle, 1825–86* (Dublin 1994), pp. 136–42.

Chapter 8

1.   This last title seems to have been a stock appellation applied liberally to various urban workmen combinations; see, for example, *Connaught Journal*, Monday 3 January 1825.

2.   Forestallers were traders allegedly monopolising supplies, in this case of potatoes, and thus profiteering.

3.   J. Bohstedt and D. E. Williams, 'The diffusion of riots: the patterns of 1766, 1795, and 1801 in Devonshire', *Journal of Interdisciplinary History*, vol. 19, no. 1 (Summer 1988), pp. 1–24. They examine how and why riots spread and explain the 'copycat' phenomenon.

4.   *The Nation*, 29 April 1876.

5.   *Limerick Evening Post*, 25 June, 29 June, 2 July 1830.

6.   *The Nation*, 29 April 1876; *Limerick Chronicle*, 9 July 1892.

7.   *Freeman's Journal*, 10, 11 April 1877; *Munster News*, 11, 14 April 1877; *Belfast Newsletter*, 10 April 1877.

8.   W. R. Le Fanu, *Seventy Years of Irish Life, being reminiscences and anecdotes* (London, 1893), pp. 31–42.

9.   Discussed in D. S. Sandhu, *Faces of violence* (New York, 2001), p. 92.

10.   See J. McGrath, 'Socio-economic conditions in St Mary's parish, Limerick' (unpublished MA thesis, Mary Immaculate College, University of Limerick), Chapter 4; the majority of city GAA clubs were weakened by the Parnellite split and the IRB *v.* clergy struggle. Many junior rugby clubs did exist in the early 1890s but lacked a competition to take part in. The city had two senior rugby clubs and two senior GAA clubs active in this period.

11. J. E. Walsh, *Rakes and Ruffians* (Dublin, 1979), pp. 12–14. The definition of the word 'rake' sometimes applied solely to the upper class, but in the Limerick context merchants' sons were sometimes classed as rakes.

12. Sarah McNamara, 'Coping with crisis: the middle-class agenda in pre-Famine Limerick', paper presented at the Economic and Social History Society of Ireland Annual Conference, 7 November 2008.

13. K. Hannan, 'Garryowen', *Old Limerick Journal*, vol. 1 (December 1979), pp. 36–8; *The Nation* [1842–1897], 7 August 1847. Fr Costelloe referred to Johnny O'Connell and the Garryowen Boys here saying, most likely in jest, that they could sweep all opponents aside in an election. The Garryowen Boys were also present to welcome Daniel O'Connell into Limerick in 1828; see *Freeman's Journal*, 12 July 1828.

14. *Munster News*, 3 August 1892. I am indebted to Sarah McNamara for economic details of those involved in the 1830 food riot.

15. *Limerick Evening Post*, 22, 29 June, 2 July 1830.

16. *Freeman's Journal*, 10, 11 April 1877; *Munster News*, 11, 14 April 1877; *Belfast Newsletter*, 10 April 1877.

17. *Limerick Evening Post*, 12, 16, 23 March, 9 April, 11, 21 May, 18 June 1830.

18. Before the 1830 riot, newspapers gave few hints of growing social unrest apart from a few solitary references to more thefts of food.

19. *Limerick Evening Post*, 10 June 1828.

20. *Munster News*, 6, 9 July 1892; *Limerick Chronicle*, 7, 9, 16 July 1892.

21. J. Bohstedt, 'The myth of the feminine food riot', in H. B. Applewhite and D. G. Levy (eds), *Women in the Age of the Democratic Revolution* (Michigan, 1990), pp. 24–6; he has detailed many earlier cases of this in Britain.

22. *Ibid.*, p. 28.

23. *Ibid.*, p. 38.

24. *Limerick Reporter,* 19 February 1841; *Limerick City Election. Minutes of evidence taken before the Select Committee on Limerick*

City Election Petition; with the proceedings of the committee 1859, p. 118, HC, 1859 (147) iv, 112.

25. *Limerick City Election Petition*, pp. 46–9.

26. *Ibid.*, pp. 118–21.

27. *Limerick Leader*, 12 September 1895.

28. *Munster News*, 25 May 1859; N. Z. Davis, *Society and Culture in Early Modern France* (Stanford CA: Stanford University Press, 1975), p. 161.

29. Fenians had a level of support from some clergy, toleration from others, but Limerick clergy were consistently strongly against combination; see also *On combinations of trades*, Knowsley Pamphlet Collection (1831).

30. *Freeman's Journal*, 1 June 1822; Bishop Touhy, the Catholic bishop of Limerick, addressed a long and powerful letter to the tradesmen of Limerick in 1822 castigating the 'Union of Trades and combination oaths' and the pan-trade dimension of the union: 'Nothing but the suggestion of Satan could invent such wicked and diabolical oaths; for what has the tailor to do with the mason, or the broguemaker with the carpenter?'

31. E. McKay, 'The Limerick municipal elections: January 1899', *Old Limerick Journal*, 36 (Winter 1999), p. 6.

32. Shortly after the 1899 municipal elections, most of the corporation marked their election to office by attending a mass in St John's cathedral. Daly left, however, after the bishop made direct and uncomplimentary references to him in the sermon. A few other councillors, some of them bakers employed by Daly, left with him.

33. E. J. Larkin, *The Historical Dimensions of Irish Catholicism* (Dublin, 1997), p. 107.

34. E. R. Norman, *The Catholic Church and Ireland in the Age of Rebellion: 1859–1873* (London, 1965), p. 89.

35. *Munster News*, 27 August 1890.

36. *Limerick Leader*, 25, 27 September 1895.

37. In this period, St Mary's Band played for St John's Temperance Society, rather than the local Sarsfield Band.

38. *Limerick Chronicle*, 29 November 1892; *Munster News*, 13 July,

26, 30 November 1892, 15 July 1895. Anti-Parnellites argued that priests had taken little part in the 1892 and 1895 elections (a claim bolstered by the absence of priests in the local press during the election campaign, apart from Fr Bannon, and by the fact that, of the votes cast for the anti-Parnellite parliamentary candidate in 1895, only one was cast by an illiterate voter. Apart from that, a St Mary's priest sought to quell a riotous group of his parishioners with little success.

39.   *The Nation*, 7, 14, 21 August 1847; *The Anglo-Celt*, 6 August 1847.

40.   L. Fenton, *The Young Ireland Rebellion in Limerick* (Cork, 2010), pp. 80–2.

41.   *Limerick Star*, 30 June, 3, 14, 17 July, 4, 7 August 1835, 18 November 1836.

42.   *Munster News*, 12, 19 May 1858; K. T. Hoppen, 'Tories, Catholics, and the general election of 1859', *Historical Journal*, vol. 13, no. 1 (March 1970), pp. 61–2.

43.   *Munster News*, 22 May 1858.

44.   *Ibid.*, 11, 14 April 1877.

45.   *Belfast Newsletter*, 10 April 1877; *Freeman's Journal*, 10, 11 and 21 April 1877.

46.   N. Z. Davis, 'The rites of violence', *Past and Present*, no. 59 (1973), pp. 51–91.

47.   The one Protestant Limerick artisan during this period who came to any sort of prominence was John Lucas, an Englishman, who made a name for himself in the 1840s with his wholehearted support of repeal.

48.   *Limerick Star and Evening Post*, 14 March 1834.

49.   *Munster News*, 12 May 1858.

50.   *Limerick City Election Petition, 1859*, pp. 52–5.

51.   T. E. C. Leslie, 'Trades' unions and combinations in 1853', *Dublin Statistical Society*, no. 74 (1853), pp. 1–15.

52.   R. Dawson, *Red Terror and Green* (London, 1920), pp. 87–8.

53.   *Limerick Gazette*, 15 August 1820.

54.   *Limerick Reporter*, 29 July 1851.

55.   My previous research supports this theory, and has shown the

domination of certain names (McNamara, Hayes, Clancy) in the 1901 and 1911 census for St Mary's parish, suggesting a Clare origin for most.

56. F. Lane, 'The band nuisance', *Saothar: Journal of the Irish Labour History Society*, no. 2 (1999), pp. 17–31.

57. B. M. Walker, *Parliamentary Election Results in Ireland, 1801–1922* (Dublin, 1978), pp. 291–3, 361.

58. J. Ridden, 'Making good citizens: national identity, religion and liberalism among the Irish elite, c.1800–1850', unpublished PhD thesis, University of London (1998), pp. 178–9, 181. Rice was disillusioned by the political capacity of forty-shilling freeholders, even though his patron Lord Limerick exerted such a strong influence on this class: 'I place no kind of reliance [on Catholics] as constituents unless indeed their own interests should compel them to come in.'

59. *Limerick Chronicle*, 7 August 1830.

60. *Limerick City Election Petition, 1859*, pp. 120–1. O'Donnell would not corroborate this allegation under questioning, but did admit that the mob aided the election victory.

61. *Ibid.*, pp. 120–1.

62. *Limerick Reporter*, 29 July 1851.

63. *United Irishman*, 22 April 1848; *Freeman's Journal*, 3 May 1848. The Mitchel article described O'Connell as 'the great aider and abettor of the English plunderers … throughout his life the upholder of "middle class" rule, in all its phases, crimes, huxteries and hypocrisies; and, on all other occasions, the mortal enemy of working man, tiller and artificer.'

Chapter 9

1. Mobilisation order to Limerick City Battalion, NLI, MS 31179, Florence O'Donoghue Papers.

2. NAI, CO 904/101, CI, MR, September 1916. [CO = Colonial Office, CI = County Inspector, MR = monthly return]

3. NAI, CO 904/101, IG, MR, November 1916. [IG = Inspector-General]

4. NAI, BMH, WS 1420: Patrick Whelan, p. 13. [WS = witness statement]
5. M. Brennan, *The War in Clare, 1911–21* (Dublin, 1980), p. 21.
6. *Limerick Chronicle*, 23 January 1917; *Limerick Leader*, 29 January 1917; NAUK, CO 903/19, 'Confidential print', 1917, Chief Secretary's Office, Judicial Division, Intelligence Notes, pp. 9–10.
7. *Limerick Chronicle*, 3, 10 February 1917.
8. *Limerick Leader*, 3 February 1917.
9. See *ibid.*, 20 October 1916, 8, 10, 12, 16 January 1917; *Limerick Chronicle*, 9, 11, 16, 18, 20 January 1917.
10. NAUK, War Office 35/94, Report by Weldon to Headquarters, Southern District, Cork, 18 January 1917; Report by Grandage to Headquarters, Southern District, Cork, 19 January 1917.
11. NAI, CO 904/102, CI; IG, MR, February 1917; *Limerick Leader*, 23 February 1917; *Limerick Chronicle*, 24 February 1917.
12. NAI, CO 904/102, CI; IG, MR, March 1917; NAUK, CO 903/19, 'Confidential print', 1917, p. 10; *Limerick Chronicle*, 31 March 1917; *Limerick Leader*, 6, 13, 23 April 1917.
13. Ernest Blythe to Madge Daly, 27 March 1917, University of Limerick's Special Collections, Daly Papers: Box 1, Folder 4.
14. Imperial War Museum, J. H. M. Staniforth Papers: 'Kitchener's soldier, 1914–18. The letters of J. H. M. Staniforth', 67/41/1, Staniforth to his parents, 14 March 1917, p. 195.
15. *Ibid.*, Staniforth to his parents, 30 April 1917, p. 198.
16. *Ibid.*, Staniforth to his parents, 4 March 1917, p. 192.
17. *Limerick Chronicle*, 5 April 1917; *Limerick Leader*, 6 April 1917.
18. *Limerick Chronicle*, 24 April 1917.
19. *Ibid.*, 21, 23 April 1917; CI, Limerick; IG, MR, April 1917, CO 904/102.
20. *Limerick Leader*, 25 April 1917.
21. *Ibid.*, 8 June 1917; NAI, BMH, WS 456: Liam Manahan, p. 25.
22. NAI, CO 904/103, CI, MR, June 1917; *Limerick Chronicle*, 14 June 1917; *Limerick Leader*, 15 June 1917.
23. NAI, CO 904/23, Sinn Féin Movement.
24. NAI, CO 904/103, CI, MR, June 1917.

25. NAI, CO 904/103, CI; IG, MR, June 1917; *Factionist*, 28 June 1917; *Limerick Chronicle*, 26 June 1917.

26. NAI, CO 904/103, CI, MR, July 1917.

27. NAI, BMH, WS 1700: Alphonsus J. O'Halloran, p. 25.

28. *Limerick Leader*, 25 July 1917.

29. *Ibid.*, 13 August 1917.

30. NAI, CO 904/104, IG, MR, September 1917; Crime Branch Special (CBS) 'Personality file' on Edward Punch, CO 904/213/363.

31. *The Times*, 6 October 1917.

32. NAI, CO 904/213/363, CBS 'Personality file' on Edward Punch.

33. NAI, CO 904/104, CI, MR, September 1917; Limerick County Council minutes, 29 September 1917, Limerick City and County Archives; Richard Mulcahy quoted in R. Mulcahy, 'The development of the Irish Volunteers, 1916–1922', *An Cosantóir*, vol. 40, no. 2 (February 1980), p. 37; J. Augusteijn, 'From public defiance to guerrilla warfare: the radicalisation of the Irish Republican Army, 1916–21 – a comparative analysis' (PhD thesis, University of Amsterdam, 1994), p. 4; *Limerick Leader*, 24, 28 September, 1, 5, October 1917; *Limerick Chronicle*, 25, 27 September, 2 October 1917.

34. NAI, CO 904/104, CI; IG, MR, October 1917; *Limerick Leader*, 15, 24, 29 October, 7, 14 November 1917.

35. NAI, CO 904/104, CI, MR, December 1917.

36. F. O'Donoghue, 'The reorganisation of the Volunteers', *Capuchin Annual* (1967), pp. 380–5; Mulcahy, 'The development of the Irish Volunteers', p. 37.

37. NAI, BMH, WS 1419: Michael Conway, p. 3.

38. *Factionist*, 24 May 1917.

39. *Ibid.*, 17 May 1917.

40. *Ibid.*, 14 June 1917.

41. *Limerick Leader*, 20 July 1917; *Factionist*, 9 August 1917; Compensation claim of Michael Gleeson, NAI, Department of Finance, 392/192.

42. *Limerick Chronicle*, 19 July 1917; *Limerick Leader*, 20 July 1917.

43.   M. Harnett, *Victory and Woe: the West Limerick Brigade in the War of Independence*, ed. James Joy (Dublin, 2002), p. 23.

44.   *Limerick Leader*, 6 March 1918.

45.   BMH, WS 1419: Michael Conway, pp. 4–5.

46.   *Nationality*, 23 March 1918.

47.   *Limerick Leader*, 20 March 1918.

48.   *Ibid.*, 27 February, 20 March 1918.

49.   NAI, CO 904/105, CI, MR, March 1918.

50.   *Limerick Leader*, 15 April, 31 May, 10 June 1918. The presence of the defendants at the making of the resolutions was not proved. A number of the defendants stated that they did not support the resolutions.

51.   *Ibid.*, 15, 17, 22, 24 April 1918; *Limerick Chronicle*, 16, 25 April 1918; *Nationality*, 20 April 1918.

52.   NAI, CO 904/105, CI, MR, April 1918.

53.   NAI, CO 904/106, CI, MR, July 1918.

54.   Harnett, *Victory and Woe*, pp. 25–7; Volunteer, 'West Limerick activities', in J. MacCarthy (ed.), *Limerick's Fighting Story from 1916 to the Truce with Britain* (Tralee, 1965), pp. 228–9.

55.   *Nationality*, 19 October 1918.

56.   NAI, CO 904/107, CI, MR, November 1918; Fr Tomas Wall to Madge Daly, 6 November 1918, University of Limerick's Special Collections, Daly Papers: Box 1, Folder 39; *Limerick Leader*, 6 November 1918.

57.   *Limerick Leader*, 4, 6 December 1918; *Limerick Chronicle*, 3, 5, 7 December 1918.

58.   *Limerick Leader*, 30 December 1918.

59.   NAUK, CO 903/19, 'Confidential print', 1918, p. 22.

60.   BMH, WS 1225: Jimmy Roche, pp. 2–3.

Chapter 10

1.   É. de Valera, 'St Patrick's Day speech 1943', quoted in C. Wills, *That Neutral Island: a cultural history of Ireland during the Second World War* (London, 2007), p. 333.

2.   *Ibid.*, p. 241.

3.   *The Irish Times*, 18 January 1941.

4.   Wills, *That Neutral Island,* pp. 241, 257.

5.   Bishop J. J. McNamee, 'Lenten pastoral', *Leitrim Observer*, 12 April 1942.

6.   Statistical Abstract, Stationery Office, Dublin, 1940–46.

7.   B. Share, *The Emergency: neutral Ireland, 1939–45* (Dublin, 1978), p. 38.

8.   NAI, DT T6/97/9/461, Department of the Taoiseach memorandum, 'Chinese Famine, 1943'.

9.   D. Ferriter, '"A peculiar people in their own land": Catholic social theory and the plight of rural Ireland, 1930–55', unpublished PhD thesis, University College Dublin, 1996, p. 33.

10.   Dáil Éireann, vol. 77, col. 921, Seán Lemass, 'Price of milk in Kilkenny', 8 November 1939.

11.   Wills, *That Neutral Island*, p. 237.

12.   Seanad Éireann, vol. 24, col. 2063, James Ryan, 'Exported Livestock Insurance Bill', 3 July 1940.

13.   *The Irish Times*, 10 October 1939.

14.   NAI, FIN S90/35/39, Emergency Powers (No. 12) Order 1939. FIN is the Finance Dept.

15.   *Ibid.*

16.   Dáil Éireann, vol. 89, col. 1013, James Ryan, 'Emergency Powers (No. 234) Order, 1942 – motion to annul', 4 March 1943.

17.   *Irish Independent*, 25 March 1940.

18.   Conacre, letting land for one season at a time, gives the tenant no permanent rights but a strong incentive to maximise yield.

19.   *Irish Independent*, 25 March 1940.

20.   J. F. Meenan, 'The Irish economy during the war', in K. B. Nowlan and D. T. Williams (eds), *Ireland in the War Years and After, 1939–51* (Dublin, 1969), p. 32.

21.   NAI, FIN S90/35/39, Interim Report of Departmental Committee on Increased Agricultural Production, 1938.

22.   NAI, FIN S90/35/39, Department of Agriculture, untitled memorandum, 4 September 1939.

23.   *Ibid.*

24.   *The Irish Times*, 19 September 1939.

25.   T. Bartlett, 'An end to moral economy: the Irish militia disturbances of 1793', *Past and Present*, vol. 99, no. 1 (May 1983), pp. 41–64, at p. 43.

26.   Seanad Éireann, vol. 23, col. 1299, Patrick Baxter, 'Compulsory tillage motion', 25 October 1939.

27.   *The Irish Times*, 13 October 1939.

28.   *Irish Independent*, 29 November 1946.

29.   *The Irish Times*, 5 October 1940, 9 January, 12 November 1941.

30.   *Ibid.*, 2 July 1942.

31.   Dáil Éireann, vol. 92, col. 1106, James Ryan, 'The Tillage Order', 16 February 1944.

32.   *The Irish Times*, 4 October 1939.

33.   See, for instance, *ibid.*, 1 April 1941.

34.   See, for instance, *ibid.*, 16 February 1942.

35.   *Ibid.*, 8 December 1943.

36.   De Valera's warning was published in *The Irish Times*, 2 March 1942. Unlike those who fell foul of censorship, farmers who failed to till enough land were never explicitly identified as 'traitors' to the Irish state, a reflection of their elevated place in essentialist nationalism.

37.   J. McGahern, *Memoir* (London, 2005), p. 29.

38.   *Leitrim Observer*, 12 December 1942.

39.   *Ibid.*, 28 February 1942.

40.   C. Townshend, *Ireland: the twentieth century* (London, 1999), pp. 7–8.

41.   T. J. McElligott, 'How the farmers can organise', *Irish Monthly* 67 (1939), p. 52.

42.   NAI, ICOS, 1088/222/4, M. Haire to Henry Kennedy, 29 May 1941.

43.   Wills, *That Neutral Island*, p. 241.

44.   *The Irish Times*, 21 November 1939.

45.   *Ibid.*, 7 July 1942.

46.   Mícheál Ó Muircheartaigh, b. 1930, Dingle, County Kerry, interviewed 12 August 2009.

47.   *Leitrim Observer*, 28 February 1942.

48. *Ibid.*
49. *The Irish Times*, 1 November 1940.
50. *Ibid.*, 18 January 1941.
51. *Ibid.*, 2 July 1942.
52. *Ibid.*, 25 February 1942.
53. Dáil Éireann, vol. 81, col. 1816, James Ryan, 'Compulsory tillage', 5 February 1941.
54. *The Irish Times*, 1 April 1941.
55. Dáil Éireann, vol. 93, col. 417, General MacEoin, 'Committee on Finance', 28 March 1944.
56. *Irish Independent*, 1 February 1947.
57. Dáil Éireann, vol. 104, col. 64, James Ryan, 'Compulsory tillage prosecutions', 22 January 1947.
58. Dáil Éireann, vol. 104, col. 64, 22 January 1947.
59. *Ibid.*
60. *Meath Chronicle*, 28 September 1940.
61. *Ibid.*
62. *The Irish Times*, 5 March 1943.
63. NAI, IND/EHR/3/C2, Dept of Supplies, 'Historical survey', part V, p. 201; part V, p. 222; part XI, p. 556.
64. James Dillon to Editor, *The Irish Times*, 1 April 1940. Dillon was at this point leader of Fine Gael and was to become Minister for Agriculture in 1948.
65. Wills, *That Neutral Island*, p. 241.
66. Seanad Éireann, vol. 23, col. 1303, 'Compulsory tillage motion', 25 October 1939.
67. *The Irish Times*, 23 March 1940.
68. Jack Magill, b. 1927, Saul, County Down, interviewed 16 April 2000, p. 6, Mary Immaculate College Oral Archive, Limerick.
69. NAI, EHR/3/15, Department of Supplies, 'Record of activities', p. 7.
70. NAI, IND/EHR/3/C4, Department of Supplies, 'Historical survey', part XI, p. 556.
71. J. W. Blake, *Northern Ireland in the Second World War* (Belfast: HMSO, 1956), p. 410.
72. *Ibid.*, p. 410.

73. *Ibid.*, p. 405.

74. NAI, IND/EHR/3/C2, Department of Supplies, 'Historical survey', part V, p. 223.

75. P67/262 (1), Seán MacEntee papers, '1936 census', University College Dublin Archives, Dublin.

76. Seanad Éireann, vol. 24, col. 2527, Dominick MacCabe, 'Compulsory tillage and guaranteed prices', 4 December 1940. This figure is slightly lower in the *Report of the Commission on Vocational Organisation* (Dublin: Stationery Office, 1943), p. 125.

77. Dáil Éireann, vol. 93, col. 487, Oliver J. Flanagan, 'Committee on Finance', 28 March 1944.

78. *The Irish Times*, 18 November 1939.

79. Pathé Gazette, 'Dig for Victory!' broadcast 22 January 1940, PRONI, Digital Film Archive, Belfast.

80. PRONI, D3004/D/29, diary of Cynthia, Lady Brookeborough.

81. UCDA, P67/264 (4), MacEntee papers, Seán Lemass, 'Memorandum on full employment'.

82. *Ibid.*

83. NAI, DT S13101 A, Seán Lemass, 'Memorandum on full employment policy', 17 January 1945.

84. Dáil Éireann, vol. 93, col. 396, James Larkin, 'Committee on Finance', 28 March 1944.

85. UCDA, P67/264 (5), MacEntee papers, James Ryan, 'Observations of the Minister of Agriculture on the memorandum by the Minister for Industry and Commerce'.

86. *Ibid.*

87. NAI, DT S13101 A, James Ryan, 'Memorandum on full employment', 14 March 1945.

88. UCDA, P67/264 (5), MacEntee papers, James Ryan, 'Observations of the Minister of Agriculture on the memorandum by the Minister for Industry and Commerce'.

89. NAI, DT S13101 A, James Ryan, 'Memorandum on full employment', 14 March 1945.

90. J. O'Neill, 'Our essential planning problem', *Studies* 33 (1944), pp. 228–36.

91. *Report of the Commission on Vocational Organisation* (Dublin:

Stationery Office, 1943), p. 45.

92. DAA, AB8/B/XVIII/51. McQuaid papers, Seán Lemass to John Charles McQuaid, 8 January 1941.

93. See Garvin's continual use of the term 'developmentalism' in juxtaposing Lemass' drive for modernisation against the perceived stasis of his more conservative colleagues in government, in T. Garvin, *Preventing the Future: why was Ireland so poor for so long?* (Dublin, 2004); T. Garvin, *Judging Lemass* (Dublin, 2009).

94. The Women's Land Army (WLA) was established by the British Government during the First World War and disbanded in 1919. It was re-formed in 1939 and disbanded again in 1950. Women did the work of male farm labourers who had left to join the armed forces or work in urban factories. By 1943 there were 80,000 women working on British farms. Most combatant nations had similar organisations during the Second World War, with the notable exception of Nazi Germany; see P. Summerfield, *Women Workers during the Second World War* (London, 1982); for a Land Girl's account, see J. Duggan Rees, *Corduroy Days* (London, 2000).

95. S. Carey, *Social Security in Ireland, 1939–1952: the limits to solidarity* (Dublin, 2007), pp. 113–33.

96. Seanad Éireann, vol. 23, col. 1121, Patrick Baxter, 'Compulsory tillage motion', 25 October 1939.

97. E. Duggan, *The Ploughman on the Pound Note: farmer politics in County Galway during the twentieth century* (Athenry, 2004), pp. 78–114.

98. See for instance, *Irish Independent*, 20 October 1939, 2 February 1940; *Connacht Tribune*, 30 March 1940.

99. Bishop Nulty of Meath, quoted in A. E. McCullough, 'The language and legitimation of Irish moral outrage', *British Journal of Sociology*, vol. 40, no. 2 (1989), p. 237. This invocation of the purity of the smallholder was made in 1871 but typifies the discursive treatment of the farmer by the church during the Emergency.

100. *Statistical Abstract* (Dublin, 1945).

101. *The Irish Times*, 18 January 1945.

Chapter 11

1.   This term is borrowed from John Bowman, *De Valera and the Ulster Question, 1917–1973* (Oxford, 1982), p. 287.
2.   D. Keogh, *Twentieth Century Ireland: nation and state* (Dublin, 1994), p. 229.
3.   See de Valera's presidential speech at the 1931 Fianna Fáil Ard Fheis, University College Dublin Archives [hereafter UCDA]; Fianna Fáil Party Papers P176/42, copy of de Valera's Presidential speech, October 1931.
4.   See de Valera speech on External Affairs estimates: Dáil Éireann debate, 24 June 1947, vol. 107, col. 84.
5.   See, for example, resolutions on partition issued at the 1926 and 1939 Fianna Fáil Ard Fheiseanna, *The Irish Times*, 26 November 1926 and *Irish Press*, 13 December 1939.
6.   UCDA, P176/276, copy of letter from Miss Ena Moore, hon. sec. of Barnstown Thomas Ashe cumann, to Lemass, 25 March 1955. This was the opinion of members of the cumann [party branch].
7.   UCDA, P176/293, letter from Seamus Babington to Lemass, 1 March 1955.
8.   UCDA, P176/286, letter from Lemass to MacCarthy, 25 January 1957.
9.   See de Valera's presidential speech at the 1954 Fianna Fáil Ard Fheis, *Irish Press*, 12 October 1954.
10. Educated in England at The Leys School, Cambridge, and Methodist College, Booth served as a captain in the Irish Army in the 1940s. Appointed to the national executive committee of fifteen at the 1954 Fianna Fáil Ard Fheis, he became Fianna Fáil TD Dún Laoghaire-Rathdown in the 1957 general election. He was managing director of Booth Poole & Co. Ltd from 1956 until he became managing director of Brittain Group in 1970.
11. UCDA, Ernest Blythe Papers P26/1366, letter from Booth to Ernest Blythe, 16 October 1954.
12. *The Irish Times*, 15 October 1954.

13.   R. English, *Armed Struggle: a history of the IRA* (London, 2003), p. 74; see also B. Flynn, *Soldiers of Folly: the IRA border campaign, 1956–1962* (Dublin, 2009); J. Maguire, *IRA Internments and the Irish Government: subversives and the state, 1939–1962* (Dublin, 1999).

14.   J. B. Bell, *The Secret Army: the IRA* (New Brunswick NJ, 1997), p. 299.

15.   Keogh, *Twentieth Century Ireland*, p. 229.

16.   *Irish Press*, 19 October 1968.

17.   *Ibid.*, 4 January 1957.

18.   *Irish Press*, 4 January 1957.

19.   When looking at the *Irish Press* coverage of the funerals it is easy to understand Freddie Boland's remark that, whatever de Valera might say in public, the *Irish Press* was edited in such a way as to 'encourage the extremist and more irresponsible elements among the nationalist minority in the North and to give the impression that Fianna Fáil agreed with them', NAI, Dept of Foreign Affairs [hereafter DFA] F132/10, confidential record of conversation between Freddie Boland and Michael O'Neill MP, sent to Seán Nunan, 3 December 1954.

20.   UCDA, John A. Costello Papers P190/683, text copy of Costello's speech, 6 January 1957.

21.   See speech by de Valera, *Irish Press*, 7 January 1957.

22.   It was Robert Briscoe, Fianna Fáil TD for Dublin South-West and lord mayor, who made this appeal, noting that such a vote should not be taken to confirm or approve the IRA's activities; *The Irish Times*, 8 January 1957.

23.   *The Irish Times*, 17 January 1957.

24.   UCDA, P176/280, letter from D. Uas. Mac Phroinsias, hon. sec. of Seán MacDermott cumann, Dublin North-East, to Fianna Fáil headquarters, 15 January 1957.

25.   *Ibid.*

26.   *Ibid.*

27.   Bowman, *De Valera*, p. 286.

28.   *Irish Press*, 7 January 1956.

29.   UCDA, P176/277, letter from E. P. Leonard, hon. sec. Joseph

Hudson cumann, Sallynoggin, to Fianna Fáil headquarters, 10 January 1957.

30.   *Ibid*; see also copy of letter from Lemass to Seán Ó Dálaigh, hon. sec. Meaghen Neary cumann, Dún Laoghaire-Rathdown, 15 January 1957, UCDA, P176/277.

31.   UCDA, P176/286, reply letter from Lemass to MacCarthy, 25 January 1957.

32.   UCDA, P176/277, copy of letter from Lemass to Seán Ó Dálaigh, honorary secretary of Meaghen Neary cumann, Dún Laoghaire-Rathdown, 15 January 1957.

33.   *Irish Press*, 21 January 1957.

34.   UCDA, Éamon de Valera Papers, P150/3095, letter sent from Donogh O'Malley to de Valera, 8 January 1957.

35.   See T. Garvin, *Judging Lemass: the measure of the man* (Dublin, 2009), p. 13.

36.   Bowman, *De Valera*, p. 287.

37.   *Ibid.*

38.   UCDA, P176/46, copy of memorandum sent by Feehan to Mullins, 20 January 1955.

39.   UCDA, 176/446, record of meeting of Fianna Fáil parliamentary party, 15 January 1957. It began at 3 p.m. and ended at 11 p.m.

40.   J. Horgan, *Seán Lemass: the enigmatic patriot* (Dublin, 1999), p. 173.

41.   *Ibid.*

42.   UCDA, P176/286, this comment was made by Lemass; letter from Lemass to MacCarthy, 25 January 1957.

43.   UCDA, P176/286, letter from Lemass to MacCarthy, 25 January 1957.

44.   UCDA, 176/446, meeting of Fianna Fáil parliamentary party, 15 January 1957.

45.   R. Fanning, '"Playing it cool": the response of the British and Irish governments to the crisis in Northern Ireland, 1968–9', *Irish Studies in International Affairs*, vol. 12 (2001), pp. 57–85.

46.   UCDA, 176/446, meeting of Fianna Fáil parliamentary party, 15 January 1957.

47. B. Farrell, *Seán Lemass* (Dublin, 1983), p. 107; Farrell records an interview he had with Lemass in which the latter noted that de Valera relied upon 'the force of physical exhaustion'.

48. Boland noted that the recent raids 'will only delay the inevitable reunion of the country'; *Irish Press*, 21 January 1957.

49. *Irish Press*, 21 January 1957.

50. Bowman, *De Valera*, p. 290.

51. See speeches by de Valera in *Irish Press*, 9 March 1957, 19 October 1957 and 19 March 1958; see NAI, DFA P203/2, record of meeting between Frank Aiken and Lord Home, secretary of state for commonwealth relations, 4 July 1958, for comments by Aiken; see also speech by MacEntee, *Irish Press*, 18 March 1958.

52. See K. Boland, *The Rise and Decline of Fianna Fáil* (Dublin, 1982), p. 106.

53. UCDA, P150/2075, copy of de Valera's presidential speech at the Fianna Fáil Ard Fheis, 19 November 1957.

54. This was the opinion of Mr Culleton, representative of the party's Mountmellick cumann, County Tipperary, *Irish Press*, 20 November 1957.

55. *Irish Press*, 20 November 1957.

56. Bell, *The Secret Army*, pp. 306–7.

57. UCDA, P150/3117, record of statement issued on behalf of de Valera, July 1957.

58. *The Irish Times*, 16 September 1957.

59. NAI, DFA P203/2, record of meeting between Cremin and Home, 27 July 1957.

60. R. English, *Irish Freedom: the history of Irish nationalism* (London, 2006), p. 331.

61. *Ibid.*, p. 333.

62. *Cork Examiner*, 12 July 1957.

63. *The Irish Times*, 31 December 1957.

64. *Evening Mail*, 21 December 1957.

65. UCDA, P176/447, record of meeting of the parliamentary party, 16 April 1958.

66. UCDA, P176/447, record of meetings of the parliamentary party, 24 October 1957, 16 April 1958 and 22 January 1959.

67. UCDA, P176/312, 'Notes for canvassers', in the constituency files for Dublin North-Central, October 1957.

68. *Irish Press*, 15 March 1959, speech by de Valera.

69. UCDA, P150/2075, copy of de Valera's presidential speech at the Fianna Fáil Ard Fheis, 19 November 1957.

70. *Tipperary Star*, 10 January 1959; see *The Irish Times* during January 1959.

71. *Tipperary Star*, 10 January 1959.

72. Seán Tracey, Labour councillor and future ceann comhairle, and G. Meskil also supported the motion; *Tipperary Star*, 10 January 1959.

73. *Tipperary Star*, 10 January 1959.

74. This was the opinion of Jack Meagher, Annfield House, Cudville, Nenagh; *Tipperary Star*, 7 February 1959.

75. NAI, DT 97/9/1273, government policy: letters of advice and criticism, 1957–9; letter from Pádraig Ó Bhrosnaeain to de Valera, 29 July 1958.

76. UCDA, P176/348, meeting of Fianna Fáil national executive, 12 January 1959.

77. *Ibid.*

78. See 'The Peter Barry papers', *Magill* (June 1980), p. 48.

79. UCDA, P176/769, record of 32nd Fianna Fáil Ard Fheis, 16–17 January 1962.

80. NAI, DFA 305/14/19 D11, letter from Seán Ó Fionn to Lemass, 23 June 1962.

81. NAI, DT S9361 K/62, letter from Rev. P. F. Malone to Lemass, 8 February 1962.

82. *Ibid.*

83. Bowman, *De Valera*, p. 287.

84. UCDA, P176/286, letter from MacCarthy to Lemass, 24 January 1957.

85. UCDA, Frank Aiken Papers P104/8812, letter from Lemass to Mr Heaney, 25 November 1961.

86. UCDA, P176/769, copy of no. 1 resolution on partition issued on behalf of the Tomás Mac Donnchadha cumann, Dublin North-Central, at the party Ard Fheis, 16–17 January 1962.

87.   UCDA, P176/286, letter from Lemass to MacCarthy, 25 January 1957.

88.   Keogh, *Twentieth Century Ireland*, p. 229.

89.   UCDA, P176/447–448, record of Fianna Fáil parliamentary meetings, 1959–66.

90.   The Earl of Longford and T. P. O'Neill, *Éamon de Valera* (London, 1970), p. 331.

91.   See T. Gallagher, 'Fianna Fáil and partition 1926–84', *Éire – Ireland*, vol. 20, no. 1 (1985), p. 48.

92.   UCDA, P176/46, memorandum for the Fianna Fáil national executive submitted by Tomas Ó Cleirigh cumann, Dublin North-East, 15 January 1955.

Chapter 12

1.   See http://www.belfastcity.gov.uk/tallships/, accessed 22 October 2009.

2.   See http://www.belfastcity.gov.uk/news/news.asp?id=1339, accessed 22 October 2009.

3.   To give an idea of the scale of violence and destruction, it is estimated that 1,820 households (1,505 of which were Catholic-owned) were displaced.

4.   See http:///www.westbelfastsinnfein.com/news/13983, accessed 31 August 2009.

5.   J. Byrne, 'Peace walls: a temporary measure', *History Ireland*, vol. 17, no. 4 (July/August 2009), p. 43.

6.   Transcription from my own recording.

7.   See http:///redbarngallery.blogspot.com/2009/06/historically unique-series-of.html, accessed 11 December 2009.

8.   See http://www.belfastedia.com/features_article.php?ID=953, accessed 11 December 2009.

9.   H. McKeown, *Ardoyne: the aftermath* (Belfast: Red Barn Gallery, 2009), foreword.

10. All were fallen volunteers of 'C' Company, 2nd Battalion Belfast Brigade, Óglaigh na hÉireann [IRA].

11. Scarman Report, *Report of Tribunal of Inquiry into violence and civil disturbances in Northern Ireland*, Belfast, HMSO (1972), vol. I, p. 222.

12. *Ibid.*, p. 222.

13. Queen's University of Belfast, Special Collections, MS 33/2/41, Scarman Tribunal Evidence, Day 164, Head Constable William Thompson, p. 25.

14. Scarman Report, *Report of Tribunal of Inquiry*, vol. I, p. 222.

15. Queen's University of Belfast, Special Collections, MS 33/2/41, Scarman Tribunal Evidence, Day 165, Head Constable Thomas McCluney, p. 22.

16. Scarman Report, *Report of Tribunal of Inquiry*, vol. I, p. 225.

17. *News Letter*, 5 August 1969.

18. Scarman Report, *Report of Tribunal of Inquiry*, vol. I, p. 225.

19. Queen's University of Belfast, Special Collections, MS 33/2/41, Scarman Tribunal Evidence, Day 165, Head Constable Thomas McCluney, p. 25.

20. Queen's University of Belfast, Special Collections, MS 33/2/41, Scarman Tribunal Evidence, Day 164, District Inspector Henry Hamilton Shute, p. 39.

21. Scarman Report, *Report of Tribunal of Inquiry*, vol. I, p. 223.

22. *Ibid.*, p. 224.

23. *Ibid.*

24. S. Farrell, *Rituals and Riots: sectarian violence and political culture in Ulster, 1784–1886* (Lexington: University Press of Kentucky, 2000), pp. 134–5.

25. J. Holmes, 'The role of open-air preaching in the Belfast riots of 1857', *Proceedings of the Royal Irish Academy*, vol. 102C (2002), p. 53.

26. A. C. Hepburn, *Catholic Belfast and Nationalist Ireland in the Era of Joe Devlin, 1871–1934* (Oxford, 2008), p. 24.

27. Farrell, *Rituals and Riots*, p. 5.

28. M. Doyle, *Fighting like the Devil for the sake of God: Protestants, Catholics and the origins of violence in Victorian Belfast* (Manchester, 2009), p. 2.

29. *Ibid.*, p. 1; see also Farrell, *Rituals and Riots*, p. 138.

30. Scarman Report, *Report of Tribunal of Inquiry*, vol. II, Appendix M.

31. C. Hirst, *Religion, Politics and Violence in Nineteenth Century Belfast: The Pound and Sandy Row* (Dublin, 2002).

32. Scarman Report, *Report of Tribunal of Inquiry*, vol. I, p. 222.

33. For an interesting selection of images of this building before and after the riots see McKeown, *Ardoyne*.

34. PRONI D3233/7/5, Vivian Simpson, draft submission to the Scarman Tribunal, p. 1.

35. Scarman Report, *Report of Tribunal of Inquiry*, vol. I, pp. 25–6.

36. *Ibid.*, p. 26. It was the landlord of the Edenderry Inn who contacted the police about the original drink-fuelled incident, but we still do not know why he did so or what he said. When the police riot squad arrived, they formed up opposite the public house. Samuel Green, an inebriated bystander, 'jokingly flicked a cigarette lighter at the drawn riot squad and said "Bang, bang, you are dead"': evidence of Fr Marcus Gillespie. Green's arrest seems to have set off the larger and wider confrontation.

37. PRONI, D3233/7/5, Vivian Simpson draft submission to the Scarman Tribunal, p. 1.

38. PRONI, D3233/7/5, Fergus McCartan to Vivian Simpson, 13 January 1970.

39. Queen's University of Belfast, Special Collections, MS 33/2/35, Scarman Tribunal Evidence, Day 136, Mr Harold Wolseley, pp. 1–2.

40. The *Sunday Times* Insight Team, *Ulster* (Harmondsworth, 1972), p. 127.

41. *Ibid.*, p. 131.

42. Queen's University of Belfast, Special Collections, MS 33/1/4/43, 'Selected messages received at RUC control room in the Commissioner's Headquarters', Exhibit (Belfast) no. 43.

43. *The Irish Times*, 7 August 1969.

44. Queen's University of Belfast, Special Collections, MS 33/3/1, 'Submission on behalf of the residents of Unity Flats and Roman Catholic residents in the Ardoyne', Scarman Submissions (Belfast), vol. I, p. 12.

45.   Queen's University of Belfast, Special Collections, MS 33/2/35, Scarman Tribunal Evidence, Day 136, Mr Harold Wolseley, p. 11.

46.   *News Letter*, 11 August 1969.

47.   Queen's University of Belfast, Special Collections, MS 33/2/41, Day 164, District Inspector Henry Hamilton Shute, p. 46.

48.   *Ibid.*, p. 51.

49.   *Ibid.*, MS 33/2/41, Day 164, Head Constable William Thompson, p. 32.

50.   Scarman Report, *Report of Tribunal of Inquiry*, vol. I, p. 26.

51.   *Ibid.*, p. 26.

52.   *Ibid.*, p. 225.

53.   J. Darby, *Intimidation and the Control of Conflict in Northern Ireland* (Syracuse NY, 1986), p. viii.

54.   E. Leyton, 'Opposition and integration in Ulster', *Man*, vol. IX, no. II, p. 185; see also R. English, *Armed Struggle: the history of the IRA* (Basingstoke, 2004), p. 100.

55.   N. Ó Dochartaigh, *From Civil Rights to Armalites: Derry and the birth of the Irish Troubles* (London, 2005), p. 1.

56.   A. Boyd, *Holy War in Belfast* (Kerry, 1971), Preface.

Chapter 13

1.   J. Habermas, *The Theory of Communicative Action*, vol. 1 (Cambridge, 1984).

2.   F. F. Piven, 'Can power from below change the world?' *American Sociological Review*, vol. 73, no. 1 (2008), pp. 1–14.

3.   L. Cox, 'News from nowhere? The movement of movements in Ireland', in L. Connolly and N. Hourigan (eds), *Social Movements in Ireland* (Manchester, 2006), pp. 210–29.

4.   G. Allen, *The Irish Times*, 17 July 2001.

5.   Dáil debates, 585/3, 12 May 2004, p. 31.

6.   'Garda pelted with bottles and glass during street row', *The Kingdom*, 6 May 2004.

7.   *Indymedia Ireland*, 27 February 2005, at www.indymedia.ie/

article/74528, accessed 20 July 2009.

8. See below for examples of such predictions by the media and gardaí of violence at the EU summit 2004.

9. A. N. Flood, 'Dublin Reclaim the Streets attacked by gardai', http://anarchism.pageabode.com/andrewnflood/dublin-reclaim-the-streets-attacked-gardai-may–2002-rts, accessed 13 March 2009.

10. W. Hederman, 'Crackdown was not a freak incident', *The Irish Times*, 10 May 2002.

11. A. Mulcahy, 'Crime, policing and social control in Ireland', in S. O'Sullivan (ed.), *Contemporary Ireland*, 2007, p. 131.

12. IMC editorial group 'World economic forum have cancelled their October meeting in Dublin' (18 July 2003), www.indymedia.ie/article/60482, accessed 13 March 2009.

13. J. Caldwell, 'May Day', *Garda Review* (2004), p. 31.

14. H. Browne, 'Consenting to capital in the Irish media', *Irish Journal of Sociology*, vol. 13, no. 2 (2004), pp. 128–41; Rosie Meade, 'Mayday! Mayday! Newspaper framing anti-globalisers!' *Journalism*, vol. 9 (2008), pp. 330–52.

15. Dublin Grassroots Network dossier, 'Ireland: Fortress Dublin?' – dirty tricks and criminalisation of protest issued 10 May 2004, www.indymedia.ie/article/64958?search_text=fortress+dublin, accessed 13 March 2009.

16. M. Raftery, 'Disturbing reflections on the gardaí', *The Irish Times*, 13 May 2004.

17. J. Humphreys, 'A May Day show of might', *The Irish Times*, 25 April 2004.

18. Browne, 'Consenting to capital', p. 140.

19. Field notes from participant observation of court proceedings after arrests at May Day 2004 'Bring the Noise'.

20. A selection of such stories includes but is not limited to: P. Williams, 'How the Shinners hijacked Rossport', *Irish Independent*, 7 October 2006; analysis, 'Writhing in the ecstasy of oppression', *Irish Independent*, 19 November 2006; R. Delevan, 'Wake up! Or else it might never happen; Ireland is plodding into the future at a sometimes embarrassing pace – no

thanks to this lot', *Irish Independent*, 24 December 2006; C. Lally, 'Policing costs mount as the Corrib clash moves closer to sea', *The Irish Times*, 20 September 2008.

21. N. Ward, 'Reclaiming the streets', *Garda Review*, November 2006, p. 10.

22. L. Siggins, 'Green Party calls for inquiry into Corrib sinking', *The Irish Times*, 12 June 2009; *eadem*, 'Ballinaboy locals hurt by jailing of fisherman', *The Irish Times*, 10 May 2010.

23. A. N. Flood, 'Prosecutions of Shell to Sea campaigners collapse', *Indymedia*, 1 April 2010, accessed 1 April 2010.

24. Cox, 'News from nowhere?', pp. 210–29.

25. D. Della Porta, A. Peterson and H. Reiter (eds), *The Policing of Transnational Protest* (London, 2006), p. 2.

26. D. Corva, 'Biopower and the militarisation of the police function', *ACME: An International E-Journal for Critical Geographies 2009*, vol. 8, issue 2.8:2 (2009), pp. 161–75.

27. An important element of the press attitude is no doubt the routine assignment to demonstrations of crime reporters – structurally dependent on police sources for their routine material – rather than political reporters.

CL184590